Also by Harold Coy

THE AMERICANS

A story about people, democracy, free schools, ice cream, airplanes, social security, penicillin, atomic energy, and all the things that make our nation great.

THE
MEXICANS

THE MEXICANS

ⓄⓄⓄⓄⓄⓄⓄⓄⓄ

BY HAROLD COY

ILLUSTRATED BY FRANCISCO MORA

Little, Brown and Company   Boston   Toronto

72938

Published simultaneously in Canada
by Little, Brown & Company (Canada) Limited

PRINTED IN THE UNITED STATES OF AMERICA

ABOUT THIS BOOK

⊚⊚⊚⊚⊚⊚⊚⊚⊚

THE MEXICANS are worth knowing, being next-door neighbors. We sometimes think to please our other neighbors, the Canadians, by saying, "You are just like us" — only to learn they would rather be like themselves. We do not tell the Mexicans they are just like us. Their path and ours have been so different.

We built our nation in the wilderness, or rather on the former hunting grounds of the Indians, and our story has been one of settlement and invention in a new land.

Mexico, on the other hand, is the story of a people regaining their ancient homeland. In a way it is an Indian success story. Long before America was "discovered," the Indians of central and southern Mexico were farmers and builders of true cities. They withstood the shock of conquest and lived to serve their conquerors. Indian historians recorded the defense of Mexico: that brave, tragic, and first great resistance of a native people to the global surge of the Europeans, then getting under way and only now ebbing.

Over the generations these disinherited people have

merged with their Spanish conquerors and those who came after into a "race of bronze" that is valorous, warmhearted, and one hundred percent Mexican. Painfully they have been winning back their country and transforming it.

If colonial status and human bondage slowed the progress of the United States, imagine their effect over a longer time on Mexico. Consider, in addition, what it meant to suffer dictatorships and invasions. Three times since 1810, Mexico has been shaken by convulsions, each lasting ten years or more: the War of Independence, the Reform, and the Social Revolution. Nine days each year the Mexican flag flies at half-mast in homage to martyred heroes.

Mexico has taken long strides yet is still a poor country alongside the United States, though it seems well-off to travelers from some lands farther south. The wonder is not that Mexico lacks our material wealth but that the Mexicans have found courage to rally from centuries of misfortune and get on with the task of building a modern nation.

Our hospitable and gracious neighbors have imagination, wit, and the gift of finding pleasure in small things. They value their own dignity and respect the worth of every race. Having suffered from foreign intervention, they lead the smaller nations in the search for peace and understanding.

Suggestions for further reading appear at the end of this volume. Most of the literature on Mexico in English is addressed to adults or to young children. The present work is intended especially for young adults. It tells Mexico's story as Beto, a Mexican teen-ager, might write it for Bob, a friend north of the border. Beto, like most Mexicans, has a lively appreciation of his country's past. Having studied in our country, he is also keenly interested in the United States.

Beto is less a fictional character than a composite of several young Mexicans whose friendship I am privileged to enjoy. To endless questions about their country and themselves they reply patiently, thoughtfully, and sometimes eloquently. Their firsthand experience has been an invaluable check on my own impressions of Mexico, gained by intermittent reading and observation over a lifetime but seen through foreign eyes. Hence to Juan, Manuel, Gilberto, Jaime, Toño, Chucho, Alfonso, Armando, and Abel, and to Luz, Carmela, Elena, Raquel, Chelo, Amelia, and María de los Angeles, this book is affectionately dedicated.

Harold Coy

México, D.F.

CONTENTS

◎◎◎◎◎◎◎◎◎

ILLUSTRATIONS

◉◉◉◉◉◉◉◉◉

THE
MEXICANS

A LETTER FROM MEXICO

Dear Bob:

How good to hear from you after so long! Your letter brings back grateful memories of your never failing friendship and generosity during our school days in Kansas. My father, you will remember, sent me there to improve my English for the sake of my future studies and career. How hard it was to comprehend the teacher! I came well drilled in the irregular verbs, but they let me down. It was your encouragement that sustained me during those first bewildering months.

We were *tocayos,* having the same name really, Robert and Roberto — Bob for short in your country and Beto in mine. Being buddies with you, tocayo, I learned to use, if not to dominate, the English tongue.

So now you are a high school senior, looking ahead to a premedical course! And me? Your servant in the Preparatoria, hoping to enroll soon in chemical engineering at the National University.

You write that your social science class is undertaking a project to "find out about Mexico and how it differs from the United States" and you do me the honor of supposing I can be helpful.

Where does one begin? If you read the baseball news, the two countries are much alike. *Cadena pegó jomrón,* Cadena hit a home run, *en su turno al bat,* in his turn at bat, *en la última entrada,* in the last inning, *con tres a bordo,* with three men on base, *deshaciendo un empate a tres carreras,* breaking a three-to-three tie, *y así el equipo de casa ganó el juego por siete carreras contra tres,* and so the home team won the game by seven to three. Oh, how such language agitates my teacher! Why say pitcher and catcher, she demands, when there are good Spanish words like *lanzador* and *receptor?* But she has to admit that *beisbol,* both the game and the word, is here to stay. And in her heart she must feel the same about hot cakes (pronounced oat káy-kaze), Orange Crush (Orench Croatch), Gillette blades and Pond's Angel Face, comic books relettered in Spanish if you can call it that, and Santa Claus (Santiclós).

My parents remember when Santa Claus first came to Sears Roebuck de México. He sat in the window, slapping his thighs and roaring with laughter for no apparent reason, but he was not so dumb, that punctual Yankee. In a few years he was delivering the toys on Christmas Eve, twelve nights before the Holy Kings made their rounds. By now the Kings (whom you call the Three Wise Men) would be unemployed except for the kids who use them as an excuse to ask for more presents on January 6.

Santa expects to find a Christmas tree, with lights winking on and off, in every home. Now here in Mexico a tree costs an eye of the face whether imported from Canada or purchased on the black market. And that's not all. Foreign trees drain the nation of money needed for bulldozers and other machinery, while trees cut illegally on our gullied hillsides threaten our remaining forests. My father has bought us a plastic tree of magenta color. It doesn't smell like a balsam fir, but it will last forever.

Happily something of the traditional Christmas remains. Colored lights illuminate the principal avenues, forming topical scenes like pilgrims in procession, searching for room at the inn, as Mary and Joseph did on the road to Bethlehem. At *posadas,* or Christmas parties, we reenact this story for old time's sake before getting on with the dancing. Posadas are joyous occasions when a boy meets many girls and vice versa. This is important, for introductions and dates are not easily arranged among us.

Except for a posada, I might never have met Chabela, my *novia;* that is, my steady girl friend. Even so, her parents and brothers were on the sidelines, eyeing me closely while we danced. Not before proving my good character could I call at her home. Chabela's father, who is given to proverbs, said, "He who keeps hens must guard them from the coyote." Dates I negotiate with Chabela's mother, who remembers when a nice girl went always chaperoned. You tell her times have changed. She says yes, but not after dark. At night only Mamá will do for a chaperon, or maybe an aunt. It's the before-supper dates that leave a mother apprehensive and uncertain. Sometimes you may go to the movies on a double date, each couple chaperoning the other, or else the little sister tags along. After being engaged a year, maybe you go unchaperoned if the mother knows exactly where you are and when to expect you.

Among the poor, old customs break down faster than in the middle classes. Where you live also makes a difference. On Chabela's saint's day, it would be gallant of me to stand under her window with my guitar at dawn and sing:

> *If you are sleeping, my love,*
> *Awaken and listen to the voice*
> *Of the one who loves you . . .*

But Chabelita lives in an apartment house among neighbors who value sleep above romance. So I phone her at breakfast time and play a recording into the receiver. Her saint's day falls on July 8, the feast of Santa Isabel, Chabela being a nickname for Isabel, like Chayo for Rosario, or Chucho for Jesús. A girl's last important birthday is her fifteenth, when she becomes a señorita and her father throws the house out the window, giving her a coming-out party. After that it's the saint's day that counts. Birthdays and saint's days used to be the same. Babies were named for the saint on whose feast day they were born. That's why my little grandmother, my *abuelita,* is Eudoxia, and her brothers are Austreberto and Frumancio. Nowadays parents prefer a free choice of any saint on the calendar.

For birthdays and romance we preserve customs inherited from Spain. And some of our customs go even further back. When picnicking at the "floating gardens" of Xochimilco, we carry what to me is a *lonche,* a lunch. My mother calls it a *bastimento* in proper Spanish. But for the little grandmother it's an *itacate,* a word as Indian as her *guacamole* of mashed avocado and tomato and chopped onions, coriander, and chili. We spread the delicious mixture on *tortillas* — Indian-style corn cakes baked on a griddle — or on sliced bread from the *supermercado.* At home, Grandmother times a boiled egg by repeating the Lord's Prayer three times. She knows the hour by the length of the shadows on the kitchen wall and feels no need to find out the exact minute by dialing 03 on the telephone.

You can see that our long past is mixed with our present. At the Home Fair, Chabela and I saw an Indian girl of ten, carrying her baby brother in a long shawl, or *rebozo*. She stood barefoot, bearing her burden as little girls have done for centuries, but watching television in color. All over Mexico, all over Latin America, people are looking up from their drudgery, wondering what the future holds for them. The little girl must be an Otomí from the Valley of the Mezquital. No one goes about there with empty hands, for idleness means hunger. People walking to market spin coarse thread from the fiber of the *maguey,* which is like your century plant. They live in huts of sticks and mud. Among them, a house of sunbaked adobe bricks is a palace. In more favored regions, people are graduating from adobes to cement blocks. Here in the capital you see the rising steel skeletons of huge housing projects. Our family lives high up over the Plaza of the Three Cultures. We look out upon the skyscraper homes of eighty thousand neighbors, a restored colonial church, and the ruined pyramids where the Aztecs made their brave last stand against the *conquistadores* four and a half centuries ago, though it seems only yesterday.

These are some examples of *how* Mexico differs from the United States. *Why* it's different is something else. If you are searching for the *why,* perhaps I can offer modest help while studying Mexican history this year. From time to time I plan to put my thoughts in writing. Then, hopefully, I shall not have to burn my eyebrows cramming for the examinations. Suppose I send you a copy of each paper as if it were a chapter in a book, putting in such special comments as might interest you and your classmates. Would that help in the project?

Congratulations to your school companions for their choice of a subject. When they tour Mexico, as nearly two million of your countrymen do every year, they will make friends easily and better understand all they see. That you may always enjoy health and happiness is the sincere wish of your friend who salutes you affectionately,

Beto

ON BEING MEXICAN

⊚⊚⊚⊚⊚⊚⊚⊚⊚ **1**

HALF OF MEXICO is under eighteen. We are young and full of *inquietudes*. But we also have long roots in the soil. Our bronze-faced ancestors were not movie Indians, hunting buffalo and sleeping in tepees, but pioneers in agriculture, mathematics, and city building. They put poems to music and danced to please both the gods and themselves. Not waiting for America to be discovered in 1492, they founded our great capital.

Those who came from the Old World are also our ancestors, though in fewer numbers. They burned our libraries, took our women, and told their children of mixed race that their Indian forebears were ignorant of writing and probably unable to count past three. In time we ourselves came to believe this. Fortunately, a few books escaped the flames. One of them contains a table of eclipses and records the phases of the planet Venus. Many old poems lingered in memory long enough to be put down in the Latin alphabet. Translated from the native tongue in recent years, they sing of finding truth through art, which the Indians, so fond of figures of speech, called "flower and song."

The corn harvest often fails for lack of rain, but the springs of poetry have never run dry. Today, even in a provincial town, a tournament brings out a score of poets to compete for the privilege of crowning the queen of beauty. Not all the verse they recite is good; it is merely necessary. We are poor in material things and must not be poor in spirit. This is not always understood. A leading writer of ours worked in his youth for a foreign company and, though a crack stenographer, was fired as unreliable for writing poetry in his spare time. Today, like many poets in Latin America, he occupies a diplomatic post.

The late Dr. Atl loved to paint volcanoes. When Paricutín erupted in 1943, he waded into the hot ashes to capture its wild beauty and lost a leg. It was hard now to climb his favorite mountains, but, as the poem says, "The bough may creak, but the bird sings, knowing what wings are for." Dr.

Atl borrowed a helicopter from the government and painted Popocatépetl, looking down on its snowy cone.

Not everyone flies so high, but what Mexican rides a bicycle without decorating it with streamers and tassels and a gay pinwheel? What slum dwelling lacks a row of potted flowers and a pair of caged songbirds, always a pair so they won't be lonesome? The tombstones in a village graveyard are pink and blue. Through the stench of the cattle market, a proud buyer leads his ox away by a brand-new halter with fluttering ribbons.

In Holy Week the religious images are draped in purple mourning cloth. Bells are silent. Children whirl *matracas* with a splintering noise as if to break Judas's bones for betraying Our Lord. Despite this gloom, flowers and tall candles are massed on the altar to commemorate the Last Supper. On Thursday evening, the faithful visit seven churches. It's an old custom.

A new custom is Mother's Day, borrowed from the United States but blown up here with band concerts, oratory, television shows, and dancing at the schools. It's not enough to send Mother flowers: those she should have all the year round. On May 10 she deserves something better than you can pay for in cash; the advertising pages are full of suggestions.

Independence Day starts on the evening of September 15, when the president gives the cry for liberty, as Father Hidalgo did in 1810, and continues the next day with a military parade. November opens with two days of homage to the dead. The graves are covered with marigolds, and the kids feast on frosted sugar skulls. Traditionally, a table is set with food and drink for the departed ones, but this custom is passing in the capital, where so few have faith in Grandfather's finding his way home through a maze of freeways and viaducts. On November 20, the anniversary of the Revolution of 1910, we who are young parade in sports attire. Christmas goes on nearly a month if you count from the feast of Our Lady of Guadalupe, patron of Mexico, to the Day of Kings.

Also there are farewells and homecomings for travelers, fiestas "without apparent motive" but just for fun, and office outings by chartered bus, everyone singing to the guitar on the long ride home in Sunday evening traffic. And don't forget weddings. Mexicans are married twice, for reasons to be told later: first, standing before a judge; then kneeling before a priest. The poor bridegroom pays for everything and grasps his only chance to save by putting on the invitations: "No reception on account of mourning." A Mexican is always in mourning, at least for a cousin. However, a baptism always calls for a feast and is a big event, since the parents and godparents become lifelong *compadres* and are from then on as close as brothers and sisters.

Not a day passes without a fiesta someplace, or many places, in Mexico, where every town salutes its patron saint with fireworks and music, masked dancers with shells swishing at their ankles, cockfights, steer riding, and sometimes a carpet of flowers spread before the temple.

That life should be beautiful is the first thing that comes to mind as I try explaining our ideals. Allied to beauty is courtesy, which means respect for human dignity. "A thing has a price," we say, "but a man has dignity." Our etiquette may seem excessive with all its handshaking, begging of permission, and courtesy titles like *licenciado* for lawyer and *maestro* for the plumber and barber. Among us, however, such deferences mark a man as "educated," no matter how little his schooling. The warmth of friendship comes out in calls on the sick and in *abrazos,* or bear hugs, when old pals meet. There is a courtesy even in names. For example, I am Roberto García Beltrán, at your orders. García for my father, Beltrán for my mother, who'd be hurt if I omitted her family name. Perhaps I may do so when she rests in peace, but again I may not, for García is like Smith among the Yankees, whereas García Beltrán will not be confused with García Romero or García Melgarejo.

A man, we say, should be serious, stern, strong, and sedate. And if he's Mexican, he's sure to be a fierce nonconformist who believes that "every man has his own way of killing fleas." There's a popular story in which a father counsels his son, "Never eat dirt, my boy, it soils the teeth and forms an adobe in the belly." Way back in Indian times, parents were giving good advice — as they still do. A newspaper runs a contest for the best "letters to my son." One letter says,

"When you grow up, machines will work for you and even think for you. But do not become a cog in a machine. Cultivate your spirit, read the history of humanity, learn from its great thinkers."

Tourists are astonished to see us calmly crossing the street instead of leaping for our lives when the red light changes, as is the custom in more advanced countries. We have the bullfighter's pride. His mouth may be so dry he can't spit, but his feet stay planted in the moment of truth when the horned beast thunders by. Cuauhtémoc, the last Aztec king, with his scorched feet, resisting his torturers, is the symbol of our nationality — not Cortés, thirsting for treasure.

Courage, fortitude, spirit — we sum them up in one word: *ánimo*. The crippled Frida Kahlo had this quality on her deathbed when she painted a still life, with a slice of watermelon as a sign of well-being and, on it, the legend, *¡Viva la vida!*, Long live life! Courage among us does not carry the promise of victory as in more favored lands where the good guy always wins. No, such does not always happen in Mexico, where we have often suffered defeats while believing ourselves in the right. This has made us wary. "Believe nothing you hear and only half of what you see," we say. We end a letter to an absent friend with a "may nothing happen to you," as if only ill could befall him. Life nevertheless goes on, and we compare it to a sweet potato: you must keep swallowing it or choke. So why not do so with grace and style? There are some, of course, who mistake bluster for courage. They boast of being *muy macho,* real he-men, and we say of them that they eat beans and belch chicken. Mexico's best defenders are her peace-loving sons, each one a soldier when foreign feet profane her soil, in the words of our national anthem written during the surge of patriotism that followed the tragic loss of half our territory in 1848.

Oh, the millions of Mexicans who have died for our country at one time or another! But now the time has come to live for our country and achieve the goals set forth in the words of another parent, full of good counsel, who tells his son, "I do not wish you an easy and comfortable life but a productive one. You will find it necessary not only to fight but to win, and your enemies, among others, will be ignorance, jealousy, intolerance, hunger, misery, sickness, hate, fear, and war."

NO COUNTRY LIKE MEXICO

◎◎◎◎◎◎◎◎◎   2

MEXICO has been called a horn of plenty, and seen on a map, tapering down from the United States, it looks like one. It lies between two continents, bridging English-speaking and Latin America. The coastline becomes longer than yours after running around the shoestring peninsula of Lower California and stubby Yucatán at the entrance to the Gulf of Mexico. Yet we have few natural harbors and live mostly in the highlands, shut off by mountain barriers. They say the conqueror Cortés held a crumpled sheet of paper before his king and told him, "This is the map of Mexico, Your Majesty."

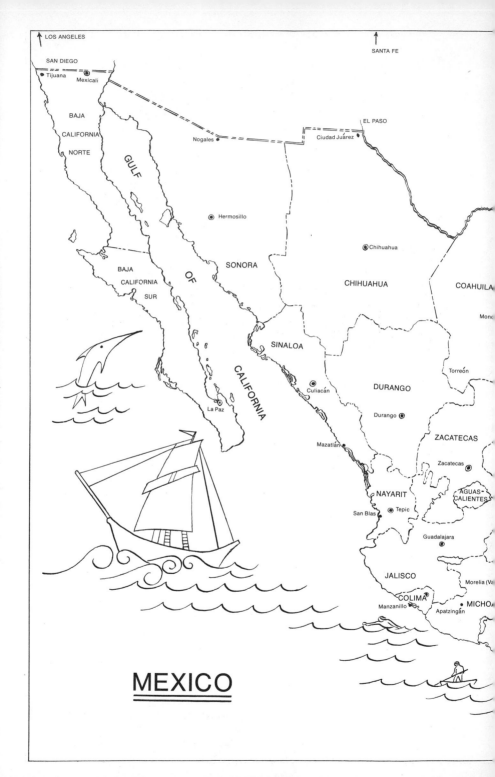

MEXICO

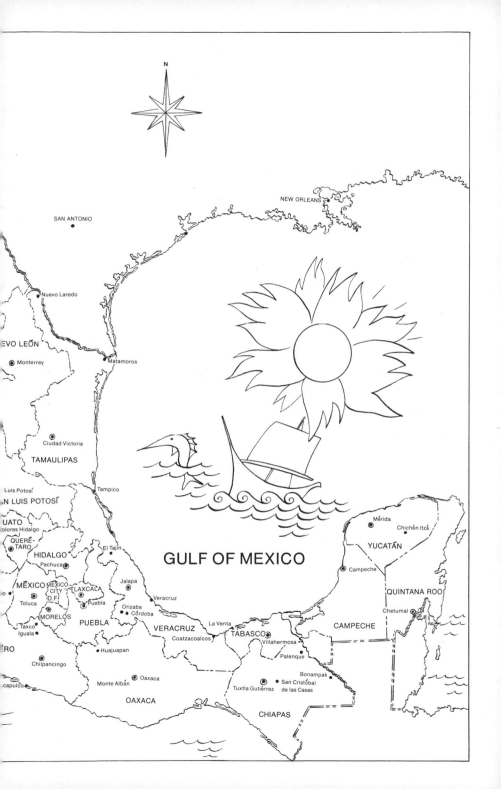

A traveler crossing Mexico climbs in and out of valleys and around the mountain ravines we call *barrancas*. There are cultivated fields so steep that a farmer can fall off his farm. Only a seventh of the land is cultivated, the rest being too craggy, too dry, too salty or marshy, or sometimes even too desolate for cattle range. Mexico will be a horn of plenty only when burros grow wings.

Water is our greatest worry. The Indians used to make offerings to Tláloc, the rain god. Now the peasants pray to the saints for rain. They harvest a good crop only once in two or three years, except where irrigation is practiced or it rains enough. Rain is peculiar. The sea breezes will spill their moisture on a mountain slope and transform the valley below into a garden, while leaving the other side of the mountain so parched that nothing but cactus and thorny acacia will grow.

The Indians counted five directions: east, west, north, south, and up-and-down. You realize that in Mexico the fifth direction can be the most important when you look down from a pine forest into a canyon lush with banana leaves. The nearest tropics are not to the south but below you. If you climb from the hot country along the Gulf or the Pacific coast, you soon come to a temperate land and then to what with some exaggeration we call the cold country — like here in Mexico City.

Our capital city lies among volcanic peaks in a mountain basin that in Indian and colonial times was partly covered by lakes. The volcanoes, all quiet now except for a rare surprise, form a belt running east and west from Mount Orizaba, within sight of the Gulf of Mexico, to Colima on the Pacific side. This belt is the dividing line between northern and southern Mexico. Running parallel to the coasts, north of the capital, are the Eastern and Western Sierra Madres. A majority of the Mexican people live between these mother ranges on a high plateau that slopes off gradually from the volcanic uplands to the United States frontier.

A few years ago my father — I called him Papi then — went on a business trip over the plateau as far as the border and let me go with him. At Querétaro we took Route 45 and drove through the corn, wheat, and strawberry fields of the Bajío, as the fertile lands along the Lerma and its tributaries are called. As we passed the statue of Christ the King on Cubilete peak, Papi said we were in the geographical center of the Republic. West of us was Guadalajara, Mexico's second city. To the south were Morelia and the lakes of Michoacán. Behind us, to the southeast, were Mexico City and the neighboring Toluca and Puebla valleys. All through this region there are cities and towns, eucalyptus-lined country roads, and green valleys at the foot of brown hills.

But after leaving Aguascalientes, we entered the dry country and followed the route of the pioneers — the Mexican pioneers who went north after silver instead of west for gold. Zacatecas had a silver boom before Shakespeare was born and is still a mining town, with steep cobbled streets only wide enough for two burros with pack baskets to pass. On we rode, and that night Papi said, "Shake out your shoes in the morning." We were in Durango, famous for its scorpions, though the hometown people claim there are just as many in other places. We continued north into the cattle country, seeing a lonely windmill now and then or a black cloud of *zopilotes,* or vultures, zeroing in on some poor animal that must have died of thirst.

The land was beautiful, believe it or not. Far off through the luminous air the mountains were lilac, purple, brown, and pink, or sometimes green, if not from vegetation then from copper ore. The sunset was crimson and fiery white over the Western Sierra, a range so massive and gashed with canyons that only one highway crosses it between Guadalajara and the border. Somewhere in that rugged fastness, where the pine boughs are heavy with snow during the long winter, live the Tarahumaras, those swift Indian runners who can wear down a deer, they say.

In Chihuahua City we visited Pancho Villa's house and saw the riddled car in which the revolutionary chieftain was slain from ambush in time of peace. What a sad destiny for the Centaur of the North, who had galloped through a rain of bullets so often on his horse Seven Leagues! Papi told me to save my sympathy for Benito Juárez, for whom Ciudad Juárez, opposite El Paso, Texas, is named. Here he held out against the French invaders and kept alive the spark of Mexican independence.

As you know, the Río Grande, which we call the Bravo, marks the boundary between our countries from this point to the Gulf of Mexico. Cotton thrives wherever water from the river touches the thirsty soil. We crossed over to the eastern side of the plateau, passing through Torreón and the Durango-Coahuila lake country, where the water from the mountains is used to irrigate vineyards and cotton and alfalfa fields. We came home on Highway 57. Between Saltillo and San Luis Potosí the road cuts through a dry forest of prickly pears and palmlike yuccas where a year may go by without rain. To live here seems impossible, yet people were out slashing their hands to gather wild desert shrubs for hard fibers and wax. Somewhere in these salt flats and limestone plains we crossed the Tropic of Cancer into the torrid zone. Yet as we climbed higher on the plateau, it grew cooler and greener, and we knew we were nearing home.

Now a little about the rest of Mexico, starting with Lower California. This long peninsula, sometimes called Mexico's withered arm, is a lonely desert except for the irrigated cotton belt in the north and a few oases and fishing ports. Yet just across the narrow Gulf of California is a broad coastal plain watered by streams that flow down the Sierra's western face. Fed by melted snow and summer rains and harnessed by great dams, they bring life to the wheatfields of Sonora and the cane and tomatoes of Sinaloa.

Farther down the coast, the mountains edge close to the coconut-fringed shore. Headlands jut into the Pacific at Acapulco, forming a magnificent harbor with beautiful beaches. On the other side of the Southern Sierra, in Guerrero and adjoining states, are the hot lands of the Balsas Valley, a hideout for guerrilla bands in the troubled past.

The coastal plain along the Gulf of Mexico is bushland in Tamaulipas, forest in Veracruz, and near-jungle in Tabasco. Oil fields rim the coast, as they do in Texas and Louisiana. The rainfall increases, going south, and the moist trade winds favor the growth of mangoes, gardenias, vanilla, and coffee on the rising slopes. You see thatched huts with walls that are merely saplings tied together with vines. Tabasco has six months of downpour and six months of drizzle. Sultry winds from the Gulf drench the mountains of Chiapas, and the water, returning, spreads out in tropical rivers like the Grijalva and the Usumacinta. More water in places than land. If only the rest of Mexico had some of it! Here is the home of alligators, hummingbirds, and mahogany forests. Orchids hang from the limbs, and creeper vines tie the undergrowth together. You need a machete to cut a path, and if you don't startle a jaguar you will surely set the parrots flying and the monkeys howling.

Around the horseshoe curve of the Gulf and up the other side is the Yucatán peninsula. Here are the seawalls of Campeche, built to keep out pirates, and the mysterious land of the Mayas. The rainfall diminishes, going north, and the trees are scrubbier. It's about the only place in Mexico where you can go anywhere without going over a mountain. Never-

Querétaro • Aculco • Pachuca • Tula • Zacapoaxtla →

PUEBLA

Teotihuacán • Ciudad Sahagún • HIDALGO

Tepexpan •

Morelia ← Tacuba • Texcoco • TLAXCALA

Azcapotzalco • Chapultepec • Tlatelolco

MÉXICO

Monte de las Cruces • Tlaxcala •

Coyoacan • Culhuacán

Toluca • Pedregal • Xochimilco

Iztaccíhuatl

DISTRITO FEDERAL

Huejotzingo •

Popocatépetl • Cholula • Puebla

MEXICO CITY
AND VICINITY

Tepeaca •

Cuernavaca • MORELOS

Orizaba and Veracruz →

Xochicalco • Cuautla

PUEBLA

Tehuacán ↘

Acapulco

theless, the outcropping rock and thorny bush make travel difficult. The streams flow in underground channels, and sometimes the roof breaks through and forms a natural well. There you will find a village, its square shaded by a spreading sapodilla, the tree from which chicle comes for chewing gum, or a ceiba, the silk-cotton Mayan tree of life. Nowadays, in the dry northwestern corner of the peninsula, near Mérida, the Mayas harvest henequen leaves and prepare a hard fiber for hammocks and twine, while the wondrous temples of their ancestors draw visitors from all the world.

From every part of the Republic, the roads lead to Mexico City. The federal highways are measured in kilometers from the monument of Cuauhtémoc, who stands with spear poised for the thrust, at the crossing of Insurgentes Avenue and the

Paseo de la Reforma. These streets are important for finding your way around. Even the taxi drivers don't know all the twelve thousand streets, squares, and alleys in the little red guide.

Insurgentes, our longest street, honors the Insurgent heroes of 1810. It starts where the highway from Laredo, Texas, enters the city and runs south through the Pedregal to connect with the road for Cuernavaca and Acapulco. The Pedregal is a petrified sea of lava that flowed from the volcano Xitle some two thousand years ago, burying the village of Cuicuilco with its temples, some of which were excavated when the Olympic Village was built for the games in 1968. Once a wasteland, the lava bed provides a spectacular setting for modern homes and the National University.

Reforma is a majestic twelve-lane avenue with shaded walks and luxury shops and hotels. It runs in a southwesterly direction, past traffic circles with monuments like the Angel of Independence. Beyond Diana the Huntress it enters Chapultepec Park, where a million people come on Sunday outings. They say Reforma resembles the boulevards of Paris. After crossing the park, it winds through Lomas de Chapultepec, a wealthy *colonia,* or subdivision, that looks like Los Angeles. It was promoted by Californians as Chapultepec Heights, but Heights does not come as easily to a Mexican tongue as Lomas, which means hills.

The older part of the city is back the other way. You turn right off Reforma at the equestrian statue we call the Little

Horse (ignoring the royal rider, Charles IV of Spain). Down Juárez Avenue, you come to the Alameda, a park and poplar grove laid out before your *Mayflower* sailed. We were burning heretics there, my teacher says, while you were hanging witches in Massachusetts. Just beyond stands the white marble Palace of Fine Arts, but it does not stand very well, having sunk in the spongy soil of an old lake bed. Over on another corner, however, is a modern engineering triumph: La Latino — the Latin American Tower — forty-three stories of silvery blue, floating safe and upright in the mud.

Farther east is the city's Spanish core, with many colonial buildings, the oldest of them fortress-palaces now decayed into slums. The heart of the old city is the great plaza, or Zócalo. It is surrounded by colonnaded shops, public buildings, and the Cathedral, whose bells have individual names like Holy Guardian Angel. The long, low building of rose-colored volcanic stone is the National Palace. It stands on the site of an earlier palace where Motecuhzoma ruled — the one we call Moctezuma and you have further changed into Montezuma. Still farther east is the airport and, beyond, the remains of Lake Texcoco, a salty puddle during the summer rains and a dust bowl in the dry season, whipped by the winds. This side of town is left mostly to the poor. Those with a choice prefer the west and the south.

A seventh of the population of the Republic lives in Mexico City, and more keep coming — a quarter of a million every year — looking for work. The largest industrial plants are in the northwestern part of the city, or beyond in the state of México. We have more than our share of factories here in the capital, but new industries are rising in Querétaro, in the cities of the Bajío, and in Guadalajara, the Pearl of the West, as well as in Puebla, Orizaba, and along the Gulf coast. In the northeast, where the Eastern Sierra Madre descends to the Gulf, is Monterrey, called the Pittsburgh of Mexico for its steel and heavy industry. We have many jokes' about its thrifty, hardworking people. It seems a Monterrey boy lost a copper five-centavo piece on nearby Saddle Mountain and didn't stop digging till he found it. That's why there's a dip in the mountain.

One reason for our industrial growth is our increasing population. Each year we have a million and a half new Mexican mouths to feed — and three million hands that will one day need work. They can't all plant corn and pick beans. Most of our good land is already in use and, anyway, what we need for a bigger yield is not more hands but more fertilizers and insecticides, and better seed. We must make jobs for the young people who are leaving the farms. We must industrialize or starve.

Besides, we Mexicans want more of such things as textiles, paper, paints, tires, toys, and radio sets. It's not easy to get them from other countries in exchange for products like coffee. Did you know that it takes two or three times as many sacks of coffee as it used to, to pay for a tractor? You see, coffee is raised all over Latin America and in Africa, too, but only a few big industrial plants in all the world make tractors. If we are to import heavy machinery, we must make everyday things for ourselves. And for this we must have nylon, acetate, polyethylene, resins, plastics, rubber — and chemical engineers. That's why one day, God willing, I shall be a chemical engineer.

Already half of Mexico lives in communities large enough to be called urban. Urban Mexico begins shading into rural Mexico in towns where the church and the municipal palace face on a plaza with Indian laurels, a monument to Hidalgo or Juárez, and a bandstand in the center. When the band plays on Sunday evenings, the boys and girls circulate in opposite directions, looking one another over, while their parents watch from stone benches. If a boy casts a meaningful glance at a girl, and she replies with a flower or even a smile, then a romance is born.

Along the streets leading from the plaza are rows of houses, one attached to another. The lower windows, so close to the sidewalk, are barred to keep the señoritas in and intruders out. You can pass a beautiful home without knowing it. Seen from the street, it's just a tinted wall, weathered by the sun and rain, unless the doorway is open and you peek through into the patio, where a fountain splashes beside blossoms and foliage. A patio is an inner courtyard and has been called a garden surrounded by a house.

Houses are simpler at the edge of town and in the villages. Often they consist of one or two rooms, along with a corncrib and outbuildings, all surrounded by a fence of organ-pipe cactus. A red tile roof and some fig trees add a touch of color, but some villages are so much a part of the brown earth that before a traveler sees them he hears the barking of the dogs.

Inside one of these humbler homes are a bench or two, a wooden chest, some pots and dishes, a griddle for baking tortillas, a float lamp glowing red under a print of the Virgin, and some *petates,* or sleeping mats. Many a poor Mexican is born and dies on a petate — and if he is *very* poor, we say he does not even have a petate on which to fall dead. Usually, though, he has a woolen sarape to keep the chill off his shoulders when he goes to the fields before dawn. And his wife has a rebozo that serves as a sling for the water jar or the baby, a head covering in church, and a shield to protect her mouth from the feared night air and winds.

The village sits among cornfields, for half of Mexico's cropland is in corn. Between the summer weedings and in the winter after the stalks have been gathered for fodder, village craftsmen make such things as painted piggy banks, lacquered jewel boxes, woven straw animals, tin and wooden masks, or candlesticks adorned with cherubs and flowers. A village may be known for its sarapes, baskets, glassware, guitars, hammered copper kettles, or shiny green and black pottery. There are places in the mountains of Oaxaca where only wild palms grow, and the people, even the children, go into damp caves and weave palm-fiber hats. Outside it's so dry that the hats wouldn't hold their shape.

On market day, merchants and craftsmen come into the plaza under loads of clay jars and towers of reed-bottomed chairs. They lay out their wares under canvas awnings and overflow from the square into the adjoining streets. Here are limes and papayas, carrots and eggplants, medicinal herbs, saddles and rope, brushes and twig brooms, and twenty kinds of chili peppers, fresh and dried, red, green, and black. You see lots of factory-made clothing, for the men are giving up their white pajama-like suits for denim and khaki, and the women are going in for one-piece cotton dresses, even in many Indian villages. They save their embroidered blouses and flouncy skirts for fiestas.

The most Indian part of Mexico extends from the country-side of central Mexico down through Oaxaca and over the narrow isthmus of Tehuantepec into Chiapas and the Yucatán peninsula. An Indian, in Mexico, is someone who lives like an Indian. He eats tortillas instead of wheat bread, wears sandals or goes barefoot, and usually speaks an Indian tongue. He is shut off in his village from strangers by mountains and desert or at least by walls of fear and mistrust. Ever since his people were robbed of their land and forced into hiding or made to work under the lash, their village customs have been a bond of union, setting them apart from a world that seemed hostile and sometimes still does.

A tenth of the people of Mexico live as Indians and are brought into the life of the nation only as their deep-rooted suspicions are slowly overcome.

If you live in a traditional community in certain parts of southern Mexico, you will have an animal companion, the one whose tracks were found in the ashes outside the hut where you were born. An anteater, for example, an *oso hormiguero,* no larger than a squirrel and half of him a tapering snout, but your spiritual double, your other self. If he fares well, you do, too, but if he is injured, you fall sick. This is only one of life's perils. If you stumble at a stream crossing, offending the guardian spirits of the place, they may rob you of your soul and not return it until a *curandero,* or witch doctor, sacrifices a turkey on the spot.

You work with your father in the fields and also have obligations to the community, like sweeping the church and cleaning the images of the saints. You help keep order in the village and, when older, sit as a judge, settling disputes. You give fiestas in honor of the saints and, in old age, you join the elders and are heard with respect. You have prestige but not wealth, for what could you do with it? To build a better house than your neighbors' would be presumptuous. They'd name you majordomo of the fiesta for the village patron saint, and after paying for food, drink, candles, music, and fireworks, you'd have to work several seasons on a coffee plantation to take care of your debts.

Being young, you are impatient with the old ways, which change so slowly. And since you can be an Indian or not, as you choose, you decide to leave the village. So you buy yourself a suit of city clothes, find a job, and enter the mainstream of Mexican life. Or is it that simple? Can you so easily cast off the beliefs in which you were nurtured? Will your animal companion feel at home where there are more paved streets than anthills? In the city you must learn the value of money and be less trusting and more competitive, not relying on neighbors for help in time of trouble. Their ways are not the ways you were taught, and you may find, too late, that you have erred. But if you go home now, your kinsmen will laugh at your city clothes, and you will no longer feel natural in a fringed woolen jacket reaching to your knees. You have changed and belong partly to two worlds but not wholly to either.

This has been going on in Mexico for four hundred years, and out of spiritual anguish a new people has been born. Gradually our remaining Indians will be drawn into the changing life about them, but I hope they will keep and treasure their folk arts and dances, their sense of duty and honor, and their habit of working together for the common good. We owe much to the Indians: the names of our towns, our delight in art, the way we feel about our history, and the way we half speak, half sing the Spanish language.

The United States became a nation in a century and a half, but our case is very different. Colonial Mexico remained an Indian land under Spanish direction, without the freedoms and opportunities that English-speaking colonists enjoyed in North America. Here both land and Indians were considered to be at the king's disposition. Great estates came into existence, and the grip of the landed aristocracy on the nation was not broken until the present century. We suffered foreign invasions, were torn apart by civil wars, and were off to a late start in building a modern nation.

Our Mexican story is that of a conquered people who refused to accept conquest as permanent. Slowly we have absorbed our conquerors and built ourselves a country. We have felt the pull of stronger nations at various times, and some of our "decent people," as they call themselves, have been ready to move into the orbit of a foreign sun. We owe our nationality to the despised ones whose simple hearts have told them to be true to themselves.

We have a saying, *Como México no hay dos,* which means, "Like Mexico there aren't two," or better, "There's no country like Mexico." Please don't misunderstand. We want to share freely in all the good things that humanity has achieved. We are happy to treat with other nations with dignity and mutual respect. But our country is Mexico, not an imitation of Spain, England, France, or even the United States, much as we admire and sometimes envy your great country.

Into our melting pot went native peoples speaking a hundred languages. There was a time when the Indians were blamed for the slow pace of our material progress and the doors were flung open to European immigrants. Yet not many came, for until old problems were settled, neither white nor bronze-faced men could make the land prosper.

The degradation of the Indians was not of their own making. Later we shall see how the quickness with which an Indian became a blacksmith, a violinist, or a Latin scholar astonished and even alarmed the early Spaniards.

Today we are not surprised. As an inscription in the Anthropology Museum says, "All men have the same capacity for confronting nature, all races are equal, all cultures are respectable, all peoples can live in peace." And there in the museum halls, before our eyes, is proof that the story of Mexico begins long before Columbus with a people who developed many of the world's basic food plants and went on to invent calendars and writing, work in jade and gold, and build palaces and temple pyramids.

LONG BEFORE COLUMBUS

⦿⦿⦿⦿⦿⦿⦿⦿⦿   **3**

TEPEXPAN MAN is only a skeleton now, named for the place where his remains were found, here in the Valley of Mexico. Ten thousand years ago, more or less, he died in the dangerous quest for food in circumstances somewhat like this: He was hiding in the rushes with a band of hunters. A herd of imperial mammoths, largest of all elephants, came down to their watering place by the lake. The men rushed out yelling, brandishing spears. They cut an elephant from the herd and drove him into the mire. Spears flew from throwing-sticks. One bold hunter — it may have been

Tepexpan man — thrust a pike into the mammoth's tough hide. Then the others drew near. The monster thrashed and bellowed. Tepexpan man slipped while ducking the great tusks and was mauled and crushed. His blood stained the water lilies, but who could stop and grieve for such a common incident of the hunt? His companions closed in with their clubs and beat on the skull of the floundering beast. Soon the hunt was over, and cries of rejoicing announced a coming feast.

For ages Tepexpan man lay in the marsh under the limestone that formed as the lake receded. In similar green muck, not far away, there were weapon points, stone knives, and huge mammoth bones, plainly showing the marks of butchering by hunters like his companions.

The ancestors of these hunters discovered America. Tens of thousands of years ago, perhaps, the first of them crossed from Asia to Alaska. Coming in small bands at different times, they spread through the Americas, following game. When elephants were lacking, they feasted on white-tailed deer, camel-llamas, bison, or horses — wild American horses that vanished a couple of hundred lifetimes before the Spaniards came riding on domesticated horses. At times they made out on squirrels and frogs. When even the smallest game thinned out, they gathered seeds and berries. They caught grasshoppers and lizards, and anyone too squeamish to eat them starved.

Eventually hunger drove them to change their whole way

of life. A story of American man's progress in the face of adversity has recently come to light in the Valley of Tehuacán, south of Puebla. There, in rock shelters and caves, the accumulated litter going back to 10,000 B.C. has been sifted and studied. Its age at various depths was calculated by testing plant and animal remains, such as charcoal from campfires and bits of charred bone. The older the sample, the less radioactive carbon is in it to make the Geiger counter click.

At the very bottom of the diggings are the leavings of early hunters who stopped to dine on birds, rabbits, and turtles. That is about all they ate for three thousand years except when prickly pears were in season. At a higher level are the remains of wild plants, including chili peppers, and the stones on which they were ground. Then, about 6000 B.C., traces of cultivated plants appear, like squashes and avocados. Man in America, with no apparent help from the Old World, had learned for himself the secret of producing food by planting seeds. Or maybe it was woman. Because for two or three thousand years cultivated foods were only a small part of what people ate. You can picture Mamá minding the babies and tending a garden, while Papá grubs for wild roots or sits in camp devising better snares and traps and waiting for the big game to come back, as surely it will if only the medicine man can improve his hunting magic.

Papá does not realize that he is destined to be a farmer. He still moves from camp to camp with his family or in a small band as the flowers blossom and the wild seeds mature.

Gradually, though, more plants are domesticated, and he is not so footloose. He is more sociable, too, since various families camp together during the growing season. And they are piling up possessions: baskets, mats, carrying nets, stone tools and vessels. About 5000 B.C. comes the great event that will lead surely, though not at once, to a settled life. A wild grass with an ear no longer than your little toe is domesticated. It carries a few dozen loosely sheathed grains and is the ancestor of Indian corn.

Thanks to Tehuacán's dry climate, a series of corncobs has been preserved. Through the centuries the ears grow larger, showing the results of seed selection and skillful crossing. The new plant spreads far and wide from where it was domesticated, which may have been hereabouts, since no older remains have been found. It changes the Indians' way of life so completely that myths in later times will say that man was not truly man until he was clothed in flesh of corn. The excavations tell the story less poetically. After 3500 B.C., tiny clusters of pit-houses — crude shelters, half underground — appear in the Valley of Tehuacán. These are hardly villages yet, but people are striking roots, like the corn they've tamed. They have gentle American dogs now and eat good black beans from heavy stoneware. A thousand years later they begin making clay pots and dishes. By its changing styles, pottery furnishes clues for dating objects with which it is found and for tracing routes of trade and travel. So do the little clay figures of women with elegant hairdos that appear after a few centuries. No one is sure why they were made: perhaps to be planted in the fields, in the belief that woman's power to bear children would also make the corn sprout.

It is clear, in any case, that the earth's fertility, on which life depends, must be quickened by water. Rain is sparse and uncertain around Tehuacán, so the cultivators go deep into the barrancas, push their digging sticks into the moist earth by the streams, drop in the seed corn, and cover it with their toes. In the last centuries before the Christian era, they succeed in coaxing water onto the drier soil. Irrigation brings about an increased yield of corn and new crops like tomatoes and peanuts. The population grows. Here and there a village raises a mound of earth for a temple platform.

Meanwhile another people, the Olmecs, have found out how to raise corn on the wet coastlands of Tabasco and Veracruz. The Papaloapan and the Grijalva are the Nile and the Euphrates of the New World, laying down rich silt year after year. And there is more cropland in the forest for the trouble of girdling the trees with stone axes, burning the brush, and planting in the ashes, though under this system new land must be cleared after a few seasons. The Olmecs imagine themselves to be descended from jaguars. This fierce cat is a symbol of the power of earth and water and the power of command over men. They paint his spots, claws, and eyebrows on their pottery. The human figures they carve in precious blue jade have the jaguar's swollen eyes and puckered baby mouth.

The Olmecs, such gifted gem-cutters and sculptors, find their stone far from their swampy homeland. As traders, or perhaps as warriors or missionaries, they plant colonies and spread their jaguar cult among other peoples. Around 800 B.C. they introduce their fashions to Tlatilco, in the Valley of Mexico, as shown by pottery figures of that time. Being well dressed calls for body paint and tattooing, ear and nose jewels, filed teeth, necklaces, bracelets, and anklets, sandals, and turbans, and a head that, in infancy, was pressed between cradleboards into a stylish shape. Clothing is just coming in: ribbons and tight skirts for women, breech-clouts for men. A ballplayer is well padded against the solid rubber ball that the opposing team will return with hips and elbows, no hands allowed. Here is a magician in a bird mask with a serpent's tongue. You all but see him leading a rain dance, followed by luck-bringing hunchbacks and musicians with drums and rattle-sticks. Looking on are the country folk, drawn into bonds of tribal brotherhood by the familiar ritual. A ceremonial center, one of many, is in the making.

The Olmecs are building a great ceremonial center at La Venta near the Tabasco coast. It takes a million days of work to carry the earth for the temple-pyramid, tall as a ten-story building, and the mounds on the plaza. Even more astonishing are the carved altars and colossal stone heads, some weighing forty or fifty tons, for the blocks of basalt from which they're made must be floated on rafts from a great distance. Into the center goes the sweat and toil of corn-growers from many villages, including their womenfolk, coming to bake them tortillas or prepare a nourishing gruel.

Someone, of course, is in charge of the works. In the early stages, it may be our friend the magician. Soon, though, he's so busy that he not only stops growing his own corn but needs full-time helpers. He is on his way to being a priest with a temple organization. His successors have even heavier responsibilities. The planting ceremonies grow more elaborate. And there must be keepers of the granaries, master builders and stonecutters, and someone to make sure each village gives its full share of labor and corn. Call him a tax collector.

This is more or less how ceremonial centers became seats of government, the kind of government my teacher calls a theocracy. Priests came to speak with more authority than village elders and to call on them for work brigades. As the centers grew more splendid, the quotas were larger and the calls more frequent. When not raising corn, the peasants were working for the glory of the gods and the good of the state. How willingly they responded we do not know, but they built temples, palaces, and irrigation works too large for a single village to undertake. The granaries bulged with corn. Clever artisans could devote themselves wholly to their crafts, working for the temple or selling their jewels and fabrics to traveling merchants. They also bartered with the peasants, who always brought produce with them to the center, as they still do in all the towns where Sunday is market day.

It is hard to imagine a marketplace without counting. Up in the temple, affairs were even more complicated. There were tallies to be kept of men at work and loads of corn received. The priests recorded the phases of the moon and the course of the sun. They told the peasants when to prepare the soil and when to plant and harvest. Counting was not enough. They had to have written numbers.

Numbers were being carved on stone six or seven centuries before Christ at Monte Albán on a beautiful mountaintop in Oaxaca. They are still there and easy to read: a dot stands for 1, a horizontal bar is 5. With them are calendar signs and hieroglyphs which can't be read but show that writing had already begun. The people of Monte Albán were related to the Olmecs, at least in their culture. Three or four centuries before Christ, La Venta was destroyed, but Tres Zapotes, in neighboring Veracruz, remained a ceremonial center and there, on a monument, a recognizable date has been found. It consists of four dot-and-bar numbers, one above another, and if the experts have read them right, they stand for September 2 of the year 31 B.C.

The Olmec culture became the mother culture of Indian Mexico. Teotihuacán, here in the Valley of Mexico, with its sun and moon pyramids, was in touch with Monte Albán and with the Mayas in the Guatemala borderlands. These and other cultures borrowed from one another and gave rise to the Classic Era, a time of such beauty and elegance that there are scholars who believe that voyagers from China and India must have had a hand in it. But the majority opinion is that the Indians, having come so far since their elephant-hunting days, were perfectly capable of building their own civilization and did so wholly or in large part.

The wise men of those days, trying to understand and control the forces of nature, put pictures together and created elaborate symbols. You may have seen pictures of a pyramid at Teotihuacán from which stone serpent heads are emerging — rows of serpents, as if to multiply their magic power. Each serpent has a ruff of feathers and the fangs and ears of a jaguar. What does this jaguar-serpent-bird combination mean? It's hard to be sure but reasonable to suppose that the jaguar is the powerful earth, joining with the serpent of rain clouds and flowing water to put forth vegetation as precious as the green plumes of the long-tailed quetzal.

Later, at Teotihuacán, the germinating power of water was personified as the rain god Tláloc. Temple wall paintings show him with traces of his past: jaguar teeth, serpent-ringed eyes, and billowing plumes. Nevertheless, he looks more human than otherwise. Raindrops fall like gems from his hands. People bring him offerings of doves and turkey eggs, as if seeking the favor of a great ruler. Priests in rich robes sing his praises. Hymns pour from their lips in the shape of scrolls edged with jewels.

Under cactus thickets, not far from the temple-lined main avenue, archaeologists are finding the remains of palatial homes with terrace roofs, open vestibules, and painted walls. They are grouped around sunken courtyards which were kept dry by means of underground drainage channels. One-story apartment buildings of masonry, with as many as 176 rooms and patios besides, seem to have housed tradesmen and lesser officials. At the edge of the city were peasant huts. Yes, Teotihuacán was a true city, the first great city of the Americas, perhaps, with an estimated population of one hundred thousand in A.D. 350, equaled by few cities in the world at that time. We are impressed by the sculptured pillars of the Butterfly Palace and the remains of paved streets and plazas, but the Indians had their own idea of what a city was, as expressed in a poem of later days:

> *Drums were set up*
> *And there was singing.*
> *They say that is how cities began:*
> *When there was music in them.*

To feed so many people, Teotihuacán drew upon the resources of a vast region by more or less peaceful means. Few warriors, at any rate, were painted and carved in these times, and many gods — corn gods; gods of flowers, music, and springtime; the bearded fire god of the three-stoned family hearth, and the earth goddess, who was the mother of gods and men.

Strangest of all were the Maya gods, carrying days, years, and other bundles of time on their backs like baskets of cocoa beans. No one in Europe had measured the year as accurately as the Maya priests in their temple observatories along the tropical rivers of the southeast. Its length, by their calcula-

tion, was 365.242 days. But they did not express it in our ten-
finger system. They used a "whole-man system" of fingers
and toes that went by leaps from 1 to 20 to 400 to 8,000.
They wrote their numbers in vertical columns, using dot-and-
bar digits. Any digit was worth twenty times as much as the
same digit in the position below it. Since an empty position
would be as confusing as leaving the zero off 10, they filled
the space by drawing a shell. They were using this zero sign,
so useful in arithmetic, ages before the Arabs brought the
idea from India to Europe.

A Maya day had two names. It might be Three Dog in the
260-day ceremonial calendar and Eight Zip in the sun calendar of 365 days. After fifty-two years, another day would
have the same double name. Similar systems were in use all
over southern and central Mexico, but the Mayas went to
astonishing lengths in their search for interlocking cycles.
Sighting the planets through a notch in a pair of crossed
sticks, their priests watched Venus return to the same position after 584 days. How exciting it was to learn that five
such cycles were equal to eight solar years! The priest-astronomers searched for hidden meanings in celestial ratios, com-
piled lists of lucky and unlucky days, and named the ceremonies due the gods to avoid sickness and famine. Their
search for the secrets of the universe, painted on strips of
bark paper, filled many books, of which only three remain.

But Maya writing survives in a thousand inscriptions on
monuments and temple walls. Some of the characters look

like human or animal heads, some are squares and ovals full of squiggles. Not even the experts can read them all, but they know that many have to do with religion, astronomy, time measuring, and the names of places and rulers. Some characters are simplified pictures, as of a knife or sprouting corn. Some are symbols: a precious jade bead means water. And some call sounds to mind, as you might draw a bee and a figure 4 for the word "before."

Maya cities and ceremonial centers rise on river terraces and hillsides or are massed around spacious plazas. Palaces and ball courts stand on raised platforms, while the temples are higher still, up the broad stairways of the pyramids. Inside the lofty sanctuaries are dark chambers that narrow to a pointed Maya arch. These were for priestly meditation. It was from below, where the people gathered, that the stone carvings, the stucco modeling in brilliant colors, and the crests of lacy stonework were admired.

One of these splendid centers is Palenque, built where the Chiapas hills dip toward the Gulf. About A.D. 700, a very important person was buried here in a secret chamber. Over it was built the Temple of the Inscriptions. In 1952, the crypt was discovered down a hidden stairway. Inside was a great stone casket. When the cover was removed, the big surprise was not the great man's remains but the jewels with which he was buried: a mosaic mask and a diadem, both of jade; a large jade stone placed in his mouth to serve as a heart;

bracelets and finger rings of jade, and a collar of nine strands with 118 jade beads.

No one knows the name of this very important person. But to be entombed so grandly, he must have been a powerful priest or king. And there were others like him. You see them in profile in sculptured panels, their sloping foreheads and aristocratic noses forming a straight line. They stand haughtily in their towering plumes, bearing the serpent staff of authority, while peasants lay offerings at their feet. These princely rulers, you suspect, have lost touch with the needs of their people. And times are no longer peaceful. Captives are pictured — abject figures, half as big as their captors. At Bonampak, deep in the rain forest, is a temple painting of a battle scene. Warriors are fighting with spears. They wear doublets of jaguar skin and helmets in the shape of fierce animals.

Trouble seems to have been boiling up everywhere. Teotihuacán was plundered and destroyed in the seventh century. The survivors scattered, some beyond Popocatépetl to Cholula and some south to Xochicalco and to other places. The Classic splendor of the Mayas continued in the southern forests until about A.D. 900; then no more temples were built, no more dates recorded. Was the burden of supporting too many very important persons becoming too heavy for the corn-growers to bear, so that they rebelled? Did warrior tribes pour in from the north? All we are sure of is that many blows were struck in anger. Temples were defaced and heads were chopped from images of priest-kings. Very unimportant people moved into Palenque, carrying their grinding stones into the temples.

Though the Classic Era was over, not everything perished. Long after Maya civilization collapsed elsewhere, the Mayas of Yucatán were still imploring the mercy of their snake-nosed rain god for their stony land. Up the Gulf coast at El Tajín was the late-flowering Totonac culture and a pyramid with as many niches as the year has days, forming sharp contrasts of light and shadow under the Veracruz sun.

In the tumbled mountains of Oaxaca, the Mixtecs were carving precious stones and learning to paint on deerskin. Some of their books still exist, and in them are real dates and real people with names. The earliest calendar sign corresponds to A.D. 692, when a chieftain's daughter was born on a day spelled out as Seven Flower. Following the custom, she was named for her birthday. Princess Seven Flower, the first person in our history whose name we know.

The three-way writing of the Mixtecs pictures events, ideas, and sounds. In the story it tells of Eight Deer Jaguar Claw, born in 1011, he comes through more alive than some Old World kings. Eight Deer wants to be a jaguar warrior, so he burns incense and undergoes tests proving his valor and endurance. He goes to Tula, where his nose is pierced for the turquoise insignia of his military rank. How splendid he looks with his spear-thrower, round shield, and gold breast-plate! He becomes a great chieftain, entertains merchants, plays ball with other rulers, travels over land and water, and marries the widows of his slain enemies. One of his wives is named Six Monkey. At the age of fifty-two, Eight Deer Jaguar Claw is captured in battle and sacrificed, a most honorable death.

It is interesting that Eight Deer went all the way to Tula to have his nose pierced. The city lay north of the Valley of Mexico on the edge of the desert plains, but its splendor was unmatched since Classic times, and its founder, the illustrious Quetzalcóatl, was of recent memory. Now Quetzalcóatl is a confusing name. It was written like Feathered Serpent and given to so many priests, gods, and natural forces that their stories are all in a tangle. But Quetzalcóatl of Tula was apparently a living man and is remembered in many an Indian chronicle. His calendar name was One Reed, and his father, they say, was Mixcóatl, who swept like a north wind into the Valley of Mexico and ruled from the Hill of the Star until slain by his evil brothers. One Reed grew up with his mother's family in the warm lands about Cuernavaca. He studied for the priesthood, perhaps at Xochicalco, and entered the service of Quetzalcóatl, a god who imposed many obligations of purity and penance.

One Reed added the god's name to his own, as was his right. Then he avenged Mixcóatl, as was his duty, and was called to rule his father's people. Tula was in its glory under One Reed Prince Quetzalcóatl. He taught the rude barbarians from the north to drink chocolate and to wear cotton garments in place of animal skins. He welcomed artists who could polish green stones and weave hummingbird feathers into shimmering patterns. Tula became a city of many peoples. Some had the rare skill of casting silver and gold and may have come from Central America.

Tula's golden age was painted in books, and its wonders grew as new books were painted in later times. The books were lost, though fortunately not before many of the stories that went with the pictures were put down in the alphabetic writing the Spaniards brought. Reading them now, we can imagine a white-haired Indian bending over a painted book, going from picture to picture, explaining what they mean. But he is speaking six centuries after Quetzalcóatl's reign, and the story has improved from many tellings. It was a time, as he reads it, when cotton burst forth in many colors, needing no dye, and an ear of corn was an armload, little ears being burned to heat the sweat baths. Man owed everything he knew to Quetzalcóatl: arts and crafts, the calendar, writing and painting, ceremonies, agriculture.

Why do we glorify the dead and fail to appreciate the living? I ask because the real Quetzalcóatl, the bearded lawgiver, had a host of enemies. The religion he brought from his mother's country was uncongenial to his father's people. They worshiped Tezcatlipoca, the Smoking Mirror, who read the secret of every heart in his polished disk of obsidian. On a few he bestowed honors and valor but to more he gave boils and the itch. He could take any form, and in his jaguar disguise he was the night sun, warming the underworld. It was as an old sorcerer that he came to Quetzalcóatl, according to a legend that must be an echo of religious strife.

Quetzalcóatl was not in his palace — rich in gold, turquoise, and rare shells — but in his fasting house, where he spent long days drawing blood from his tongue with a maguey thorn and taking cold baths at midnight. Tezcatlipoca found him here and held a mirror before him, saying, "I come to let you see yourself and know yourself." Quetzalcóatl saw the warts on his eyelids, and his sunken eyes and swollen face, and moaned, "If my people see me, they will run away." He covered his face with a turquoise mask. But it was no use. He could not hide from himself and broke into a song of lament. Tezcatlipoca meanwhile had sent for maguey honey and brewed a batch of pulque. He held out a cheering bowl, but Quetzalcóatl said, "No, I am fasting."

"Try it with your little finger," urged Tezcatlipoca. Oh, why did the good man let himself be tempted? That one sip led to five deep draughts, and then Quetzalcóatl summoned others, and a wild party was on in the house of fasting.

Imagine the remorse, the self-accusation, of the morning after! Quetzalcóatl had failed in the example he owed, and knew he must go away. Many followed him to the red and black land where day merges with night, and some say that on reaching the Gulf he sailed east on a raft of twined serpents, promising to return someday. But others declare that he built a funeral pyre and cast himself into the purifying flames and that songbirds rose from the ashes and his heart became the morning star. What history records is that Quetzalcóatl, or some of his followers, went on to Yucatán and built the great civilization of Chichén Itzá.

In the myths that filtered into Quetzalcóatl's story, he was the wind in a bird mask, a symbol of breath and life. He had robbed a giant's bone from the underworld and sprinkled it with his own blood to create the present race of men. And he had given them corn for their sustenance by turning himself into a black ant and going into the hiding place where the precious grain was kept. His name of Feathered Serpent could also be read as Precious Twin, and as such he was Venus, now the morning and now the evening star.

Maybe Quetzalcóatl was raised to the heavens because there was no room for him on earth. He was the last of the great priest-kings. It was time to make way for the warrior chieftains whose valor is exalted in the tall figures in battle dress that you still see in Tula. The figures marching across temple panels are warriors, too, processions of warriors in human form or as jaguars and eagles. And the broken columns that remain once supported the roof of a spacious hall where warriors met in a ceremonial fellowship more to their taste than lonely meditation in the dark.

What can a peace-loving Mexican say for these Toltec warriors? That they were drawn from the hungry north into a land grown soft on idleness and pulque. That they took tribute in feathers and foodstuffs but maintained order and promoted commerce and the arts over an area extending from Sinaloa to Yucatán and Guatemala.

All this is true, but add to it that Tula lived and perished by the sword. Internal dissension never ceased. It is written that Tezcatlipoca came as a seller of green chilis, who bewitched and married the king's daughter; that he came as a musician, inspiring such frenzy that the dancers tumbled into barrancas and fell on crags; that he lay as if dead in the marketplace, spreading pestilence, and strong men with heavy ropes could not budge him.

For such stories to be handed down, it must have been a dreadful time. And worse was to come, for the Chichimecs were pressing on the northern frontier. They were bow-and-arrow warriors of many tribes, though some spoke like the Toltecs and were in fact their poor relations. They came asking for land and offering to fight as mercenaries, but as their numbers swelled they poured through in war bands, taking whatever they found.

In the end the Toltecs were as spoiled by luxury as those who preceded them — or so it seems from the story by which their last king is remembered. His name was Huémac, and being fond of playing ball, he arranged a match with the little rain gods who ride the black clouds, sprinkling water from their pitchers and hitting them to make thunder. The loser was to pay a forfeit of precious gems and feathers. The players butted the ball back and forth with their shoulders and hips, and Huémac won. The rain gods, who were perhaps remote descendants of the Olmec jaguar children, came to him with the prize: a handsome ear of corn. Its pearly rows were precious gems sheathed in fine green feathers, as the king should have known. But he insisted on jade and quetzal feathers. "O.K.," said the rain gods, or words to that effect, but what they meant was, "You asked for it." They pelted Tula with hail till the stones were knee-high. They scourged the orchards with frost. Then for four years they passed overhead without even tipping their pitchers. Plants withered, stones fell apart. And the king who had despised corn fled to Chapultepec and hid in a cave.

The bow-and-arrow warriors, pushing southward, destroyed Tula late in the twelfth century. The upside-down stone serpents that had held up the temple roof with their tails lay in the dust, and the surviving Toltecs sought refuge in the Valley of Mexico beside the lakes and on the Hill of the Star. But the Chichimecs were not far behind. In the years after 1200, they overwhelmed the valley and imposed their rule on the towns. So many Chichimecs, and more always coming! Who in that upset thirteenth century had time to notice the arrival of a pitiful band of stragglers with dizzy ambitions, who called themselves the Mexica but are better remembered as the Aztecs?

WHO WERE THE AZTECS?

⊙⊙⊙⊙⊙⊙⊙⊙⊙   **4**

THE VALLEY OF MEXICO was so full of Chichimecs that no vacant land remained when the Aztecs came, dressed in the fibers of the desert. They were not welcome. "Everywhere they were reviled, nobody knew their face," says an old chronicle.

The Aztecs had been wanderers for many lifetimes. Though known sometimes as "water Chichimecs," they did not really belong to the club. Their legendary ancestral home was Aztlán, off somewhere in the northwest among the lagoons, and that is why we call them Aztecs. But they called themselves Mexica, or Mexicans, and have given their name to our country. They were more civilized than they seemed. During their long migration, their scribes recorded the years in proper calendar signs. They noted down in phonetic picture writing the towns through which they passed, many of which are still there, bearing the same names. No ordinary Chichimecs had such learning. Perhaps the Aztecs were returning to the land of their ancestors, abandoning a frontier that had been settled in Classic times and could no longer be held against the advancing barbarians.

Anyway, they had the gift of adaptability. During frequent stops of a year or more they turned to farming. If they paused by a lake, every Aztec knew how to float in among the ducks with his face hidden under half a gourd, and grab one by the legs. Sometimes two. And he hunted like a Chichimec, going with bow in hand, always looking, while his wife followed, laden with gear. In camp, he stood well back from the barbecue pit, for smoke hurt his eyes and might expose him to the humiliation of having to shoot a second arrow at a rabbit.

Chichimec war bands laid claim to the land, and the Aztecs hated to share their plump tomatoes and roasting ears with some chieftain for his consent to use it. This they called tribute. Rather than pay, they moved on, or they paid in warrior fashion, helping one chieftain fight another. When not fighting strangers, they quarreled among themselves, for at first they were not so much a unified tribe as a loose group-

ing of separate clans, traveling together for safety in dangerous times. A legendary moon priestess made them a lot of
trouble, sending her scorpions and centipedes to bite tired
warriors in need of rest. Maybe she was only performing
planting rites. We don't know her side of the story, for it was
the sun people who won out and later painted the pictures.
They were followers of Huitzilopochtli, a great chieftain
who became a god. His name means Hummingbird on the
Left. To the poetic Aztecs, that was another way of describing the resplendent sun, bearing to the south of the Mexican
sky.

Though short of stature, Huitzilopochtli had a grim mouth
and a glaring eye. Four warrior-priests bore his figure over
crags and gullies in a little house. He spoke to them in
dreams and promised that the wanderers should have a
home, along with precious stones and feathers, gold, chocolate, and cotton. But he added this warning: "It will cost
sweat, toil, and blood, much blood, and they must obey me
alone."

On the journey, the moon people were intimidated or left
behind. Huitzilopochtli was in full command when the tribe
neared the valley. On the Hill of Serpents, he was born as the
sun, youngest child of Coatlicue, mother of the gods. His
sister, the moon, and his brothers, the stars, were jealous. So
jealous that they put on battle dress and charged up the hill,
paper streamers flying, copper bells at their ankles, bent on
slaying him and his mother, too. But they'd picked on the

wrong baby. Huitzilopochtli, in blue and yellow war paint, hurled a fire serpent and struck off the moon's head. Then he took after the stars. Four times he pursued them round the hill. As they fell, pierced by his shafts, he stripped off their bells and streamers and made them his own. A younger brother's sweet revenge!

When a wise Indian retold this story from an old picture book, four hundred years ago, some Spaniard must have wondered how Huitzilopochtli could be born after he'd already led his people halfway across Mexico, because the narrator explained, "Huitzilopochtli was born again, after the other times he was born, because being a god he could do as he pleased."

To thirteenth-century Aztecs, it was plain as day that the sun is born anew each morning after struggling with night. He was the invincible father of a tribe that had been hardened like a planting stick in the fire. They came into the valley as brothers, lean and wiry, tough, frugal, able to hunt, fish, farm, and fight.

The Chichimecs, as we know, were already there. Some of them were now sleeping in houses instead of caves and eating tamales in place of raw meat. Who had taught them these social graces? Their wives, naturally, Toltec girls of aristocratic old families. The children of these unions had their mothers' refinement and their fathers' audacity and were fast taking over the rule of the valley.

The unwelcome Aztecs speared salamanders in the northern lakes and furtively grew a little corn. After some years, they ventured south to Chapultepec, a wooded spot with a running spring that seemed like the promised home. Huitzilopochtli, however, sent down word: "This is not the place, though it is near. Meanwhile, prepare for trouble."

Trouble came in the shape of the magician Copil, son of the moon priestess. He came to avenge slights and wrongs to his mother and went around telling everyone that the Aztecs were stealers of women. At Huitzilopochtli's command, a priest ambushed Copil on an island near the present airport. He cut out the troublemaker's heart and hurled it as far as he could. It splashed down near the present National Palace. A good throw.

But Copil had done his work. The valley towns, fearful of the Aztecs' growing strength, united their forces and overwhelmed Chapultepec, leading prisoners away for slavery and sacrifice. Some were sent to perish in Tizapán, a horrid place crawling with rattlesnakes. But when next heard of, the Aztecs were having a fiesta and the snakes were bubbling in their cooking pots.

The king of Culhuacán hired the hardy Aztecs as mercenaries and sent them against Xochimilco, where they vaulted over ditches on staves and pursued the lake dwellers from seedbed to seedbed. Such feats won them respect. They began marrying Culhuacán girls and moving from the snake pit into town. Better for the children, they said.

Better for them to grow up as little Toltecs? Huitzilopochtli was not pleased. He had another destiny in mind for his people and brought about an irreparable break between them and Culhuacán. Exactly what happened is not clear, for we are barely coming out of myth and legend into the light of history. One story is that Huitzilopochtli's priests asked the ruler for his daughter to be their goddess. The king, though he should have known better, let her go. Poor girl, she was taken to Huitzilopochtli's temple and flayed, and a priest put on her skin and danced before her horrified father. My friend Carlitos, a medical student, doubts this. You can skin a coyote or an ocelot, he says, but not a princess.

Anyway, the Aztecs fled Culhuacán in a rain of arrows and hid in the reeds of Lake Texcoco. The warriors lashed their shields together with lances to make rafts for the women and children and made their way north through the shallows. They floundered in the ooze and halted on mudbanks to quiet wailing babies and find firewood and food.

After weary weeks of this, a pair of scouting priests waded through a canebrake and found an island with a spring running swift and fresh under leafy trees. Huitzilopochtli spoke to them that night. They had seen the place where Copil's heart fell when cast into the lake. It was the home he'd promised his tired people — and he gave a sign by which they would recognize it.

Next morning the priests led the way to the lovely spot. They came upon a nopal cactus, rising from a stony mound and spreading like a tree, heavy with heart-shaped prickly pears. Aloft an eagle grappled with a serpent, like the sun with darkness.

This was indeed the place! The Aztecs wept for joy and named it Tenochtitlan, meaning "by the hard prickly pear." This, by tradition, is how our capital was founded in 1325 and why our flag bears the eagle and the serpent.

Gratefully, the Aztecs built Huitzilopochtli a hut of sticks and mud. As soon as they could trade birds and fish in the lakeside towns for stone, lime, and wooden beams, they erected a more fitting temple. From this *teocalli,* or god house, they marked off a wide straight road in each of the four directions. The watercourses of the low-lying island, and the footpaths beside them, became the lesser streets. Freight moved by canoe, and every house and hut had its boat landing.

Those who had traveled together lived side by side in clan neighborhoods, though some settlers were dissatisfied with the land assigned them and moved to the neighboring island of Tlatelolco. The elders of each clan chose a "grandfather" to teach the young men and an "elder brother" to keep land records and assign community tasks. Everyone owed some service, like dredging the canals or cultivating the fields that supplied grandfather and elder brother with provisions. And everyone had a right to a piece of land for a corn patch and an orchard. It was necessary to take land from the lake. The new fields spread out in "floating gardens" as the roots of slender willows anchored mud-covered mats in place.

From behind their natural moat, the Aztecs kept an eye on their powerful neighbors. Texcoco was rising on the eastern shore of the lake as the Chichimec capital. To the south was the unfriendly Culhuacán from which they'd fled. On the western shore, and very near, was Azcapotzalco, ruled by wily Tezozómoc. The Aztecs needed his friendship. They sent him canoes laden with frogs and marsh-fly eggs, calling them gifts, a nicer word than tribute.

Tezozómoc liked these delicacies but preferred military aid, and the Aztecs did not mind helping him add Culhuacán to his growing city-state. For this and other services they were allowed to elect their own kings. Acamapichtli, Tenochtitlan's first king, was descended from Quetzalcóatl. His royal blood raised Tenochtitlan from a fishermen's hideout to a recognized city whose bravest warriors could aspire to the jaguar and eagle brotherhoods. But it was far from wealthy. The best houses were of adobe, and the king himself wore coarse maguey. His son Huitzilihuitl went courting a Cuernavaca princess and was rebuked by her father for not wearing cotton. He won the girl, anyway, and when he was king, after his father's time, he campaigned with old Tezozómoc, and they made Cuernavaca pay a tribute in cotton and were able to dress better.

Huitzilihuitl had many wives, as was his duty, it being good public relations to form alliances with other ruling houses. He married, among others, Tezozómoc's favorite daughter and, while the old man lived, Tenochtitlan's tribute was very light. Chimalpopoca, the next king, was either their firstborn son or Huitzilihuitl's kid brother. Authorities differ, as they do on other royal relationships. At any rate, Chimalpopoca came to the throne as a child and ruled with Tezozómoc's favor and protection until the old man died in 1427, at the age of a hundred and something. Two sons wanted to step into the great man's sandals. Chimalpopoca backed the loser and paid with his life. Maxtla, the winner, then imposed a staggering tribute on Tenochtitlan.

The freedom, the very existence of the city was at stake. Some hoped to soften the tyrant's heart by going before him in procession, carrying Huitzilopochtli. Some wanted to flee from the marshes. In this crisis, Itzcóatl was called to the throne. He stood in the royal line on his father's side, but his mother had sold vegetables in the market. This did not matter now. He was needed for his valor.

Two of his nephews also were destined for fame. Tlacaélel undertook a dangerous mission to Maxtla. He offered peace and, that failing, performed the ceremony of declaring war. This consisted of dressing his enemy's hair with feathers and anointing him as one does the dead. Then they exchanged arrows and shields, and Maxtla let Tlacaélel out a secret door so he could go safely home — a courtesy that even a tyrant owed a brave foe.

Moctezuma, the other nephew and the first of that name, was the son of the Cuernavaca princess who'd made cottonwear fashionable. She must have been proud when they told how he marched against Azcapotzalco and saw the enemy massed from the shore to the hills, shields gleaming, tall in their plumes. At his command, his men rushed upon them, whistling, yelling, closing in combat. Now they surged forward, now they were pushed to the water's edge, but when Moctezuma felled the opposing commander with a mighty blow, Maxtla's army melted away. The Aztecs found the tyrant cowering in a sweat bath and cut him down. Some said Moctezuma himself delivered the blow that made Tenochtitlan free and independent.

This was the story they liked to remember. Actually, the struggle was long and hard, and Tenochtitlan received help from over the lake and beyond the volcanoes. Leading the allies was Nezahualcóyotl, Texcoco's rightful king but a fugitive since that dreadful night when he was a child hiding in a tree and saw his father slain by warriors from Azcapotzalco. They were after him, too, and he grew up like a hunted animal, owing his life to villagers ready to hide him under a pile of husks or a fiesta drum. Having so many friends, Nezahualcóyotl was of great assistance to the Aztecs.

When victory came, Nezahualcóyotl and Itzcóatl pledged themselves to work together in peace as in war. Joining with Tacuba, they organized the Confederation of Anáhuac, meaning "around the water" — a league of independent city-states, one in the lake and one on either shore. Tenochtitlan, however, spilled over onto the mainland where Azcapotzalco lay in ruins. There the clans received small strips of land and the war heroes, larger ones. The biggest piece was put in the king's name to help meet the expenses of the palace. You can see in the paintings that Itzcóatl is not like the rulers before him. He sits on a throne of woven straw, robed in celestial blue, and wears a turquoise diadem that rises in front to a golden peak. The speech scroll coming from his mouth means he's the speaker. He speaks for the great men who sit in council, deciding what shall be done. He's like a king, but Tlacaélel is a sort of chief justice and prime minister, sitting at his elbow and counseling him.

Under Itzcóatl, and then Moctezuma I, temples and stone palaces rose. Causeways were built to the mainland, with openings for canoes, spanned with light bridges easy to remove in case of invasion. It being a rule of the Confederation for one city to help another, Nezahualcóyotl built a long dike in the lake just east of Tenochtitlan, with floodgates to pass high water and stop the backflow of salt water. They say he also designed the aqueduct that brought water from Chapultepec to the city's fountains, and planted the water cypresses that you see in the park today. He was the great engineer of his time and a poet who mused on the vanity of earthly treasure, saying, "Not for long are we here, only a little while."

But the sons of the war heroes were not philosophers. They clamored for copper bells from the Southern Sierra and Mixtec jewels cast in gold. Their wives wanted polychrome Cholula ware and Totonac blouses in butterfly designs. Merchants catered to these expensive tastes in a great market at Tlatelolco. For money the shoppers used pieces of cloth, quills of gold dust, and T-shaped copper blades. Cocoa beans were small change, and you could also drink them in a beverage.

Food had to be imported for the valley's growing population. In the years of frost and drought after 1450, the supply fell to a trickle. Granaries were empty, and the lake was fished out till hardly a water beetle remained. Coyotes prowled the city and vultures circled overhead in 1454, these things being pictured in the chronicles under the One Rabbit year sign.

The next year, Two Reed, marked the end of a calendar cycle. All fires were put out on a certain night, and the frightened people wondered whether the sun would ever rise again. Priest-astronomers kept an anxious watch on the Hill of the Star till the Pleiades reached their highest point, then jubilantly rekindled a flame. Torchbearers hurried over the valley with the New Fire. It was a promise of fifty-two years more of life and sunlight. That year the rains returned, but the rabbit remained in memory as a symbol of hunger.

People thought in symbols and talked in them. The blood you drew from your earlobe with a cactus thorn was jewel water. It came from the heart, that restless symbol of motion and energy. You nested the reddened thorn in grass and laid it before the temple as your tiny contribution to the force that moves the sun and the cosmos.

Even war's ugly face was veiled in poetry. A warrior was a dancing flower. His prowess was measured by the prisoners he took, not by the men he killed. The winning side gained many captives. But what should be done with them? Free them to fight again? Enslave them and fill the valley with dangerous enemies? No, let them be messengers to the sun. Place a banner in each captive's hand, paste him with eagle down, rub him with chalk until he looks like a god — and *is* almost one — and grant him the death he missed on the battlefield. Let him join the heroic dead in the palace of the sun and return as a hummingbird to sip nectar from flowers.

Another name for this is human sacrifice. Tourists ask us about it, and we like to oblige, but how much do we know for certain? It was long after the Spaniards came that the most horrifying of those tales of hearts ripped out wholesale on the sacrificial stone were told. Some were told by Indians, it is true, but did they relate what they had seen with their own eyes? As for the Spanish accounts, the later they were written, the bloodier they read. How much did the conquerors exaggerate to excuse their own cruelty? Only one thing is sure. When our Indian ancestors offered the gods the gift of human life, they acted in the same reverent spirit as all the Old World peoples who did the same not so very long ago.

When we come to the year Three House in the chronicles, we see a picture of water splashing against a face. This is a phonetic way of writing Axayácatl and is the name of a new king. He has a year-old son who is fated to rule as the second Moctezuma. Poor child, born on the unluckiest of days!

Axayácatl's immediate concern was Tlatelolco. His sister Jade Doll was unhappily married to the king of that neighboring city, who claimed she had bad breath and made her sleep in the kitchen. It's an old Mexican custom to take up for your sister, and Axayácatl did, though perhaps not for her sake alone. Two cities, Tenochtitlan and Tlatelolco, were growing where there was barely room for one. Each was set for war, but Axayácatl had better reports from the enemy camp, since sulky Jade Doll told him everything she knew. He struck by surprise, and the battle reached its climax on Tlatelolco's highest pyramid. There the two kings fought hand to hand, and Axayácatl sent his brother-in-law's body rolling down, the body of Tlatelolco's last king. Tlatelolco passed under military rule, and the two Aztec cities became practically one, though their old rivalry lived on. Axayácatl also made war on the Tarascans in the west, but they turned him back with their copper-tipped weapons and remained a hostile independent power. Another enemy, little Tlaxcala, lay to the east in the Valley of Puebla, tenaciously resisting absorption by Tenochtitlan and its allies.

Axayácatl, and after him his brothers Tizoc and Ahuízotl, adorned their city with monuments. Everyone knows the Sun Stone, that great disk carved with fire serpents, calendar signs, and the story of man — how he was eaten by jaguars, destroyed by hurricanes, pelted with hot lava, and drowned in a flood, but came back after each catastrophe and tried a little harder. The signs of these past ages come together on a sun god's face and form a diagonal cross. This is the Four Motion sign of our present age. It began when the gods leaped upon burning coals to give us sunlight and will end by earthquake, but no one knows when, for that depends on how we behave ourselves.

And then there is Coatlicue in her serpent skirt. Her feet are eagle claws, and her head, if you can call it that, is formed by two snakes rubbing noses. She wears a necklace strung with hands, hearts, and a skull with wide-awake eyes. Coatlicue is the sum of life and death. She pushes up the tender shoots and sends forth the sun, the soaring eagle; she gathers in the stubble and the eagle that falls. You might call her Mother Earth.

Sculptors worked in the Toltec tradition, adding their own bold vigor. Craftsmen fashioned jewels for noble ears, noses, chins, necks, wrists, and ankles. They made sandals for important feet from deer and jaguar skin. They embroidered the sash that a well-dressed man tied about his waist and loins, and wove feathers into the cape he knotted at his shoulder. Feather tassels dangled from his hair band, and when he wore battle dress cascades of feathers ran down his back. His father had been content with white heron feathers, gray eagle feathers, and black turkey feathers. But the fashions of the 1480's called for the hot-country touch. Searching for the plumage of the spoonbill and the quetzal, merchants "climbed up and down canyons and mountains on elbow and knee," in the words of an old chronicle, and circled the coast-lands as far as Guatemala.

The Confederation of Anáhuac now reached from ocean to ocean and from the rain forest to the rainless desert. In hundreds of valley shops, craftsmen made jewelry and fabrics for distant markets. Into the valley, by trade and tribute, came precious stones, metals, and feathers, as well as paper, incense, tobacco, warrior costumes, and rubber balls. Each of the founding cities — Tenochtitlan, Texcoco, Tacuba — had allies and tributaries among smaller towns, and they, in turn, took tribute from surrounding villages. Little federations, grouped around various valley cities, had a voice in the councils of the great Confederation. It is sometimes described as an empire based on conquest, but new regions were drawn into its orbit by trade treaties and marriage alliances as well as by war. Tribute was light when paid by friends and allies, but if an enemy town robbed a merchant caravan and refused to make the losses good until defeated on the battlefield, its land might be seized and the inhabitants forced to work on it as tenants. They were not, however, disturbed in their customs and religion.

The tribute that passed from lesser to greater places kept the machinery of government running. There were advantages in belonging to something bigger than a village or town. The Confederation built roads and dams, and preserved internal peace. Honest judges settled disputes over land boundaries and water rights. Doctors set broken limbs, cured battle wounds, and knew the uses of medicinal herbs.

Couriers carried messages between cities, and travelers rested in hostels, speaking the Aztec language and being understood wherever they went. In the Confederation of Anáhuac were the seeds of our nation.

Tacuba was famous for its crafts and Texcoco for its learning, but Tenochtitlan was America's greatest city. México-Tenochtitlan, it was often called, or just México, as it is today: a city of scribes, song composers, and public officials, of priests in god masks, and warriors who were walking jewels, and merchants who dressed plainly to hide their wealth from envious eyes. Beside the canals, the clan brothers still tended their gardens, but the "grandfather" now went to the palace daily to hear the king's pleasure.

In Eight Reed, or 1487, a new and greater temple was dedicated. A double stairway led up the pyramid to the sanctuaries where Huitzilopochtli and Tláloc lived companionably side by side, one drawing up moisture by solar heat, the other returning it as fruitful rain. Huitzilopochtli had grown tolerant as his people prospered. Around him, in lesser temples, were the gods of other places, all children of a supreme God who exists beyond time and space and, like night and wind, cannot be seen or touched.

Outside the sacred precinct were palaces, public buildings, and houses with whitened walls gleaming like silver, and terraces planted with flowers. Canoes glided through the city and over the lake. "México spreads out in ripples of jade, a quetzal plume shimmering in the light," said a poet. Poetry sought to speak true things in the language of symbols. In Eleven Rabbit, or 1490, Anáhuac's greatest poets gathered at Huejotzingo to search for the meaning of truth. Each was of a different mind, but all agreed that at least the hearts of our friends are true.

Then came Twelve Reed and Thirteen Knife, when "nothing happened," according to the annals of Tlatelolco, one of the places that kept a running record of yearly events. But something did happen on another small island, this one out beyond the Gulf of Mexico. There a bold explorer stepped from a Spanish ship and found himself among gentle and trusting Indians. "If anything be asked of them," he said in his report, "they invite you to share it and show as much love as if their hearts went with it." Already a dark thought must have entered his mind, because on October 12, 1492, he wrote in his journal: "These people are very unskilled in arms. With fifty men they could all be subjected and made to do all that one wished."

OUR SPANISH ANCESTORS

◉◉◉◉◉◉◉◉◉◉ **5**

WHO WERE THE STRANGERS who appeared in the New World in 1492 and after? Why were they able to conquer Mexico within a generation? To understand what happens during the next three centuries, we need to know them.

In the Spain from which they came, men once hunted the wild boar and the big-horned ibex. They painted bison and wild horses on the walls of their caves to bring themselves luck. Then around 7000 B.C., in Spain as in Mexico, the climate changed and big game became scarcer. In both lands, people turned after many hardships to farming as a way of life.

So far, the two stories are much alike. It was Spain's good fortune, however, to lie on the land and sea ways from the Near East, where Old World civilization began. Intruders, even if unwelcome, brought useful plants and animals and new skills. Compare them with the desert nomads who poured into central Mexico with only their empty stomachs, causing turmoil until their grandchildren were reconciled to raising corn.

Settlers moving westward on the Mediterranean shore planted vineyards and olives on the warm Spanish coast and sowed wheat on the high plains. They introduced wool-bearing sheep, milk cows, and oxen and donkeys to draw plows and carts. We had none of these in Mexico. It used to be said that the principle of the wheel never occurred to us. You have only to look at pictures of the toy animals on wheels that have been found to know that isn't so. What we lacked were wagons and animals to pull them. Our leather was deerskin. Sandals, a luxury here, came to mark a Spaniard as poor. Spanish horsemen became knights. Seagoing vessels carried Spanish tin to Near Eastern bronze foundries three thousand years before metalworking reached Mexico.

Our Spanish ancestors include native Iberians, Celts who came in from central Europe with iron swords, Greeks and Phoenicians who colonized the coast, and Carthaginians who opened silver mines in the interior but lost them to invading Roman legions.

The Romans spent several centuries conquering Spain and making it into a Roman province. Their historians wrote that the natives worshiped earth goddesses and bronze bulls and that some of them practiced human sacrifice. They told of tribesmen in the northwest who resisted to the last and who, when taken prisoner and crucified, died on the cross singing. For such people the Romans had two adjectives: heroic and undisciplined. They supplied the missing discipline, building roads, aqueducts, schools, and towns. They married local girls, and their sons spoke Latin and became Roman citizens. Two thousand years later we speak a Latin language and are Latin Americans in our own Indian way.

Two faiths became deeply rooted in Spain: that of the Jews, recently scattered from their homeland, and Christianity, nourished on the blood of martyrs. When Rome declined, the Visigoths, a Germanic war band, invaded Spain and became a landed aristocracy. Though heretics at first, they found themselves unable to govern without the help of the Catholic clergy and entered into an alliance with the Church that was to have profound consequences in Spain and Mexico.

In the eighth century, Moors in turbans and robes came from North Africa and conquered most of Spain, bringing with them their Moslem faith. Anyone could become a Moslem by agreeing that there was no God but Allah and that Mohammed was his prophet — and Spaniards of weak faith did so to avoid paying tribute. But perhaps they should not be called Spaniards at this early date. The proud Spain that conquered Mexico was forged in eight centuries of religious war.

In the northwest, a handful of Christians resisted the Moors as their forefathers had defied the Romans. Rude and simple men, they herded pigs in the oak forests, harassed the enemy, and took refuge in caves. The hardiest were guerrilla chieftains and came, in time, to be counts, dukes, and little kings.

It was a Moorish custom to ride into battle shouting, "Mohammed!" At Compostela a bishop discovered the tomb known as that of Santiago, or Saint James the Apostle, and the Christian warriors used Santiago's name as a rallying cry. Some told of seeing a celestial figure on a shining steed, leading them to victory. Santiago Matamoros, they called him, Saint James the Moor Killer. The apostle had been a humble fisherman, but these were fighting times when bearded churchmen rode to war beside kings.

Among the Christian kingdoms emerging in the north was Castile, named for the castles from which men in mail rode to battle and to which they returned to feast and hear minstrels relate valorous deeds. No hero was more celebrated than El Cid. He wrested Valencia from the infidels and tossed his foes into a roaring fire. But he did not personally hate the Moors and had in fact served an emir in battle against a Christian count. It was not dishonorable for a fighting man to cross religious lines to earn his bread. The men in the castles wrote their own rules. "We are as good as the king, but he is richer," they would say.

The Moors of those times were in touch with the bright world of the Arabian Nights. They brought peaches and citrus fruits to Spain, raised cotton, rice, and sugar cane on irrigated land, and were the cowboys of their day, famous for Arabian horses. Their lace, silk, and leather were the finest, and their writing paper took the place of parchment.

At Córdoba, Moorish and Jewish scholars taught the old wisdom and the new sciences to students from Paris and London, and even to a future pope. But after Toledo fell to the Christians in 1085, the struggle entered a more bitter phase. There were raids into enemy territory to lay the land waste and to capture prisoners for ransom.

As Spain was reconquered, the desolated land was claimed by great nobles and knightly and religious orders, and turned into sheep pasture. Towns grew and prospered behind walls, enjoying the king's favor and supporting him in his quarrels with unruly nobles. They sent their representatives to sit with lords and bishops in the Cortes, or parliament. For the times, this was very democratic, but do not imagine there was one law for all. Nobles settled their disputes by duel. Churchmen were tried in their own courts. A poor man was tried by ordeal. If he could grasp a red-hot iron without being scorched, he was innocent.

In the thirteenth century, the Christians broke through the last mountain barrier and took all of Andalusia except Moorish Granada. The saintly Ferdinand III strove for reconciliation among Christians, Moors, and Jews, and was called the King of the Three Religions. His son Alphonso the Wise codified the laws and banned such punishments as tearing out an offender's eyes or pushing him over a cliff.

Strolling minstrels catered to a wider public, including townsmen and their ladies. They sang of El Cid, but now he was a Christian gentleman, charitable to lepers and nearly as fond of his wife as of his horse Babieca.

Knighthood came to full flower in the tales told of Amadís de Gaula, who went about slaying dragons on enchanted islands for his lady's love. If only real knights and nobles had been like him! Instead they grew insolent, defied the king, levied tribute on the peasants, and let their sheep over-run the fields on the drive between the summer and winter pastures. Poor boys abandoned the farm, took service under a lord, and robbed traveling merchants. But if caught, they were tied to a pole and shot with arrows. This sentence was carried out by the brotherhood which the towns organized to make travel safe. Town dwellers resented the king's failure to protect them and the high taxes he imposed on them while the lordly estates paid nothing. To silence protest, the king sent his own men into the towns and set limits on municipal self-government.

Fourteenth- and fifteenth-century kings remained on their unsteady thrones by playing one group against another. They married their daughters to neighboring princes and gave their friends noble titles. When friends proved ungrateful, they chose their counselors among lawyers and churchmen. The Jews had successfully raised money for the Reconquest, and to them went the unpopular job of collecting higher taxes. Then came the Black Death, claiming one Spaniard in three. The ignorant were ready to believe a rumor that the

Jews had poisoned the wells, and from that time on, the Jewish quarters of the cities were never safe from pillaging by mobs. Sometimes the victims were forced to choose between death and Christian baptism. Those who submitted were called New Christians but were always suspect, for who knows the heart of a man converted against his will?

Old Christians were anxious to prove their "purity of blood," so they would trace their family tree for a hundred years — but no further, or they'd surely find a Jewish or Moorish ancestor. People came to be tagged by their callings. Blacksmiths, stonemasons, and grocers were Moors. If a boy went into commerce or medicine, people would assume he was a Jew or at best a New Christian. It was safer to choose the career of arms or take holy orders.

Mistrust spread. A child's illness would be laid to the glance of an old woman who carried the curse of the evil eye, or to a spell cast by an evildoer who had signed a blood pact with the Devil. Death was a familiar figure. Wandering actors represented him moving in a ring of dancers, laying a fleshless hand on peasant, bishop, beggar, and king — a model of fairness in troubled times.

It was then that our Spanish ancestors learned to bear hardship with patient dignity. For every swaggering grandee there were many lean plowmen who made bread from stones, as the saying goes, and tireless women in black shawls who lowered their eyes from modesty, not lack of pride. These austere people had courtly manners and shrewd wisdom.

"Speak neither well nor ill of the great," father told son, "for if you speak well you lie, and if ill, you place yourself in danger."

Conditions were never worse than when Princess Isabella was born in 1451, a rosy-cheeked baby whose hazel eyes were to see more than was good for a child. She learned to embroider and to cast javelins at wild boars and — after her brother's sudden and painful death — to eat nothing until her taster nodded his approval. At eighteen she was married in great secrecy to Ferdinand of Aragon. He came to the wedding in a mule driver's costume, slipping by a gang of lawless nobles out to kill him.

As support rallied to the gallant couple, the crown of Castile was placed on Isabella's auburn head. The union of her kingdom and Ferdinand's marked the birth of the Spanish nation. The royal couple offered the hospitality of their court to the high-spirited nobles and pressed the invitation home by demolishing a few castles with siege guns. The guests could wear their plumed hats in the royal presence, joust at tourneys, fight bulls, and write poems in the fashionable Italian style. They could enlist for the coming campaign against Moorish Granada, but under royal command. No more private armies.

Isabella was determined to unify Spain. It was necessary, she believed, for every Spaniard to profess belief in the Catholic faith. Heretics were traitors, to her way of thinking, and to punish them she and Ferdinand established the

Spanish Inquisition. Its first prisoners were New Christians who claimed they were no longer Jews, but how could you believe them when they wore clean clothes on Saturday and never ate pork? Soon so many suspects were in custody that children began playing inquisitor and prisoner. The queen woke from a siesta one afternoon just in time to stop Prince John from strangling a playmate.

To keep the Church Spanish, Isabella insisted that Rome grant the crown the right to nominate bishops. She made Friar Jiménez de Cisneros, her father confessor, an archbishop. He was so true to his vows of poverty that he wore an itchy hair shirt under his rich robes and slept on the floor. At Granada, he rallied the men for the final assault, going on ahead with a silver cross and planting it on the Alhambra watchtower as a sign that all Spain was at last under Christian rule.

Marching in the victory parade after Granada's fall was a foreigner, ill at ease in his new clothes. For all his white hair, he was only thirty-seven, like the queen. They'd met before, Isabella and this tall man of the sea named Columbus, who wanted to sail west to a terrestrial paradise where unicorns guarded mountains of gold. Wise men had pronounced his ideas impossible and vain, but here he was again, asking for help. You may have read that Isabella pawned her jewels and gave Columbus his chance, but my teacher says that it was Ferdinand's treasurer, a man of Jewish lineage, who raised the money. While the arrangements were being made, professing Jews were on four months' notice to change their faith or leave Spain. Columbus went to sea on the tide that carried the last of them into exile.

When Columbus returned from the West Indies with his green parrots, golden trinkets, and frightened Indians, no one doubted that he had reached the edge of the Marco Polo country, where temple's were roofed with gold. Looking on at the Seville city gate was Bartolomé de las Casas, a teen-ager who was to write much of what we know about the great explorer. Columbus crossed Spain to pay his respects to the court and, while returning for a second voyage, passed through the western sheep country. Among the admiring throngs must have been Hernán Cortés, a rickety child who scarcely looked his seven years. He was a problem to his parents, always listening to the ballad singers and planning, despite his delicate health, to be a soldier like his Old Christian ancestors. At fourteen he was too weak to work in the fields, so they sent him to Salamanca to study law.

Hernán was a dropout after two years, and his exasperated parents decided he might as well seek his fortune in the Indies. They arranged for him to sail in 1502, but he tumbled from a high window while keeping an unchaperoned date, broke his bones, and missed the boat. The fleet that sailed without Cortés carried Bartolomé de las Casas, who was soon to be ordained as a priest. Cortés finally reached Santo Domingo in 1504, the year Isabella died, pleading in her will for justice and kindness to the Indians. An old friend told him how to get a plot of land, but the nineteen-year-old new-comer drew himself up proudly and said, "I came to seek gold, not to till the soil like a peasant."

For one man to be rich, many Indians had to toil constantly, washing gold from the stream beds. They quickly died of disease and overwork, yet every Spanish caravel brought a new flock of adventurers, all claiming to be of noble rank and deserving of Indians.

The search for Indians led on to Cuba. Cortés went there as secretary to the governor, Diego de Velázquez. Las Casas was chaplain to the conqueror Pánfilo de Narváez and carried to the grave the painful memory of a day when the Spanish soldiers fell without warning upon a crowd of curious Indians, killing many of them with the excuse that they looked suspicious and that the example would help to pacify other villages.

Both Cortés and Las Casas received grants of Indians. Cortés prospered, married, grew a beard to cover an ugly knife wound, and became mayor of his town. Father Las Casas was troubled in spirit. Was it not sinful to hold peaceable people in bondage? Convincing himself that it was, he freed his Indians and called on his parishioners, without success, to do the same. In Spain he pleaded so eloquently that young King Charles named him Protector of the Indians. To their defense, Las Casas devoted the rest of his ninety-two years, preaching, writing, working within the Dominican order, and risking his life in Chiapas, where he was bishop for a time.

There is a Las Casas monument by the Cathedral in our capital with this inscription: "Stranger, if you love virtue, stop and venerate. This is Brother Bartolomé de las Casas, Father of the Indians." We think that Las Casas does honor to the name of Spain for having awakened the consciences of so many of his countrymen and even of the king. Not all our Spanish friends agree. They say his harsh attacks on the conquerors started a "black legend" of Spanish cruelty that lives on in the English-speaking world. But we say conquest is always cruel. Have other nations a better record? "Only we Indians have a right to throw stones," says my teacher. She claims the Indians fared worse in English-speaking America than under Spanish rule. But please don't take offense. I didn't say it. She did.

I guess no nation can go back very far in its history without running into pirates and brigands. Today's Spaniards, so courteous and dignified, are not to blame for Cortés. He belongs to a time when Spain was full of idle soldiers and boys too young to have fought at Granada, but thirsting for glory, and when war against infidels was the high road to honor and wealth.

In 1517, an expedition sailing from Cuba to look for a fresh supply of Indians came upon the Mayas of Yucatán but found them too well armed to be subjected. The following year, another expedition explored the Gulf coast, trading glass beads for gold, and heard about México-Tenochtitlan, a fabulous city high in the mountains. Governor Velázquez then assembled ships and supplies for a great voyage of discovery and put Cortés in charge.

Never was a man so persuasive as Cortés, decked out in velvet and braid and wearing a big feather in his hat to look taller. To some he promised fame and glory; to others, land and Indians in a country richer than Cuba.

The governor's suspicious relatives warned, "This man will make away with the fleet and never come back." Velázquez tried, too late, to change the command. Cortés raced along the coast, signing on recruits even among those sent to arrest him. In February, 1519, he sailed for Mexico in command of eleven vessels, a hundred sailors, five hundred swordsmen, gunners, and crossbowmen, and sixteen horses that were to be worth their weight in gold.

TWO WORLDS MEET

⊙⊙⊙⊙⊙⊙⊙⊙⊙   6

TWENTY-SEVEN YEARS after Columbus came upon the New World without knowing it, Hernán Cortés rode into its greatest city and stood face to face with Moctezuma II. Such a meeting can never happen again unless it happens in space.

The story of these two men has often been told and goes something like this: Moctezuma mistook Cortés for a god and tried by gifts and enchantments to turn him away. But the little band of intrepid Spaniards scaled the sierra and boldly entered the Aztecs' island fortress. Moctezuma's nerve failed him and he gave over his treasure and his kingdom to the bearded men. His own people stoned him for his cowardice, and he died, a tragic figure.

The trouble with this story is that it nearly all comes from what Cortés said and wrote. He sent his king five letters describing the Conquest. In the first one, written from the Gulf coast, he promised to have Moctezuma "dead or a prisoner or subject to Your Majesty's royal crown." Cortés had made away with the governor's fleet but hoped by great deeds to be forgiven and richly rewarded. After winning fame, he related his exploits to his chaplain, López de Gómara, who put them in a book. Bernal Díaz del Castillo read it and boiled, for it glorified Cortés and slighted men like himself who had fought at his side. To put the record straight, Bernal Díaz wrote a "true story" of the Conquest, adding colorful details, as old soldiers do. But he was so tired and nearly blind that he copied Gómara more than he realized. And so, directly or indirectly, the story comes mostly from Cortés.

Until recently, no one paid much attention to the Indians' side of the story. Yet there are several accounts of the Conquest as they saw it or heard it from the lips of their elders and the traditions of their people. They drew pictures, wrote of it in Aztec and Spanish, and told their story to missionaries. Your Mr. William H. Prescott knew some of these accounts, but Indians were redskins and bad guys when his book came out in 1843. Today we can compare the Spanish and Indian versions and try to see the Conquest as it really was.

One mystery remains. Did Moctezuma, a warrior renowned for his bravery, really turn into a coward? An answer to this question would answer others. The clues, though few, are worth searching for.

Moctezuma was named for his famous ancestor. His name means Frowning Lord, an Indian way of describing the sun behind a veil of clouds. His upbringing must have been like that of others who attained high office. Custom was strong, and the proper things for parents to say and do were so well known that long after the Conquest, old men could repeat them word for word. Moctezuma's mother must have called him "little dove" and "quetzal feather," but it was Axayácatl's duty to be firm and give his son advice like, "Don't eat with all your fingers — only three fingers, and use your right hand," or "Be off promptly on errands; don't jump once like a toad and sit looking." When Moctezuma was ten or twelve, his father must have taken him aside to explain that he could not expect to live by his nobility alone.

"My well beloved son, more esteemed than any precious stone or rich feather," we can imagine Axayácatl saying, "take care to learn some honest trade like the plumary art and be sure to plant some magueys and fruit trees. You, my son, don't you like fruit? Where will you find it if you don't plant and raise it? Though our ancestors were rich, we do not inherit their wealth or power. No one who is haughty and discourteous is elected to high office, no one who says whatever comes to his mouth.

"Here in this world we travel a steep and narrow road and, if you wander a little to one side or the other, you will fall into a deep barranca. This world is a place of troubles, but so that we should not go about whining our Lord has given us laughter and sleep, food and drink, and the power of generation."

In every neighborhood there were schools for boys and girls, but Moctezuma probably went about with tutors who sharpened his powers of observation in the countryside and marketplace, and prepared him for college, that is for the Calmécac, "the place of sorrows where rulers are formed." There in the sacred precinct, behind the Wall of Serpents, he kept fasts and vigils, swept the temples, and placed smoking incense before the gods. He slept on a mat, exposed to the cold, or went alone at night to a mountain cave and drew blood from his tongue. His teachers sang the pictures that were painted on strips of cloth and flipped the pages of the books and made them speak. Repeating after them, Moctezuma memorized the deeds of men and gods, elegant metaphors, laws, and calendar computations. He danced in the fiestas, carried supplies to the battlefield, and left the Calmécac with a "wise face and a firm heart."

Then Moctezuma proved himself as a warrior. His rise was marked by the splendid costumes he was permitted to wear. At twenty-two he won fame on the Jade Coast of

the Gulf. As a result, Ahuízotl, the hardest-driving of all
rulers, gave him the command of the campaign that opened
the long trade route to Guatemala.

Ahuízotl died in 1502, and the electors met to choose a
ruler among his nephews. Moctezuma excelled them all in
virtue, judgment, and courage. His nose was pierced for the
amber rod; the turquoise crown was placed on his head.
Knowing his burden would be heavy, he prayed, "Grant me,
O Lord, a little light, though it be no more than the glow of
a firefly in the dark, to guide me in this dream of life that
lasts a day."

He was thirty-four, slender and sinewy, with a wispy beard
and grave but loving eyes. He could be stern or magnani-
mous; unfriendly writers make him vain and cruel. Cortés
wrote that Moctezuma never wore the same garment twice
nor ate from the same dish, and that six hundred great lords
attended him in bare feet. Six hundred other men tended
waterfowl in tanks of sweet and salt water and the birds of
prey, snakes, and wild animals that he kept in cages. Other
writers copied Cortés and added touches of their own: that
Moctezuma chose his food from among four hundred plates,
that he sipped chocolate from a golden vessel and smoked a
tobacco tube while jesters amused him, that he had three
thousand wives and dancing girls. Everything was believed
in Europe, everything but the incredible story that Moctezuma bathed twice a day.

Moctezuma must have found it just as hard to sift fact

from fancy as the first rumors of the coming of the Spaniards reached his ears. He was crowned in the year when Columbus, on his final voyage, seized a Maya merchant canoe off the Honduras coast and carried away the captain. Such an unheard-of event must have been talked about as far away as Campeche, where the Mayas traded with the Aztecs. It is hard to believe that Moctezuma did not hear of it or of the Spaniards who were shipwrecked in Yucatán in 1511 on a voyage from Central America. The uneasiness that these reports would cause may explain the omens for which these years were later remembered: a tongue of fire in the sky, an unseen woman wailing for her children, and a bird with a mirror in its head, in which Moctezuma was supposed to have seen armed men riding on deer.

By 1518, at the latest, Moctezuma's agents on the coast were sending him drawings of three-masted ships and bearded men in armor. Early in 1519, they picked up the trail of Cortés, perhaps in Yucatán, where two of the Spanish castaways were still alive. Cortés took Jerónimo de Aguilar aboard, but Gonzalo Guerrero refused to be rescued. He was a chieftain now and the father of three children. "Look how pretty they are!" he said — and we share his pride, for the children of Guerrero and his Maya wife were our first Mestizos.

What an amazing battle report must have come to Moctezuma from Tabasco, where the horses were taken ashore — the first horses to set foot on Mexican soil since the age of the mammoth! Cortés shouted, "Santiago, and at them!" and his horsemen scattered the Indians. Some of the Spaniards reported that Santiago himself led the charge, as he had so often in the Moorish wars. "It could be so," comments Bernal Díaz, "and that I as a sinner was not worthy of seeing him." For the Indians, the horses themselves were a miracle. They ate men, the Spaniards declared, unless restrained with bit and bridle. The Indians had no name for them but deer and no way to draw a picture of their neighing except as many little speech scrolls bursting like soap bubbles.

After receiving a peace offering of twenty Indian girls, including one who would be known as La Malinche, Cortés went on to the Jade Coast in his houses that moved on the water. It was the year One Reed, and this was Quetzalcóatl's calendar name. Did Moctezuma think Cortés was Quetzalcóatl, returning to claim his ancient throne? Most Conquest stories say he did. From Columbus on, it had pleased Europeans to imagine that the natives took them for gods. Why should Moctezuma be different? And if Cortés was a god, might not even the brave Moctezuma feel powerless to fight him? The Quetzalcóatl story explained what was otherwise inexplicable. Spanish and Indian writers picked it up and passed it along. Who am I to say they were wrong? I am duty bound, though, to report what the historian Ixtlilxóchitl, of the royal Texcocan line, wrote on the subject. He said that no one believed that Cortés was Quetzalcóatl except simple people and Toltecs.

In any case, Moctezuma was not one to fail in hospitality to a distinguished guest. He sent messengers to the Gulf coast with gifts worthy of a god. When Cortés dropped anchor, they paddled to his flagship and climbed aboard. Bowing reverently, they adorned him with plumage, jewels, and a turquoise mask. They piled rich gifts at his feet. "Are these all?" asked Cortés. The messengers replied, "This is all with which we came, our lord." Then Cortés, as the Indians tell the story, had the reception committee put in irons and the great cannon fired. He thrust swords into the messengers' trembling hands and challenged them to a tourney. "But we came only to welcome you," they explained, hurrying away as soon as they could and carrying as fearful a story to Moctezuma as Cortés could have wished.

The Spaniards went ashore on Good Friday and pitched camp on the dunes. Indian bearers came with food. On Easter Sunday, a high official called with Moctezuma's compliments and a chest of gold. In an Indian picture that has come down to us, Cortés sits with a long cloak covering his bowlegs, while at his shoulder, twice as tall, stands La Malinche. She is his invaluable "tongue," speaking two languages. Cortés says he is the ambassador of a great emperor and bears a message he must deliver in person to Moctezuma. The casta-way Aguilar puts his words into Mayan, and La Malinche translates them into Aztec.

Cortés knew that Moctezuma had his artists watching them, and put on a show. We have an Indian description of the scene — a stone ball leaping from a cannon in a rain of fire amid ear-splitting thunder and foul smoke that hurts the head; a tree blown into splinters, a hill falling apart; men in iron clothes, with faces of plaster and black or yellow eyes, borne on deer as tall as rooftops; dogs with floppy ears and blazing yellow eyes, gaunt bellies, tongues hanging out, panting, always panting, spotted like jaguars.

Cortés sent Moctezuma a red cap for a present, along with a wooden chair and a gilded helmet. But he asked for the helmet back, full of gold nuggets, because "we Spaniards suffer from a disease of the heart for which gold is the only cure." Moctezuma honored the request and sent for good measure a golden sun and a silver moon as big as cartwheels. He advised Cortés not to attempt the steep and tedious journey to his capital but did not actually forbid it.

Why such generosity and indecision? Did he hope the Spaniards would be satisfied and go away? Was he afraid, so afraid that, as one account has it, he cried out, "My heart burns as if immersed in chili sauce"? It could be he was stalling while taking counsel. Ixtlilxóchitl mentions a debate on the question of receiving the Spaniards. Moctezuma's brother Cuitláhuac advised him, "Don't admit anyone to your house who may throw you out." But Cacama of Texcoco said, "You have brave warriors to defend you in case of double-dealing. Let them come before they discover the secrets of the land."

Cacama prevailed, but it was too late to hide the secrets.

The Totonacs of the coast, who paid tribute to Anáhuac, already were pouring their troubles into Cortés's sympathetic ear. At his instigation, they cast off the burden and tied the tribute gatherers with wooden collars. They had only Cortés to protect them now. He, for his part, freed the prisoners, hoping Moctezuma would put all the blame on the Totonacs.

Moctezuma must have seen through this double game, but he may have been puzzled by the quarrel going on in the Spanish camp between those who wanted to return to Cuba and those like Cortés who were here to stay. Cortés encouraged his followers to found a Spanish city, the first in Mexico. They called it Veracruz and elected him their chief justice and captain general. He silenced his enemies by hanging two men and softening the hearts of others with gold. To make sure no one departed, he had the ships run aground and bored full of holes.

In the last days of August, they all set out for México-Tenochtitlan, except for a small garrison left at Veracruz. There were Totonacs to show the way from the tropical coast and carry the baggage in the driving sleet of the pass between the Perote badlands and Mount Orizaba. This choice of route must have dismayed Moctezuma, for it went by way of Tlaxcala, an enemy state. The Spaniards arrived there hungry and made no friends at first, for they raided the outlying villages, which, it happened, were colonized by Otomí warriors. During a skirmish, an Indian struck off a horse's head with an obsidian blade. Native historians make much of this event, which served to prove that horses were only mortal after all. But if Cortés fought a great battle with 149,000 Tlaxcalans, as he claims, they fail to mention it. Whatever happened, the rulers of Tlaxcala reached a fateful decision. They saw a chance to even scores with their old enemies in the Valley of Mexico, invited the Spaniards in and, amid feasting, became their allies.

Now that Cortés had the Totonacs and Tlaxcalans on his side, it looked bad for Moctezuma. And the news that soon came from Cholula made it even worse. Cortés had summoned the Cholulans to the temple courtyard, accused them of treacherously plotting against him, and ordered an attack on them in which three thousand perished. Moctezuma received pictures as frightful as the one you can see in the Tlaxcalan account of the Conquest, in which legs, arms, and heads are flying off and bodies are tumbling from pyramids.

Why Anáhuac's rulers let the Spaniards into the valley after this is hard to say. Perhaps it seemed easier to deal with them in the city, where the bridges could be removed, than in the open country. From this point on, Moctezuma's courage was put to a hard test. One account says that a band of sorcerers went to the mountain to head off Cortés with their magic and that Tezcatlipoca appeared to them as a drunkard and asked, "Why do you come when México is gone forever?" They turned where he pointed and seemed to see the city in flames. Moctezuma, hearing this, sat with bowed head and asked, "What can we do, my brave fellows, but face what may come and do honor to our Mexican line?"

The Spaniards passed between the volcanoes in a November snow flurry and enjoyed the warm hospitality of the valley towns rising from the lake. At the other end of a long causeway, the towers of Moctezuma's city shone in the clear autumn air. To Bernal Díaz it was like an enchantment in the book of Amadís. But to Cortés the towers were mosques, and the people he saw wore flowing garments like Arab burnooses. He was going, as it were, to the land of the Moors.

There's an Indian account of the procession entering the city. Four Spaniards rode ahead, scanning the rooftops. Dogs ran with noses to the ground, sniffing and panting. Swordsmen flashed their blades. Whinnying horses with bells ajingle bore riders with lances atilt and pennants flying. Harquebusiers went by with handguns. Crossbowmen with quivers of iron bolts tested and sighted their weapons. Cortés came with his captains around him. He was followed by Indians carrying crates and dragging cannon by ropes. Tlaxcalan warriors with feathered arrows brought up the rear, screeching and slapping their mouths. Into the city they all came, an astonishing diplomatic mission.

Cortés was the self-appointed ambassador of a Spanish king who that same year became emperor of the Germanies as well. Moctezuma ruled México-Tenochtitlan at the height of its splendor. They approached each other on what is now Pino Suárez Avenue. Cortés was coming in the wrong direction, as traffic flows today. A one-way street where two worlds collided four and a half centuries ago.

Moctezuma stepped from his litter, Cortés dismounted,

and they came face to face, or nearly so, for the pictures show La Malinche between them, arms folded and rather smug. She knew Spanish now, and this was her day.

"Are you not Moctezuma?" asked Cortés.

"Yes, I am he. You are tired from your long journey, but now you are in your city and here are your houses and palaces."

The Spaniards crowded round, staring at Moctezuma and clapping him on the back. Cortés took his hand, and they went with their entourages to the palace of Axayácatl, which was dressed in green boughs to serve as a guesthouse.

There are two versions of what happened next. The one you may have heard is that after some pleasant days of sightseeing, Cortés induced Moctezuma to move in with the Spaniards. There was the matter of an attack on the Spanish garrison at Veracruz to clear up. After the guilty Indians were brought to Tenochtitlan and burned in the plaza, Cortés treated Moctezuma with honor and respect and a deep friendship sprang up between them.

That is the usual story. But there's a strong Indian tradition that Moctezuma, and other leaders with him, were treacherously seized and put in chains at the very moment they were showing their guests into the palace. The story is not merely an Indian legend, there are hints of it in Spanish accounts. Brother Francisco de Aguilar, a onetime conqueror, did not deny it when a monastery companion questioned him long after, but said, "If it were done, it was for the security of the captain and his men." The custom of taking hostages, after all, was as old as the Moorish wars. But Cortés would naturally put the affair in a better light, knowing that men like Las Casas had the ear of the king.

If Moctezuma was an unwilling captive, trapped by a ruse, then it can no longer be taken for granted that he was a coward. We see him from November to June only through the eyes of his jailers. The Spaniards declare that he received visitors freely and continued to rule. But the Indians speak of cannons firing from the Spanish quarters. No one dared enter; it was as if a wild beast were there. A picture shows La Malinche calling down from the palace roof, scolding a man for not bringing food and fodder for those inside. She's cross and he's talking back, because the speech scrolls curl down.

Everyone knows the story of the sealed room with Moctezuma's treasure. It is opened, and Cortés says, "My men are a little mischievous, please don't mind." Moctezuma replies, "You are welcome to the gold, just leave the feathers." That is the Spanish version. The Indians tell it differently: you see Spaniards looting everywhere, crowding, shoving, tearing gold from shields and devices, "behaving like animals, so glad is their heart." And the precious green feathers they heap in a patio and set afire.

More treasure comes from mining expeditions, or by torturing captives, depending on what you read. It remains only to possess the land. Moctezuma is now convinced, Cortés informs his sovereign, that a great lord who formerly ruled the land has sent the Spaniards to take it back. So he calls in his vassals, and all swear fealty to the emperor of the land where the sun rises.

We do not have Moctezuma's side of the story. Did he first hope that the Spaniards would get their fill of gold, and leave? Did he later try to reach a peaceful agreement, realizing that stone weapons could not resist steel? Or was he a chained and defiant captive for seven agonizing months?

The long arm of Spanish justice reached out for Cortés in the spring. Narváez landed on the Gulf coast with a thousand men, a hundred horses, and orders to take Cortés to Cuba in irons. A formidable force, but Cortés had weapons of gold. He sent his agents ahead to soften hearts, then marched to the coast with part of his men, leaving the others with Pedro de Alvarado. The battle was quickly over. Poor Narváez lost one eye and through the other had the misery of seeing his men go over to Cortés.

Tenochtitlan was preparing for the fiesta that heralds the coming of the rains. The Indians, with Alvarado's permission, set up a figure of Huitzilopochtli in the temple courtyard: a paste of ground seeds spread over mesquite branches and adorned with the god's costume. Chieftains and warriors came for the traditional dance, unarmed and richly costumed. They were circling and swaying to a rising drumbeat when Spanish soldiers moved in. One of them struck off the drummer's hands, a signal for three hours of horror in which six hundred dancers were cut down and stripped of their jewels. A few hid among the dead, but the flower of the Aztec nobility perished.

The massacre touched off a desperate revolt, led by young warriors like Cuauhtémoc, hardly out of their teens. Sappers in relays battered the walls of the Spanish quarters and started fires. Darts and stones fell on the patios. Even with the reinforcements from the coast, the Spaniards could not venture from the palace without heavy losses.

Cortés had promised the men of Narváez showers of gold, and they had not a tortilla to eat, for the market was closed. Turning on Moctezuma, he exclaimed, "Go to for a dog who will not even keep open a market!" Moctezuma reminded Cortés that everyone with authority to remedy matters was a prisoner. Cortés then reluctantly freed Moctezuma's brother Cuitláhuac, who instead of opening the market took command of the besieging forces.

Years later, at a judicial hearing, one of the conquerors testified that about this time Moctezuma sent out word telling the warriors to attack the Spanish quarters without regard for the fate of the hostages inside. It may have been Cuitláhuac who carried the brave message.

So we have at least one bit of evidence that Moctezuma's courage had not failed him.

What did he say, if anything, when Spanish soldiers hauled him to the roof and ordered him to pacify the surging crowd below? I like to think that he remained silent. The Spanish version is that when he opened his mouth, the people booed and stoned him and he received a fatal blow on the head. But the Indians say that Moctezuma died by Spanish hands, strangled or stabbed. This was also the fate of the other hostages, as related by the friar Aguilar in his old age. Forty years had passed, but the old Dominican remembered a night when he kept watch on the palace roof and saw the bodies carried out and women with torches searching for their husbands and "raising such a wail it put fear in the heart."

That night, or one soon after, was the Sad Night of June 30, 1520, when the Spaniards slipped out under cover of darkness and rain, laden with treasure. They were making for the Tacuba causeway when a woman drawing water gave the alarm. A trumpet blast from the great pyramid summoned the warriors. "Come with your canoes and cut them off so that not one may be left alive!" cried a battle commander.

The fugitives carried a portable bridge with them but trampled it to pieces in the rush to gain the causeway. At the next opening, canoe-borne warriors closed in from both sides, showering them with missiles and climbing to the narrow causeway for toe-to-toe combat. The Spaniards had blades of steel but were weighed down with gold. Some fought with one arm, holding fast with the other to their yellow bars. Even when pushed into the water, they refused to let go, but as Cortés was to put it, "They died rich." Tlaxcalan bearers tumbled into the breach in such numbers that Spaniards passed over the bodies of their Indian friends, owing their lives to a seeming miracle. Cortés fought his way through and, circling the lakes, took refuge in Tlaxcala. He had lost more than half his army — and all of Moctezuma's treasure, he claimed, though Bernal Díaz never believed him.

The Tlaxcalans had so many sons to grieve for that they debated whether to receive their beaten allies or seek an advantageous peace with the Confederation. The young chieftain Xicoténcatl pleaded for a reconciliation of the two peoples, so alike in speech and customs, but his elders overruled him. They were still betting on the Spaniards.

After a month, Cortés was back in the field with more Tlaxcalans and a new strategy of conquest by encirclement. This audacious man was fond of comparing himself with Julius Caesar, perhaps with reason. But do not expect me, a Mexican, to paint our conqueror as a hero.

Tepeaca, on the road to Oaxaca and the Gulf, was the starting point of the campaign. From there, Cortés wrote to the Emperor Charles, likening the rugged highlands to a New Spain. Before opening hostilities, he observed the legal forms. While the Tepeacans stood among the corn and magueys, he had a proclamation read to them in a notary's presence. In a language they did not understand, he commanded them to submit to an emperor of whom they had never heard. Taking their bewilderment as rebellion, he gave the order for attack. Tepeaca was destroyed. The survivors — mostly women and children — were branded on the cheek with *G* for *guerra,* or war, and distributed as slaves to console the conquerors for the loss of the gold.

Fear of the branding iron forced every town to choose between heroic resistance and surrender. Cuitláhuac defended the Confederation and tried to hold the people's loyalty. But misfortune followed misfortune. Smallpox, unknown before the Spaniards came, swept Anáhuac in the fall. Many were left blind or with pitted faces, and many more died, Cuitláhuac among them.

Cortés was coming from the east with tens of thousands of Indian allies and mercenaries. On the last day of 1520 he marched into Texcoco. The loyalists fled over the lake, and he named a puppet ruler and prepared to close in on Tenochtitlan.

In these tragic circumstances, Cuauhtémoc was called to the throne. He had been in command at Tlatelolco. Now he undertook the defense of the city as a whole. Bernal Díaz describes him as gracious and handsome "for an Indian." The people called him Young Grandfather, as we do today. He fought knowing he must lose but affirming the will of our people to live. His name means Falling Eagle, and you might say he was the last Aztec and the first Mexican. He tried to unite the native peoples, friend and foe, against foreign invasion. It was too late, or too early.

Breaking the strong hold of custom, Cuauhtémoc prepared for a conflict that would go on day and night over many weeks on several fronts. He stored food and arms, sent the aged out of the city, deepened the canals, and had captured Spanish swords fastened to long poles for use against horses. He harried the Spaniards wherever they went and delayed the city's encirclement until May.

It was finally brought under siege by means of a fleet of thirteen single-masted, flat-bottomed scows. Cortés had them built in Tlaxcala, carried in pieces over the sierra, and assembled at Texcoco. He called them his brigantines. Fast sailers with mounted guns, they scattered the war canoes and commanded the lake. The invaders smashed the aqueduct, and no food or fresh water came into the city except in supply canoes slipping through at night.

Three Spanish columns advanced along the causeways under cover of the brigantines. Each cut had been converted into a deep pit with earthworks on either side to stop the horses. Stones rained on the invaders from every rooftop. By day they inched forward, demolished houses, and filled the breaches with rubble. But at night the Mexicans removed the fill and raised new barriers. Cuauhtémoc inspired them. He seemed to be everywhere, leading a silent raid one night and striking, the next, in the light of temple fires and the din of trumpets and drums. He knew the insults that would provoke the allies of Cortés into rash action and the sober truths that would cool their ardor.

"Go on, destroy the city!" the Mexicans would shout. "If we win, you will rebuild it for us; if the Spaniards win, you will rebuild it for them."

In mid-June, Cortés raided deep into Tenochtitlan. Horsemen with lances couched under the right arm rode through to the plaza and set temples and palaces afire. Alvarado was crowding in from Tacuba, and Cuauhtémoc was obliged to withdraw to Tlatelolco.

June 30 came. It was a year since the Sad Night. Cortés ordered the three columns to move simultaneously into Tlatelolco and meet in the great market. Cuauhtémoc sent the first wave rolling back into a street on which Cortés was advancing. The two Spanish forces collided at a poorly filled gap and tumbled into the water. The Mexicans were instantly upon them, peering through the jaws of animal-head helmets and swinging truncheons and clubs. Four grim Tlatelolcans laid hands on Cortés and dragged him off, a prisoner. By killing him right then, they might have won the war. In fact, by Indian rules the war *was* won, for the chieftain had been taken. But the Spaniards played by their own rules and rescued their captain. Upon withdrawing to bases outside the city, they found they'd lost eight horses, seventy of their countrymen, and who knows how many Indians.

So great was the defeat that many Indian friends abandoned Cortés. He was eighteen days preparing a new offensive, but time was on his side. His encircled enemies were gnawing roots and drinking brackish water. They were too weak to prevent a landing on Tlatelolco's eastern shore. The ring tightened. A story of the last days comes from the pen and lips of Tlatelolcans whose names we do not know. They exalt their own heroes and disparage the Tenochtitlan refugees who once lorded it over them and now huddled at their doors in the rain. But when La Malinche called out to the Tlatelolcans to lay down their arms and "let the others perish by themselves," they hesitated only a moment, for "we could not abandon them."

These narrators remember four horsemen circling the market and lancing the chieftains, and the fighting about the stalls where incense for the gods was sold. "We ate the stalks of the coral tree, we chewed marsh grass, lizards, mice, lumps of clay." As men died, women put on war insignia and pursued the enemy, clutching their skirts high. The defenders were pinned to such a narrow shoreline that some stood in water with their children on their shoulders. "We had no shields, no obsidian blades, nothing to eat, and all night it rained on us."

On August 13, Cuauhtémoc launched his last attack and became a prisoner. The Spaniards say he was taken in flight on the lake, but according to the Indians he gave himself up, hoping to spare his people more suffering. Brought before Cortés, he touched the hilt of the conqueror's dagger and said, "Kill me, since I can no longer defend the city." Cortés answered with loving words and promised him the honor due a brave warrior.

The three-month siege was over. Spaniards went among the pestilential ruins with linen cloths pressed to their noses. Our Tlatelolcan narrators picture the desolation: "litters of broken darts, tangles of hair, roofless walls spattered with brains, worms swarming, salty water stained with blood."

"Our heritage," they say, "was a net full of holes."

On the Plaza of the Three Cultures there is a plaque at the site where Young Grandfather held out for a way of life. It bears this inscription: "On the thirteenth of August, in 1521, Tlatelolco, heroically defended by Cuauhtémoc, fell to Hernán Cortés. It was neither a victory nor a defeat. It was the painful birth of the Mestizo people, who are the Mexico of today."

LIVING TOGETHER

⊙⊙⊙⊙⊙⊙⊙⊙⊙   **7**

Now I shall ride in a golden saddle!" shouted a horse-
man as Tenochtitlan fell. But when the booty was divided —
a fifth for the emperor, a fifth for Cortés, and more for expenses — his share came to eighty pesos. And he owed ten
times that much for his horse!

Where was Moctezuma's treasure? Everyone clamored to
know. Did Cortés have it hidden away? No one dared ask.
Did Cuauhtémoc throw it into the lake before his capture?
To find out, he was put to torture in Coyoacán, where the
Spaniards were staying. His feet were rubbed with oil and

held over a pan of burning coals. Beside him, the lord of
Tacuba was undergoing the same ordeal. He turned to
Cuauhtémoc as if the agony was too much to bear. Cuauhtémoc silenced him by asking, "Am I in a pleasant bath?" And
to this day no one knows what happened to the treasure.

Mexico's real wealth was its people. They alone could
redeem the extravagant promises of Cortés. So he gave his
captains provinces to conquer and consoled his men with
grants of Indian towns. It was the Indians, too, who built
Mexico City on the ruins of Tenochtitlan. They came from
many villages, bringing their food and dragging timber.
Seven thousand cedar beams went into a house for Cortés.
Where ten Indians were needed, a hundred were put to work.
They fell from trestles and were buried under falling debris.

For three years Cortés was governor of New Spain. The
emperor was putting down unrest at home, and it was no
time to quarrel with a man who was winning him a new
kingdom.

Cortés decreed that every Spaniard was to instruct his Indians in religion, keep horses and arms, and send for his
wife. If unmarried, he must marry. Cortés believed that every
man but himself needed a wife's steadying influence. His
own wife came uninvited from Cuba and died with marks of
violence on her throat, according to malicious tongues.

Power began slipping from his hands in 1524, when he set
off for Honduras to assert his authority. He took Cuauhtémoc
with him under guard but became suspicious of him while

wandering lost in the jungle and hanged him, "most un-justly," says Bernal Díaz. Cortés returned to Mexico City after two years and found his enemies in control. He appealed to the emperor and was put off with twenty-two towns, twenty-three thousand Indians, and the title of marquis. He found himself a highborn Spanish wife, built a palace in Cuernavaca, and had many sugar plantations, but his dreams were still of cities ripe for plundering. He searched the Gulf of California for Amazons, those fabulous women warriors, and looked in vain for a passage between the oceans that would open a way for conquering Asia. When not exploring, he was suing the crown's officials for meddling with his property. He took his grievances to Spain and died there, a disappointed man, asking to be buried in Mexico. His remains lie in a church by the spot where he met Moctezuma.

Among the conquerors who spread over the land, none tried harder than Nuño de Guzmán to outdo Cortés. He put Calzontzin, the Tarascan king, to horrible tortures for his gold and then cast him into the flames. Moving into the west, he conquered a region that was to be known as Nueva Galicia and founded Guadalajara, though not where it is now. He left a trail of blood along the Pacific coast as far as Sinaloa, then crossed over to the Gulf of Mexico and branded many slaves for sale in the West Indies, where the natives were now almost extinct.

It seemed likely that Mexico's Indians, too, were doomed.

Some had lost the will to live. One Spaniard's Indians, according to a story typical of those times, went into the woods to hang themselves. Their master found them tying ropes to the trees. "We are going to a better world," they told him. He said, "I will go with you, for I cannot live without my Indians." As he looked for a rope for himself, the gloomy Indians had a change of heart and decided that if the Spaniard would always be with them, they might as well remain in the present world.

There was once a general in your country, so I've heard, who said the only good Indian was a dead Indian. But to a Spaniard, the only good Indian was a live Indian. His Indians owed him tribute and paid it by cultivating his fields. The fates of the two races were linked. They had to find ways of living together.

The emperor also preferred live Indians. Dead ones were "a burden on the royal conscience" and brought forth books like *The Destruction of the Indies* by Las Casas that horrified good people in Spain. But live Indians paid a yearly tribute to the crown, unless given away so that petty conquerors could live like great lords. Charles figured that one Cortés was enough. Working through his Council of the Indies, he sent an Audiencia to New Spain to sit as judges, and a viceroy to govern in his name. He made wise and good laws for the protection of the Indians, but not even the great viceroy Antonio de Mendoza could enforce them all. When the conquerors heard that after one lifetime their grants of Indians would pass to the crown, they cried to high heaven that an ungrateful monarch was abandoning the sons of his most loyal subjects to the most absolute poverty. So exceptions were allowed, and some grants lasted two centuries. Tribute, however, came to be paid in money and grain. It was collected by the local Indian ruler. He was called the *cacique,* and he spoke for his people but dared not speak very loud or the Spaniard would name a new cacique.

The true intermediaries between the races were the missionaries. They taught the conquered new ways of life and worship, and reminded the conquerors that Indian and Spanish souls were equally precious. It was impossible to convince some Spaniards that Indians had souls, but they had bodies, no question of that, and the missionaries would ask, "If you finish with them, who will serve you?"

It wasn't easy, at first, to convert the Indians. Some of the early friars disputed with the Aztec priests after the fashion of European universities and were told: "Our ancestors taught us that we live by and through the gods. We ask them for rain so that the plants may take root and grow. We know to whom we owe life and how to pray. Do not make us do what will cause our destruction."

But the missionaries — Franciscans, Dominicans, Augustinians — were persistent and had been prepared in a strict discipline. "They go about poor and barefoot as we do," said the Indians. "They eat what we do, sit down among us, and speak to us mildly."

No one knew the Indian languages at first. But Brother Pedro de Gante noticed how quickly Spanish and Indian children learned to converse. He was not too proud to pick up native words by playing at straws and pebbles. When fluent in Aztec, he opened a school and taught crafts and the use of iron tools. His Franciscan brothers were astonished to see him perfectly at ease, for when among them he stuttered in any language.

The friars put the Ten Commandments to music and spelled out the Lord's Prayer in phonetic picture writing. The Christian rule of one God and one wife was the hardest to teach. A man with many wives found it impossible to remember which he'd married first — and he'd put a crucifix among his idols as if it were merely one more god. Children were the easiest to convince, and the friars, in their zeal, led them on idol-smashing raids. But the friars respected dancing as an Indian way of praying. All they asked was that the Indians dance to please the saints or to give thanks for the victory of the Christians over the Moors.

They taught the new religion by means of plays. Indian audiences watched Adam scrape the spines from nopal pads, while Eve made him proper shirts and trousers and the grieving angels sang, "Oh, why did she eat the forbidden fruit?" At Christmas, caroling angels spread the tidings that a Savior was born to Mary. The Holy Kings knelt by the corn husks where the Christ Child lay, calling Him "precious jewel" and "quetzal feather."

Indians were more easily drawn to the Christ Child and his Blessed Mother than to the bearded saints who looked so Spanish. Late in 1531, according to venerated tradition, Our Lady appeared in shining raiment to a poor Indian on Tepeyac Hill at the far end of the northern causeway. Speaking to him in Aztec, she said, "My dear son Juan Diego, whom I tenderly love, go to the bishop and ask him to build me a church here so that in it I may give my help and protection to the Indian people in their sorrows and calamities." Juan Diego obeyed but was not believed. So the Virgin sent him up the hill, where only prickly pears had grown before, and there he filled his cape with red roses of Castile. When he poured them before the bishop, his garment was seen to bear an image of the Virgin of Guadalupe as he had seen her, dark-featured and gentle. She became Our Mother to the Indians, or La Morenita, the Little Dark One.

In the 1530's and 1540's, the Indians began to feel comfortable in the new religion, and nine million were baptized. As there were not churches for so many, the friars preached in walled courtyards and sang the mass in open chapels. They taught the converts to take stones from the pyramids and build vaulted churches and monasteries with cloister walks. Native artists painted the walls with Old World designs or let their imaginations run free, as at Ixmiquilpan, where you can see centaurs with quetzal plumes prancing in Indian sandals.

Any member of the horse family fascinated the Indians.

Spanish gentlemen rode horses. Their ladies rode mules and so, for humility's sake, did clergymen. Indians had nothing to ride and heavy burdens to carry. Knowing this, Bishop Juan de Zumárraga brought a herd of burros from Spain. They multiplied, and people said, "God made the burro to give the poor Indian a rest."

In Michoacán, Bishop Vasco de Quiroga is affectionately remembered as Tata Vasco. Tata for Grandfather. No one else could have induced the Tarascans to come down from the hills after Nuño de Guzmán's bloody march. Tata Vasco brought them cows, chickens, and bananas. He had read Sir Thomas More's *Utopia* and started a community where everyone worked at common tasks and enjoyed a six-hour day. The Indians were unselfish enough to live like the early Christians, said the bishop, and apparently they did, as long as they had his love and protection.

The conquerors had such an unfeeling way of likening the Indians to animals that Bishop Julián de Garcés of Puebla could endure it no longer. He persuaded the Pope to declare that "the Indians are truly men and should be converted to the faith of Jesus Christ by preaching the word of God and by the example of good and holy living."

At Tlatelolco there was a school for Indians, Holy Cross College. The teachers soon discovered that their pupils were not only human but as smart as Spanish boys. A couple of students from Xochimilco prepared an illustrated treatise on herbs with a text in Aztec and Latin. It has been published in

the United States as "America's first medical book." Brother
Bernardino de Sahagún organized his advanced students into
a research team. They asked many questions of venerable
men who remembered the times before Cortés, and they
helped their teacher collect material for a dozen books:
customs, beliefs, occupations; names of plants, animals, and
minerals; even three thousand medical terms. Young scholars
like these, at home in both worlds, might have smoothed the
way for the races to live in harmony. But to admit that Indians had not only souls but minds was more than some
Spaniards could bear. A high official warned the emperor that
to let the natives read and write was "as harmful as the
Devil."

Bishop Garcés and Brother Motolinia, who had taken the
Aztec name for Poor Man, were the founders of Puebla, on
the way to Veracruz. It was to be a Spanish city. Since the
Spaniards did not always set a good example of Christian
behavior, it was better for them to live apart until the Indians
were stronger in the faith. Each settler received a town lot
and a good farm and was supposed to live by his own work.
No Indians. But alas, before you could say Iztaccíhuatl, the
first families of Puebla were forcing Cholulans, Huejotzin-
gans, and Tlaxcalans to work for them and build them
houses!

Everyone arriving from Spain expected the privileges the
conquerors had fought for, including Indian servants. There
were not enough Indians, especially after the fevers of 1545.

Newcomers had to be content with vaguely bounded land on which livestock could be raised with little labor. Their sheep and cattle multiplied astonishingly and overran the Indians' gardens and cornfields.

A Spaniard coming to New Spain also expected to eat good wheat bread. The Indians were slow to raise wheat. They had no plows and no idea what prayers were pleasing to the wheat gods. So wheat was grown on Spanish farms with forced Indian labor. Each cacique rounded up a weekly quota of workers and delivered them to the principal town of the district. A Spanish magistrate parceled them out to the wheat farmers. On Saturday night the Indians went home with their small wages — or without them, if the magistrate made them buy something they didn't want, like spurs for the horses they were forbidden to own.

Indian labor was as necessary in the city as in the country. The Very Noble, Notable, and Very Loyal City of Mexico — as was the capital's proud name — boasted of a printing press, a hospital endowed by Cortés, and a university chartered by the emperor and the Pope. Along the finest street were splendid houses with battlements all of the same height, for Spaniards were very touchy in such matters. Beyond the Spanish city were the marshes, where the Indians were supposed to remain. Exceptions were made, of course, for Indian servants and for all the tradesmen whose work, though vile, was necessary. In practice, the Spaniards found it impossible to shut the Indians out. Neither could they shut themselves in, for the city grew and they had to fill the marshes and move in among the people they did not wish to live with but could not live without.

European colonists never came to Mexico in great numbers, as they did to the United States. What happened was that a few Spaniards ran the country, telling the Indians what to do. Our frontiers were opened not by pushing the Indians back but by playing Indians against Indians. The Montejos were twenty years trying to conquer Yucatán and only succeeded after they enlisted the Xiu family against the Cocomes. Viceroy Mendoza used an army of Aztecs and Tarascans to put down an Indian uprising in the west. These former enemies liked the country around Guadalajara and settled down there as neighbors.

The big frontier was the north, and the rush started when silver was discovered in Zacatecas in 1546, and a boomtown sprang up in a windy mountain canyon. Soldiers rode beside the wagon trains that went there, for hungry Chichimecs were lying in wait to butcher the mules. Querétaro and San Miguel were forts and stopovers along this route, while a turnoff on the left led to the great mining camp of Guanajuato.

From Zacatecas, explorers pushed farther north to new silver mines in Durango and Chihuahua. Ranches supplied food for the miners and wool for warm clothing. In some there were patios where mules were driven around in a goo of ore and quicksilver to prepare the amalgam from which silver was separated.

A fifth of the silver belonged to Philip II, who came to the Spanish throne in 1556 and made the mine owners mad by declaring quicksilver a royal monopoly and charging a high price for it. The conquerors' sons were also disgruntled. Philip would not promise them their Indians for all time to come, and they cried out for a Cortés to right their wrongs. It happened there was a Cortés — Don Martín, the conqueror's son, born in Cuernavaca and reared in the Spanish court, a haughty fellow with a fierce black beard and dainty hands. He returned to Mexico and took up with a crowd who were fond of costume parties and sham street battles that kept the town awake. One morning a procession halted at his doorway with smoking incense pots. He came out in his father's costume and accepted an imaginary kingdom from Alonso de Avila, who was dressed like Moctezuma.

The conquerors' sons had found a new game called conspiracy. They went muffled in their cloaks to secret meetings and spun a plot to proclaim Martín I king of New Spain. Of course, it would first be necessary to knife the viceroy and the Audiencia judges.

The viceroy knew all about it and found the naughty boys amusing. What a pity he died, for the judges lacked his sense of humor. They summoned witnesses and had papers notarized. When the pile of papers was high enough, they sent the constables to bring in the traitors. Alonso and his brother Gil were the first to die. Too noble to hang, they lost their heads on the chopping block on a fine summer evening in 1566. Don Martín got off to Spain in the nick of time. He was in disgrace for a while, but he missed the grim investigator Muñoz, whom the king sent to root out rebellion in New Spain. Screams came from the torture chamber where this remorseless man presided. Early risers would often see a mule and a crucifix at the prison gate at dawn and know that another conspirator was going to the scaffold.

After two years the terror ended. The conquerors' sons were now as meek as lambs, and a new viceroy was due from Spain. Five vessels sailed into Veracruz and were mistaken for his fleet. Actually, they were English pirate ships. In command was Juan Aquines — the one you call John Hawkins. He'd come from Africa and was selling contraband slaves. The viceroy arrived right after him. A norther was blowing up. No one fools with a *norte* at Veracruz, and the viceroy made a truce with Hawkins to take shelter from the storm. But when safe in port, he weighed the faith he owed his king against his promise to a pirate. The king won, the viceroy opened fire, there was a battle, and Hawkins escaped with only two ships. One was captained by young Francis Drake, who swore to make the Spaniards pay dearly. We call him El Draque — and to this day his name means boogeyman.

The other vessel was so unseaworthy that Hawkins put a hundred men ashore near Tampico. Luis de Carvajal, a Spanish official, sent them under guard to Mexico City. One of them, Miles Philips, went home after many years and wrote his story "in the plain Stile of an English sailor." He told of doing menial work and then of going to the mines, where he might have done well except that the Inquisition was set up in New Spain and chose the Englishmen "to make a Beginning."

"We were committed to Prison in sundry dark Dungeons," he relates, "and were often called before the Inquisitors alone and there severely examin'd on our Faith." In 1574, during Holy Week, Miles and his companions marched to the great plaza, carrying unlighted green candles and wearing "Fools Coats with red Crosses upon them before and behind." Three of them were sentenced "to be burnt to Ashes," sixty to be whipped and sent to the Spanish galleys, and some, like Miles, to serve in monasteries.

He spent five years among kindly friars who treated him well and quietly despised the Inquisition. Great monasteries were rising, and the first stones of the Cathedral were being laid. Miles managed a crew of Indian workmen and found them to be "a courteous and loving kind of People, ingenious and of great understanding." He also came to feel for the Africans in bondage, though he had hunted down slaves a few years before. Perhaps if he'd known what was happening in his own country in those cruel times, he might have found a place in his heart for the Catholic priests who were dying in the Tower of London.

While Miles was with the friars, a great plague swept New Spain. A nosebleed, three days of high fever, then death. Two million Indians died. A bare million now remained. A missionary, seeing the empty churches, exclaimed, "How the multitude has diminished and there are few to unite in dancing!" In many villages even the cacique died, and the Spaniards came in with their sheep and took over the land.

In Tlatelolco, Sahagún, still at his writing, penned a gloomy chapter with á trembling hand. He remembered his eager students of forty years before and asked himself why students no longer wanted to learn, nor friars to teach, and where the Spaniards had gone wrong. It had been a mistake, he believed, to try to make the Indians live as in Spain. As their culture was destroyed, they lost their self-respect and became apathetic or turned to drink. No one attended them in sickness now, and they died miserably.

Sahagún never saw his great work in print. The king, warring on heresy in the Netherlands, would not tolerate a book on heathen Indian customs. The manuscript, our richest mine of information on the Aztecs, gathered dust for two centuries and a half before being published in Mexico in 1831.

The plague was hardly over when El Draque burst into the Pacific and ravaged the coast. The king and his viceroys took steps to tighten Spain's hold in the north and protect the silver mines. They promised wealth and glory to military explorers who would plant colonies in Sonora, New Mexico, and the northeast. Carvajal, the official who had arrested

Miles Philips, was made governor of Nuevo León and brought many kinsmen to the country around Monterrey. It was their misfortune to be New Christians and suspected Jews. The Inquisition reached over the desert for them. Carvajal died in prison, and six of his family perished in flames.

Missions and forts marked the new frontier. Many of the Indians were hunters who did not take readily to a settled life. The friars' work was made no easier by soldiers who considered the natives incapable of civilization and went after them in *sangre y fuego,* in blood and fire. Everyone was surprised when the Chichimecs along the Zacatecas road, after forty years of fighting, abandoned their nomadic life. They accepted a ration of meat and clothing, went to live in towns, and died rapidly from the white men's diseases.

Not even the Indian farmers back in the hills could live as in Spain. At the end of the sixteenth century, thousands of isolated families were moved into tight communities where they could be ruled, taught, and taxed more easily. They died in such numbers that it was said, "The Spaniard's very shadow kills the Indian."

You will read in some books that to the average Indian the Conquest meant only a change of masters. How can that be true when the average Indian was soon dead? In the old days, he had a place in his clan and a part in a rich ceremonial civilization. Even his enemies had customs much like his own. The Spaniards were different. They demanded all his working strength and robbed him of his dignity as a man.

You will read in other books that the Spaniards repaid the suffering Indian by bringing him plants, animals, tools, and the culture of the Mediterranean. Though it's true that the Old World civilization came to Mexico by way of Spain, the average Indian is still waiting for a plow and a yoke of oxen. It was the Mestizo who came into the Spanish inheritance — and what a long, long struggle he waged to get it!

The Mestizo's lineage goes back to the time when the conquerors married into the Indian nobility or took Indian concubines. If such a union lasted, the children were considered Spanish. But if a Spanish father went to the mines and never returned, or came back a rich man with a Spanish wife, then his half-Indian children became despised Mestizos, cast adrift to live by their wits or do menial work. The only tenderness they knew came from a mother too weak to spare them humiliation. The boys hated their neglectful father, yet imitated his masterful ways. The girls became too meek and submissive. This is part of our heritage as a conquered people.

Lowliest of all were the African slaves, picked for their youth and strength and brought in after the plague to the mines, farms, and sheep ranches. When possible, they married by Indian custom in a nearby village. Then their children were not slaves but grew up with their mother's people as Indians and shared in the common land.

Most black slaves were men, unlike Juana Petra, a house-keeper in the capital. They say she never lost her patience except with Felipillo, the spoiled child of the family. Little Philip's parents had faith he'd change for the better, but Juana Petra would always say, "Felipillo will be a saint when the fig tree turns green." She meant the tree in the patio that was all dry sticks. After Philip became a teen-ager, he was expelled from two monasteries and failed as an apprentice silversmith. Even his father lost hope and sent him to the Philippines, far away. There the wild youth repented and took the Franciscan habit. One morning in 1597, the fig tree burst into leaf, and Juana Petra ran screaming, "Felipillo is a saint!" Months later word came that Philip had died as a Christian martyr in Japan, speared while chained to a cross. Though the tree is only a legend, Philip did become San Felipe de Jesús, our first and only Mexican saint. So far.

The religious persecution was a thing of the past in 1614, when some two hundred Japanese diplomats visited us and were entertained in the House of Tiles, now Sanborn's restaurant. Trade with the Orient had grown in the half century since a Spanish expedition set out from Mexico and conquered the Philippines. Now the Manila galleon left Acapulco with silver bars, cocoa beans, and a red dye made from cactus bugs. It came back with silks and spices, porcelain vases, ivory fans, and often a few slaves known as Philippine Indians or Chinese, though they might have been from Malaya. Part of the cargo remained in Mexico, and the rest crossed to Veracruz by packtrain and was shipped to Seville, along with Mexican silver, tobacco, sugar, tallow, and hides.

Agricultural products for export, and for sale in the cities and mining towns, came mostly from large holdings known as *haciendas*. In their growth they were swallowing wheat farms and sheep ranches, encircling Indian villages, and spreading out along watercourses. The owners needed full-time hands, and paid Indian workers small but steady wages. The ablest hacienda managers were the black-coated Jesuits. They lived frugally by the rules of their order but received rich gifts and were able to buy choice land, operate sugar mills, run great flocks of sheep, and support schools for the colonists' children. The one thing they left alone as too risky was mining.

The silver pouring from our mines impoverished Mexico without enriching Spain. The Hapsburg kings who had ruled Spain since the Conquest wasted their treasure in endless European wars. And when Philip III expelled the New Christian Moors, Spain lost her best craftsmen and turned to other countries for the goods she sold us. Spain became a funnel through which Mexican pesos flowed to northern Europe, quickening trade there and giving rise to the saying, "The Spaniards are *our* Indians."

Prices in Spain were five times as high as before the Conquest — and they doubled again in Mexico when the cost of fighting pirates was added, along with sales taxes, port charges, and customs duties. Our silver bought less and less but cost more to mine as the surface ores gave out. Many mines were abandoned and, by 1630, when your country was off to a good start, ours was going into a century of depression.

The haciendas had fewer buyers for their beef and wheat. But as long as there were Indians to shoe horses, mend wagons, shear sheep, and do every kind of work indoors and out, a hacienda could attend to its own needs. The owner lived behind high walls in a kind of fort or castle. He had armed retainers to fight cattle rustlers, horse thieves, and wild Indians. Thirty or forty sat at his hospitable table, including travelers. He raised fine horses and was fond of saying he could ride from sun to sun without leaving his property. He never dreamed of selling it and was likely to pass it on undivided to his oldest son. Some of his Indians were refugees from the drainage works in the Valley of Mexico, where men were forced to toil and die in the seemingly endless effort to breach the northern rim of the basin and save the capital from floods.

The lord of the hacienda protected his Indians from forced labor. He did not drive them to raise more than could be eaten or sold. They came from their huts and heard mass with him in the chapel of the big house. He let them have small loans for saint's day fiestas and the tribute they owed the king. It was hard to repay him out of small wages, but he was patient and came to regard his Indian debtors as belonging to the hacienda, like his flocks and herds.

Hacienda Indians became lifelong children of the conquering race. They had no choice, perhaps, yet "poor are the people who kiss the sword that wounds them." Richer were the Indians who lived on the poorer soil of free villages or who took refuge in a mountain valley, by a desert stream, or in the Yucatán bush, and built themselves a new life from half-forgotten ancestral ways and half-remembered ways taught by the friars.

These Indian communities put themselves under the protection of a patron saint. He stood in the temple, painted and gilded, an imposing figure, with Virgins and other saints to keep him company. His people worked a field in common to buy him candles and dress him in neat native costume. All were secure within their common poverty. Parents followed and strengthened the Spanish custom of choosing godparents to sponsor their children in baptism. When life is uncertain, a child needs a spare mother and father. The parents and godparents became compadres, and so, whenever a baby was carried to the baptismal font, new ties were formed to replace clan ties now lost.

In the Maya country, the old gods lived on as goblin-like spirits of trees, hills, wells, and cornfields. They expected a prayer and a little honey from the man who robbed the hive. They made him no trouble for burning the brush if he courteously explained that he was clearing only enough land for his family's needs. In Chumayel, as in other towns, a jaguar priest kept a sacred book in the Mayan language. He wrote of the happy days before the Conquest when, he supposed, there were no aching bones and no chests on fire from consumption. The white men came as "mountain lions loose in the towns, bloodsuckers of the poor Indian. For their flower to live, they destroyed the flowers of others. It was the beginning of tribute, church fees, fighting with firearms, debts based on false witness, and strife between individuals." In 1640, the jaguar priest ventured a bold prophecy when he wrote, "We shall not lose this war, here in our land, for this land will be born again."

In their various ways the Indians fought to survive, and by 1650 they had reached a standoff with death. Their numbers held steady for many years, then slowly increased. The long retreat was over. The will to live had triumphed.

There were then Spaniards in Mexico, five generations removed from Spain, who still talked of making a fortune and returning to the mother country. But when one did, he found he was an *Indiano,* a stranger from an Indian land. His showy clothes and lavish entertaining offended the frugal Spaniards. He missed the long horizons, large horse herds, and plentiful servants of his native land and usually returned to it, a Spaniard still but now an American Spaniard. Not a European Spaniard.

American Spaniards came to call themselves Americans or Creoles, and finally Mexicans. Attitudes changed most quickly in the north, where many settlers were Spaniards only by courtesy. Mestizos went there to better their lot, Indians to escape bondage. Once an Indian forgot his ancestral ties and mother tongue, he was accepted as a Mestizo, too.

Between the frontier and Mexico City was the Bajío, a fertile valley supplying the north with foodstuffs, clothing, and horse gear. This region in and around the present state of Guanajuato became the Mestizo's land of opportunity. If he opened a shop, no jealous Spanish artisans put obstacles in his way. What he most wanted, though, was a ranch of his own and a life in the saddle, riding herd on his Longhorn cattle. He pictured how he'd look from Santiago's image in the country church. For Santiago, in this country, was a cattleman, handsomely attired in a sombrero with a silver cord, a braided bolero jacket, a silken scarf and sash, silver-buttoned riding breeches, gleaming boots, and big spurs, with a rope hanging from his handtooled saddle.

Some achieved their dream, but more became *vaqueros,* or cowboys, and wore ranch working clothes: a pointed hat of woven palm, deerskin jacket and pantaloons, goatskin chaps, sarape over the shoulder. They moved restlessly from ranch to ranch or roved the countryside in bands, feared for their long curved knives. They had a bad name for killing stock and selling the hides and tallow to the mines but were sought after at the roundup when range cattle were separated by brands. "It is bad to have them but worse not to have them," said the ranchers.

The common ambition of rancher and cowboy was to be "a good bullfighter, a good rider, and a good lover." By exhibiting their riding and animal-handling skills, they pleased the ladies and themselves. Sometimes they fought bulls from horseback in the knightly Spanish fashion and drove lances through small rings while riding at full speed. Oftener they performed feats learned from their daily work, roping a steer by the fore or hind feet or racing alongside a bull and throwing him by the tail. Great-grandsons of Indians who trembled before "deer as high as rooftops" now proved their manhood by breaking wild horses. The Bajío was a melting pot for a valiant race of bronze. It has been called the birthplace of our Mexican nationality. It was to be the cradle of independence.

THE CREOLES GO MEXICAN

◉◉◉◉◉◉◉◉◉   **8**

THE WAILING WOMAN was apt to appear after the ten
o'clock curfew — a ghostly figure, brushing the low roofline
with her vapory garments and luring men into the canals. She
was said to be the soul of La Malinche in torment, haunting
the city she had betrayed.

Fearful shapes peopled the dark streets. No one was for-
getting Don Juan Manuel, and how he used to speak out of
the shadows to ask a passerby the time. Having his answer,
he'd draw a dagger from his cloak and drive it to his victim's
heart, crying, "Fortunate is he who knows the hour of his

death!" One night a band of angels carried him to the gallows to pay for his crimes. But others were still about under cover of darkness, doing the Devil's work.

The Ave Maria from the church towers announced the blessed dawn. Bells called the people to masses and prayers, rejoiced over the fleet's safe arrival, implored protection from earthquakes and hailstorms, and doubled for the dead. They rang out in anguish night and day in 1624, while the archbishop and the viceroy were locked in struggle. A fugitive had found asylum in a church, and the viceroy was bent on taking him. One thing led to another until the archbishop excommunicated the viceroy — cast him from the ranks of the faithful — and put the city under an interdict. Religious services were suspended. The bells tolled unceasingly. The people mourned. Angry men gathered before the Palace. They cried, "Death to the Lutheran!" This was the worst name they knew to call the viceroy. They hurled paving stones through his window and finally set the Palace afire. It was his turn now to ask asylum. He ran for his life and found safety among the Franciscans.

In calmer times, cows waited on the plaza and were milked for customers, spicy foods simmered in the food stalls under palm-leaf awnings, blind men sang psalms for copper coins, and trumpeters announced royal decrees that only the barking dogs heeded. A pair of slaves in silk livery might be seen bearing a lady of quality in her sedan chair through a swarm of Indians and Mestizos. The wellborn called these idlers "people without reason" and sneered at their rags but were annoyed when one of them presumed to dress in Spanish clothes. Social distinctions vanished momentarily when the sacristan came with his handbell — *tin, tilín, tin, tilín* — clearing a path. For then all fell to their knees: the gentleman in his stiff white neckcloth, the lady in her lace mantilla, the rancher clutching his wide hat brim, the gowned student, the pickpocket, the beggar. While they knelt, a carriage passed, drawn by mules and followed by friars with lighted candles. A priest was taking the Holy Eucharist to a dying parishioner.

South of the Palace, behind the market, was the Cross of Forbearance. A poor widow might lay her husband's body at its foot and ask alms for his Christian burial. Across the square, in a covered passageway, the letter writers penned declarations of love, in verse if desired. The Cathedral, half completed, was already in use. The town hall stood on the other side of the plaza, beyond a canal. A boat with pennants flying was often seen passing under the flower market on the bridge, carrying the viceroy to the theater. The canals were not as clean as in Aztec times. Nor were the streets, where slop was thrown with the warning, "Water coming!"

It was better to lift one's eyes to the blue and yellow tiles on the shining cupolas of the new baroque temples. The twisting columns and luxuriant foliage about the doorways were the work of Indian sculptors. Inside were golden altars and images with miraculous histories. People believed that the Virgin of Afflictions slipped out at night in time of flood and held the gates of the dike against the rising water. Since she was back on her pedestal at dawn, no one would have known of her concern, except for her muddy skirts. Our Lord of the Rebozo had gone out on a rainy night to comfort a dying nun, and she, like a solicitous mother, had wrapped her rebozo about him before he returned to his chapel. These stories were the despair of scholarly theologians, but friars of simple faith saw no harm, and sometimes much good, in carrying holy images and relics to sickrooms where bleedings and purgings had failed to cure.

A friar's bare feet were a sign of obedience to a vow of poverty, but an Indian, as Bishop Juan de Palafox pointed out, was poor without a vow. Guards were posted to turn him away from the Alameda, where gentlemen on horseback saluted ladies in coaches during the afternoon promenade. How these American-born Creoles loved pageants and parades! No viceroy was too disliked for his saint's day to be celebrated with fireworks and cockfights. On August 13, riders in bright attire carried the banner of the Conquest to the site of the Sad Night amid volleys of cannon fire. On Good Friday, black-hooded penitents dragged chains through the streets, whipping themselves for their sins till blood ran from their shoulders.

At other times these men were fiercely proud. Two Creoles once met head on in their carriages in a narrow lane. Neither could back out without conceding precedence to the other.

There they sat, three days and nights, servants bringing them food and blankets, and they might be there still but for the viceroy, who commanded both to back out at the same time.

A Creole had courtly manners and, however poor, put the noble title of Don before his name. If rich, he had a military escort to accompany him through the peaceful countryside from his hacienda to his city mansion. Being a man at arms with no one to fight, he amused himself by making verses with labored figures of speech. Or he ruined himself by gambling for high stakes, which led to the saying, "Father merchant, son gentleman, grandson beggar."

To a Creole, a European Spaniard was a Gachupín. No one is sure what this originally meant. Something insulting and not very neighborly, for though Spain sent us her worst rascals, she also sent her best sons. Many a poor Spanish boy of those times left his ruined country to seek his fortune among us. He took a humble position and rose by hard work. His employer gave him his daughter in marriage, happy to have an industrious Gachupín for a son-in-law and to know that the family fortune would be safe for another generation.

By working fourteen hours a day, the Gachupines built little grocery stores into big ones. One of our educators has said, "The grocer and not the conqueror is the true Spanish father of Mexico." An old Creole poem makes fun of a Gachupín who "used to sell needles and pins on the street and is now a count." But the Creoles, too, bought themselves titles and public offices. Spain was in such distress that the king would sell almost anything. If a Mestizo had money and disliked his dark skin, he could buy a certificate from the king declaring him to be white.

The king was surrounded by deserving courtiers who recited their merits and wearied him. The cheapest way to reward them was to send them to rule over us, especially since he did not trust his American subjects to fill the high positions in government and the Church. The Creoles resented this discrimination. The men who were placed over them regarded a Creole as more than an Indian but less than a Spaniard. They had a pet theory that no native living thing — plant, animal, or man — could reach full maturity in the New World climate. Hence it was necessary for Europeans to rule.

Now it is hardly fair to blame all the Creoles' shortcomings on the climate, when the mother country excluded them from so many occupations. Oaxaca had a thriving silk industry until the king ordered silkworms and mulberry trees destroyed, fearing they would hurt the sale of goods carried in Spanish ships. For the same reason, Creoles were forbidden to raise olives and wine grapes, weave high-quality cloth, or have their own merchant fleet. They were supposed to buy from Spain, yet one Spanish coat cost them a hundred cows. And the taxes! A Creole even had to pay a tax for a clear title to land his great-grandfather had taken from the Indians. It was robbery!

Tithes — a tenth of the crop — were collected like taxes.

Most of the proceeds went for church purposes, but the king often used his right of patronage to impose an unwanted canon on a bishop when the money was needed for poor parish priests. The Church was very close to the daily life of the people. Young Creoles attended religious schools and often became friars or priests. Travelers lodged in monasteries. The hungry were fed at convent doors, the sick cared for in hospitals. Frequent religious holidays gave the poor time out from monotonous toil, and made the rich grumble over the interruption of work.

A man of means had many cares. One of his few satisfactions was to complain that the clergy were pampering beggars and lazy Indians. But when he neared the end of his days and felt the weight of his sins, he would leave something to a religious order. He might go further and provide for the support of a priest to say masses for his soul. He could do this by mortgaging his land. His obedient children did not mind the small yearly payments. It was only after they, and their children, piled new mortgages on the old that the burden became heavy. Then there was nothing to do but persuade a poor and studious relative to take holy orders so the money could remain in the family.

Some Creoles, without waiting to die, mortgaged their property and lived beyond their means. Religious orders lent money at five percent and did not ask for it back if the interest was paid. They invested this income, and the gifts they received, in land and city houses, which they seldom if ever sold. In 1683, the councilmen of Mexico City complained that a third of the property in New Spain was in the hands of church organizations. This meant there was little land on the market for sale. It was a new problem here but not in Spain, where for centuries Catholic kings had been forbidding people to sell or give land to the Church. Nevertheless the practice continued. Who else would support schools, hospitals, and convents? Not the king certainly.

A convent served many purposes. It was a place where a widow without a family found refuge and a merchant traveling to the Philippines left his wife for safekeeping. A woman who lived alone was obviously a witch. The exception proving the rule was La China Poblana, the Chinese girl of Puebla, who was not Chinese. She was kidnaped in India, sold in Manila, carried to Acapulco, and adopted by a kind Puebla couple. Outliving them, as well as a husband, she devoted herself to nursing the sick. She must have dressed plainly, but legend has confused her with the *chinas* of a later time, who made their own living and wore what they pleased. From these self-reliant women of mixed race comes the China Poblana costume worn in the Mexican hat dance: an embroidered white blouse and billowing red and green skirt, sparkling with sequins.

La Mulata de Córdoba, the mulatto woman of Córdoba, was the true witch type. She had the gift of being in two places at once and could find husbands for "difficult cases," though she did not care for one herself. The fact that she helped the poor and went regularly to mass did not explain away the whiff of sulphur that came from her house. At least one person of good repute had seen her flying in the night sky with red glaring eyes. It's not surprising that the Inquisition came and took her to Mexico City. Her fate remained a mystery until a story reached Córdoba, long after, that fitted her character like a glove. It seemed that on the evening before she was to carry the fearsome green candle and hear her sentence, she drew a three-masted ship on the wall of her cell. The picture looked so real that she asked the jailer if anything was missing. "Only for it to move," he replied. "So be it," said La Mulata — and she hopped aboard and sailed off through the dungeon walls. To Manila, they say.

Since not every father had such talented daughters, he took care to provide them with dowries. A girl needed one to marry well. If she failed to marry, so many men having gone to the north, she needed a dowry to enter a convent and have food, shelter, and spiritual comfort as long as she lived. The rector of the University mortgaged everything he owned to put eight daughters and his mother-in-law into convents. Let us hope he made a wise selection. There were convents for women whose vocation for a religious life ran so deep that a bare cell seemed a fitting place in which to share the sufferings of Our Lord. And there were others, less strict, that let a girl furnish her quarters to her taste and wear a favorite piece of jewelry or keep a servant or two.

Our great poet Sor Juana de la Cruz was not meant to be a

barefoot Carmelite and sleep on a sack of straw. She left the cold, damp convent of Santa Teresa la Antigua after three months, a very sick girl, and took her final vows in San Jerónimo, which had a milder rule. Her passion was study. As a child, she'd begged leave to attend the University, disguised as a boy, and her mother had to explain that a girl was educated when she could sew, say her prayers, and play the harpsichord. Despite this, Juana read through her grandfather's library and was a teen-age prodigy, the talk of the viceroy's court. Suitors admired her staring black eyes but could not win her heart. She became a nun because, she later said, "it was the decent thing to do."

Sor Juana's cell at San Jerónimo was crammed with chemistry flasks, terrestrial globes, and four thousand books. She received visitors in the social room and often talked through the wooden bars with Carlos de Sigüenza y Góngora, who collected Aztec picture books and watched the stars. He was also known for the triumphal arch he had designed to welcome a viceroy. No one had seen its like. The allegorical figures representing the "political virtues" were not Zeus and Athena, as you'd expect, but Axayácatl, Moctezuma, and Cuauhtémoc. He had charted the path of Halley's comet and disputed with the famous missionary Father Eusebio Kino, who believed, like other learned men, that comets were omens of evil. Sigüenza boldly asserted, "Dogma has no place in science, only proof and demonstration." But a series of disasters convinced people that Kino was right. Pirates sacked Veracruz, the French occupied the Mississippi, the Indians rose up from Durango to New Mexico, and a solar eclipse started the roosters crowing and filled the churches. Sigüenza remained on the empty street, sighting his telescope and "thanking God for letting me see what so rarely happens."

Sor Juana was meanwhile writing plays and poems. Every Mexican knows her famous lines about "silly men who accuse women of frivolity and are themselves the cause of what they blame." It worried the mother superior to have a duckling among her chicks. She told Juana to forget her books and work in the kitchen awhile. But Juana could not stop studying. She found herself asking why an egg coagulates when fried in oil but separates when placed in syrup. In 1691, she replied to a bishop who had gently reproved her for writing on theology. "God knows," she said, "that I have begged Him to dim the light of my understanding and leave me only enough to keep His law, for they say anything more is superfluous in a woman." But she did not mean these words too seriously. Her letter was a vigorous defense of the right of women to learn and teach.

That summer it rained and rained. Houses collapsed. Mildew infested the wheat. The price of grain soared in the hungry season before the next year's harvest. Sigüenza watched a mob gather in the plaza, men of all races, even poor Creoles. He heard them shout, "Death to the Gachupines who eat up our corn!" and "Long live the king and

death to the bad government!" They set the public buildings
afire. Sigüenza rushed into the town hall and saved armfuls
of historical documents. Most of his own writings have been
lost, there being no one to pay for printing them. Sigüenza
lived before his time, like Sor Juana, who came under increasing criticism and at last gave away her library. She
nursed her convent sisters in the 1695 plague and took sick
and died. Sigüenza spoke at her funeral and died five years
later, in such pain that he asked his doctors to do an autopsy
and see with their own eyes where the trouble lay. They
found a stone as big as a peach seed in his right kidney.

A few weeks later, the Hapsburg line ran out in Spain
with the death of Charles the Bewitched. The new Bourbon
kings found the black costume of the Spanish court too
dreary to endure. Their French tastes appear in the portraits
of the viceroys they sent to rule us: men in long wigs and
bright coats with heavy braid and frilly sleeves. The Bour-
bons took over a bankrupt Spain that no longer had the ships
or goods to supply her colonies. When an English merchant-
man entered a Mexican port, the customs officials looked the
other way, especially if the captain was generous with his
samples. We liked English goods, and the English could not
do without our silver. Smuggling was an easier way to get it
than piracy, they said. And fairer, we agreed.

A packtrain was a month on the road from Veracruz to
Mexico City and six months more to upper New Mexico or
over the long trail through San Antonio to the forts in east

Texas that kept watch on the French. Between 1748 and 1755, José de Escandón occupied Tamaulipas on the Gulf coast, rounding out Mexico as it exists today. New Spain then recognized no northern limit short of the imaginary but still sought-after passage from ocean to ocean. The horses were moving ahead of the explorers now, running north in wild herds and being traded among the Indians from tribe to tribe. The Apaches and Comanches were becoming such skilled riders that they could defend their hunting grounds and even raid the Spanish settlements. When pursued, they vanished into the mountains and lived on game. Horses had made the Conquest possible and now, except in California, were bringing it to a close.

Silver mining flourished once more, supplying the needs of the world's growing commerce. José de la Borda struck it rich in Taxco and built a church with lacy stone towers on the highest hill. "God gives to Borda, and Borda gives to God," he said. Antonio Obregón became the Count of La Valenciana, named for his Guanajuato silver mine. At the mouth of the mine he built a rose-tinted church in the exuberantly Mexican churrigueresque style. The Count of Regla, a former muleteer, took five million pesos from a mine at Real del Monte and gave us the Monte de Piedad, where we now pawn our wristwatches and television sets for the sake of a merry Christmas.

Charles III came to the throne in 1759, and ruled as an "enlightened despot" for three decades. He cleaned out corrupt local magistrates and divided New Spain into intendancies that correspond somewhat to our present states. Needing his troops for wars with England, he left our country's defense to a colonial army. The Creole and Mestizo officers fought Indians, gained military experience, and grumbled about the Gachupines.

Charles sought to bring the Church under tighter royal control and had a showdown with the powerful Jesuit order. The Creoles admired the Jesuits for their Lower California missions and loved them for their schools, so much better than the University, whose professors believed that all knowledge came by reasoning from the words in ancient books. The Jesuits held that things mattered more than words. The earth could move around the sun without disturbing their religious faith. They knew about Benjamin Franklin's electricity and realized that other changes were coming. Mexican independence, perhaps.

The king feared the Jesuits' influence. In 1767, he hastened what he feared by having them arrested and exiled. Riots broke out in the Bajío and elsewhere. The Marquis of Croix, the blunt-spoken viceroy, declared, "The subjects of His Majesty should know once and for all that they were born to obey and not to meddle in the high affairs of government." He put down the demonstrations with whippings and hangings. A score of Jesuit schools closed their doors. Miguel Hidalgo, in the second year of his studies at the Colegio de San Francisco Javier in Michoacán, had to go home, like many others. He was fourteen years old.

Father Francisco Javier Clavijero, who had taught there,

was in his thirties. Going into exile in Italy, he grew more Mexican with the passing years. He recalled his childhood in the sierra among the Indians, his teen-age discovery of Sor Juana's poems, and his delight in studying Sigüenza's Indian manuscripts. Drawing on his memory and the libraries of Italy, he wrote the *Ancient History of Mexico,* affirming in it that the Indians are endowed with the same faculties as the other children of Adam.

No sooner were the Jesuits gone than the king needed missionaries. The Russians were moving down from Alaska, and he wanted to occupy upper California before they did. It was Indian country that no Spaniards except navigators had ever seen. Friars as well as soldiers had to prepare the way for settlement. The royal inspector José de Gálvez and the Franciscan Junípero Serra formed an alliance "for the service of both Majesties," God and the king, and founded San Diego in 1769. Soon there was a chain of missions, besides Spanish towns like San Francisco and Los Angeles. Father Serra went up and down California on his lame foot — he'd been stung by a scorpion years before — and looked after the planting of wheat and the great herds of cattle. He and his Franciscan brothers took to California the vines and fruit trees the Moors had brought to Spain centuries before.

In the years after 1770, New Spain enjoyed its greatest prosperity. The rules of trade were eased, and people half forgot old grievances. When you had your revolution in the United States, Charles was fearful that your success would set us a bad example. But the chance to strike at the English was too good to miss. Bernardo de Gálvez, José's nephew, took Baton Rouge, Natchez, Mobile, and Pensacola. Galveston in Texas was named for him. Becoming viceroy of New Spain, he built Chapultepec Castle and was one of a line of notable viceroys who filled the stagnant canals, erected the Cathedral towers, and beautified the city.

The Second Count of Revillagigedo banished the terrors of the night by installing turpentine-burning streetlamps. He had sidewalks built and stray animals picked up. The city had clean streets and a botanical garden for the first time since Moctezuma. The Indians were ordered to dress more decently, but not even the great Revillagigedo was wise enough to tell them how to do so without money.

A century had passed since Sor Juana's time, and now a relative of hers, José Antonio Alzate, was publishing a scientific journal. It carried pictures of new instruments and machines, and reports of advances in medicine, agriculture, and mining. Alzate had a house full of laboratory animals, apothecary's jars, and mineral specimens. He went wherever his curiosity led him: after the migratory swallows or up Izta to see if it had a crater like Popo. It didn't.

All the talk at the new School of Mines was of pumps and mills and the need for chemists and metallurgists. Respect for old ways was breaking down. Young people sang ballads at novenas and danced the fandango. Their elders said the French Revolution was to blame.

Charles IV, who now ruled, was as incompetent as the later Hapsburgs. He imposed heavy taxes on the colonies for his wars with France and England and forfeited whatever goodwill his father had earned. The Creoles posted scurrilous verses in public places and recited a mock prayer with lines like, "Deliver us from evil and the Gachupines." The Inquisition prepared a list of forbidden readings and put the United States Constitution on it. Mexicans being what they are, everyone tried to find out what was in it.

The taste in churches and public buildings was changing from the fine frenzy of former times to the cold dignity of the neoclassic style as taught by the architect and sculptor Manuel Tolsá in the new San Carlos Academy. His equestrian statue of Charles IV is a famous landmark. We call it El Caballito, the Little Horse, out of disrespect for the royal rider. Tolsá cast it in bronze and lost his teeth from the fumes.

The dedication of the Little Horse, in 1803, was a big event. Baron Alexander von Humboldt, the German naturalist, made a speech. Standing beside him was the charming María Ignacia Rodríguez de Velasco y Osorio Barba, better known as La Güera Rodríguez, the blonde Mrs. Rodríguez. Men admired her beauty and flashing wit. She was so lovely, so clever, and so rich that no one expected her to enter a convent when any of her three husbands died.

Baron Humboldt passed a year among us. We love him because he loved Mexico. He measured the latitude and longitude of our cities and the height of our mountains, observed our plants and animals, studied our resources, and believed in our people. His *Political Essay on the Kingdom of New Spain* opened the eyes of the world to Mexico. He lived to be ninety and never forgot us. What he remembered best in his later years were "those majestic snow-capped peaks, rising in the midst of tropical foliage," and La Güera Rodríguez, "the most beautiful woman I have ever seen."

THE CRY OF DOLORES

⊚⊚⊚⊚⊚⊚⊚⊚⊚ 9

THE YOUNG SEMINARIAN Miguel Hidalgo won friends and enemies in Michoacán for his paper on the true method of studying theology. "I see you towering over many old men who call themselves doctors but are mere spinners of cobweb arguments," the dean of the Cathedral told the junior professor from the Colegio de San Nicolás. The venerable churchman's colleagues did not feel flattered. After a lifetime of hair-splitting disputes on the meaning of words, they resented his praising a novice who sought truth by studying the Scriptures and the church traditions in the light of history.

A new bishop came to Valladolid that year, and his aide, Manuel Abad Queipo, became Hidalgo's close friend. The two scholars enjoyed the same books — some, it was whispered, on the Inquisition's forbidden list. Their talents were alike but not their prospects. Abad Queipo could aspire to be an ecclesiastical judge, a canon, even a bishop. He was a Spaniard. When Hidalgo, a Creole from the Bajío, was made rector of the college sometime later, his enemies did not rest till they had him banished to a small parish at the far end of the diocese.

For eighteen years, Hidalgo remained a country priest. His hair whitened and fell away, except at the temples, and he went about with a walking stick, stooped from study but jaunty and sociable. He shared the parish house with sisters and cousins, and welcomed his parishioners — Creole, Mestizo, or Indian — to evenings of dancing and conversation. His democratic establishment at San Felipe was called "Little France." There he staged plays by Molière, his green eyes dancing in his expressive dark face as he coached the amateurs in their parts. The chief character was sure to be a miser or a hypocrite, and the spectators delighted in recognizing some rich Gachupín of the neighborhood.

The poorer folk at this dry rim of the Bajío called themselves ranchers. Pushed from richer soils as the haciendas expanded, they pastured a few animals and raised some corn if the rainfall permitted. Mestizos or Indians, they were equally wretched unless they cheated on the king, selling contraband tobacco or transporting silver on which the royal fifth was unpaid.

When Hidalgo took over the nearby parish of Dolores, his reading turned to the industrial arts and soon he was organizing a cooperative enterprise. A religious brotherhood donated a lot, an order of nuns lent money for equipment, and there were plenty of hands to build workshops and pottery kilns. Taught by their padre, the workers made tiles, fabrics, and leather goods for sale at village markets. They set out saplings and vines by a stream, hoping to sell olive oil and wine, but the Spanish authorities put a stop to that, explaining that such products must come from the mother country.

The ban did not extend to unbleached cotton for country wear or woolens for uniforms. From time to time, Hidalgo visited his classmate, Miguel Domínguez, now magistrate, or *corregidor,* of Querétaro, a busy textile center. The Indian weavers toiled behind locked doors, except for a Sunday furlough, and were whipped for falling short in their tasks, a practice that elsewhere had led to bloody insurrections. Domínguez was trying to improve their lot and keep the looms running so the growing colonial army might be properly clothed. It had the mission of protecting the coasts. The loss of the Spanish fleet at Trafalgar made Mexico a tempting prize for the British or the French or Aaron Burr's filibusters in the Mississippi Valley.

Spain needed the loyalty of her overseas subjects but was deaf to their grievances. More than once the rising dignitary

Abad Queipo communicated with the king, picturing for him "the clashing interests of those who have nothing and those who have everything." The crown officials, he warned, were so corrupt that the clergy alone had the people's trust. But Charles IV was usually at war with either France or England and wished only to extract money from his colonies. He even called the benevolent funds into the royal treasury. These were pious gifts placed with religious bodies to produce income for charities, such as dowries for poor girls. They were invested in farm mortgages. The king's order led to forced sales that ruined many landholders — and the money went to Spain, never to return, not even the interest on which the good works of the Church depended.

The bells rang joyously in 1808, at word that Charles had made way for his son Ferdinand to rule. But the tidings were two months out of date. Ferdinand was in France, a prisoner of Napoleon Bonaparte, who had invaded Spain and placed his tippling brother Joseph on the throne. Pepe Botellas — "Joe Bottles" — the royal intruder was called. Some Spaniards supported him while others joined guerrilla bands to fight him or formed *juntas,* or local committees, loyal to Ferdinand. Out of this confusion came the movements in Spain's American colonies that led over a trail of blood to independence.

The unfolding story came to Hidalgo from travelers and in the columns of a capital newspaper. There was no mention of independence at first, only how to save New Spain for

Ferdinand VII. Juntas were springing up in Spain to rule in his name — why not in Mexico? The issue was hotly debated at the capital among judges, canons, and councilmen, with Viceroy José de Iturrigaray in the chair. Francisco Primo Verdad, the city recorder, asserted that in the absence of a legitimate king, the sovereignty of Mexico had returned to the people. "Seditious and subversive!" shouted the public prosecutor. "Outright heresy!" cried the chief inquisitor.

Popular sovereignty meant that the Creoles, not the Gachupines, would rule. But the Creoles needed the viceroy on their side. Iturrigaray saw a chance to stay on indefinitely in the captive king's name. He refused to recognize any of the juntas that claimed to speak for Spain and might send another viceroy in his place. He then joined with the friar Melchor de Talamantes in plans for a national congress. The Gachupines became suspicious and menacing, so the viceroy called for the troops on the coast. Before they came, five hundred armed Spaniards invaded the Palace by night, dragged him and his family from their beds, and installed a puppet viceroy of their own. They killed Verdad and flung Talamantes into a Veracruz dungeon to die of yellow fever. The lesson was not lost on the Creoles. The Gachupines had taught them that the person of a viceroy was no longer sacred and had set them an example of taking the law into their own hands.

Late that year, Captain Ignacio de Allende of the Queen's Dragoons was sent home from his post, the Gachupines fearing armed Creoles more than foreign invaders. He was a handsome man except for a broken nose, the price of his daredevil riding. And he was furious over a Spanish officer's taunt that no Creole was fit to be a captain. At San Miguel he began drawing his companions into an anti-Spanish conspiracy. On a visit to Dolores he met Father Hidalgo and confided his plans.

Hidalgo, now in his mid-fifties, considered them well and reminded Allende that "the authors of such enterprises seldom harvest the fruits." But after committing himself, he was firm in his purpose and resolved the religious scruples of others. Mexicans had been taught that rebellion against Spain was an affront to God — but who now represented Spain? Napoleon and "Joe Bottles," those profaners of convents? The Seville junta, now calling in defeat for the help of English heretics? Gachupín parasites, sucking Mexico's blood and ready to deliver her to France, England, or the Devil to save their possessions? Who else than the Mexicans themselves could defend their faith?

The craftsmen of the cooperative were strong for their padre. Hidalgo asked one of them, an orphan boy reared in the parish house, "If I let you in on an important secret, would you betray me?"

"No, sir."

"Listen, then. It is not right that we Mexicans, having a rich and beautiful country, should remain under the rule of the Gachupines. They treat us as slaves; we cannot speak freely or enjoy the fruits of our soil, for they own everything. Doesn't that seem unjust?"

"Yes, sir."

"All right, we must all unite and run out the Gachupines. What do you say? Will you take arms and join me? Will you give your life, if necessary, to free your country?"

"Yes, sir."

"Well, then, not a word, not even to your companions."

In Valladolid, the conspirators had trusted the Creole lieutenant Agustín de Iturbide, to their sorrow. Leading families and high churchmen were involved when he tattled, so the affair was hushed up. Abad Queipo received a scolding from the viceroy for knowing more than was good for him to keep to himself. But he must have made peace with the authorities, for he'd been named bishop-elect when Hidalgo saw him at Guanajuato during the 1810 New Year fiestas. They talked harmlessly of silkworms, a hobby they shared. The bishop's had done poorly, but Hidalgo promised him more worms than he'd know what to do with. A casual remark, seen later to have another meaning.

People were joining the conspiracy now almost as a patriotic duty. The French had overrun Spain, bringing resistance to an end, except for daring guerrillas like young Javier Mina and a regency that sat at Cádiz under the protection of British naval guns. Mexico's conspiratorial juntas met in parish houses and mechanics' shops and, in Querétaro, in the Municipal Palace, with the corregidor and his high-spirited wife taking part. The general plan was to raise the banner of revolt late that year, seize the Gachupines, and use their wealth as a war fund. After victory, each local junta would send delegates to a central governing junta in Mexico City. And the Spaniards would be expelled with no more mercy than they'd shown the Jesuits in 1767.

On two points, Hidalgo and Allende were not agreed. Allende did everything in Ferdinand's name, in order to reassure those too timid for a clean break with Spain. Hidalgo was for outright independence but made no great ado over a king who might never reign again. What worried him was Allende's reliance on the Creole officers in the coming struggle. True, they were valuable professionals, able to manage guns and men. How many, though, would risk their bright uniforms and regular pay and turn their weapons against the Gachupines while the civilians merely looked on? Hidalgo favored arming masses of people with anything at hand: machetes, slings, bows and arrows, lances with iron points that a blacksmith could forge.

By September, three thousand were in the conspiracy. Inevitably there were leaks, secret accusations to the authorities, and barber-shop gossip that one night soon every Gachupín was to have his throat slit. Captain Joaquín Arias, on whom Allende counted to bring the Querétaro garrison into the rebel camp, panicked and told all to save himself. To the corregidor Domínguez came an order to search a certain house for a cache of arms. This was an embarrassing situation for one in on the secret, but at least he knew where *not* to look. Before going on the search, he locked his wife in, knowing that women are apt to do silly things.

Vain man, giving himself so much credit and his Josefa so little! Because of the corregidor's bungling, an assistant found the arms. But his wife's cool head won her fame as La Corregidora, whose stately likeness you may see on coins and banknotes. Acting quickly to warn Allende that the plot was discovered, she stomped three times with her sturdy foot, a signal prearranged with the jailer Ignacio Pérez in the room below. He ran up and put his ear to the keyhole. Doña Josefa communicated the message on which the country's fate depended. Pérez leaped to the saddle, a Mexican Paul Revere, and was off to San Miguel. He learned that Allende was with Hidalgo, but Captain Juan de Aldama, another conspirator, was in San Miguel, and the two men rode on to Dolores on that memorable night of September 15, 1810.

At two A.M. they pounded on Father Hidalgo's bedroom window. He heard the news calmly and went for chocolate while they joined Allende. The dining room soon filled with the padre's armed relatives and neighbors. The two captains lamented the lack of time to alert their commands and said that unless the conspirators went into hiding they'd be arrested by morning. Father Hidalgo, pulling on his stockings, looked up and said, "Gentlemen, we are lost, there is nothing to do but go hunting for Gachupines." Taking charge, he sent squads to arrest the Spanish merchants and officials, then marched with his workmen, pistol in hand, to the jail. Out came the prisoners, in went the Gachupines. By five A.M., Hidalgo had collected eighty recruits. It was Sunday, and people were coming in from the country to hear early mass and do their shopping. After the church bell was rung long and loud, Hidalgo climbed to the temple doorway and there, under richly carved columns, he raised the *grito,* the cry of Dolores:

"Friends and countrymen, you are the sons of this land, yet have been for three centuries in bondage. The Europeans have everything. We propose to end their rule. Come march with us for country and religion. Long live America! Death to the bad government!"

"Death to the Gachupines!" came the reply.

That day eight hundred volunteers set off, the first Insurgents, Hidalgo with them on a little black horse. A girl called from a window, "Where are you going, Father?"

"I am going to free the people from their yokes, my daughter."

"Careful, Father, that you don't lose the oxen while you're about it."

Hidalgo could take or make a joke but knew that deeper feelings move men to fight and die. At a roadside sanctuary he raised a painting of the Dark Virgin on a staff and shouted, "Long live our Holy Mother of Guadalupe! Long live America!" His men fell to their knees, sobbing.

Then on to San Miguel, the Guadalupe banner at their

head. Allende's dragoons joined them here, smartly turned out in yellow tailcoats. What a contrast with the peasants in flimsy cotton who fell to looting a Gachupín shop! Allende dispersed them with his sword. Hidalgo remonstrated with him, holding it necessary to tolerate some excesses. These people were tasting liberty after three centuries under masters who had never troubled to teach them civics. They were needed for the force of their numbers to overrun towns and countryside.

Ranch hands, weavers, and miners swelled the Insurgents, who marched to Celaya four thousand strong, with Spanish hostages and chests of gold, and paraded before a cheering throng. The informer Arias was there, watching. He'd been sent to talk the leaders out of their mad scheme but seeing their success, joined them, concealing his treachery.

Before the month was out, twelve thousand Insurgents invaded Guanajuato, second city in the land for the silver in its hills. José Antonio Riaño, who governed this province, had fortified Granaditas, a thick-walled granary, and put the Gachupines and three million pesos inside it. Outside were the miners who on ordinary days earned eighteen centavos and a ration of corn for carrying ore sacks of twice their own weight. Today they were gathered on the sloping hillsides, as in a stadium, waving Guadalupe prints from poles and waiting for the show to begin.

The Insurgents came shouting, singing, storming the trenches before Granaditas with sticks and stones. Riaño died

with a bullet through his head while bringing reinforcements
to his soldiers. They withdrew into the granary and fired
from the windows and roof on waves of Indians breaking
against heavy doors that would not give way. A boy miner
called El Pípila covered himself with a flagstone, crept
among the strewn bodies, clenching a torch, and set the
portal afire.

Seeing the barrier tumble, the Spaniards tossed gold coins
from the windows to hold back the tide and ran up a white
flag. Firing nevertheless continued from various points. The
Insurgents swept in, giving no quarter, the miners following
after. Gachupín shopkeepers begged on their knees for time
to confess their sins and died in a welter of spilt corn and
silver ingots. Granaditas and all its treasure fell at five
o'clock.

By torchlight, burial teams carried many Spanish bodies to
the cemetery and many more Indian bodies to trenches by the
river. Lucas Alamán, a teen-age son of wealthy Creoles,
heard axes crashing into Spanish shops and cries of "Death
to the Gachupines!" The memory stayed with him all his life.
The Insurgents had won their first battle, sweeping everything before them and frightening the good Creoles of
Guanajuato, who liked a little revolution but not so much.
Hidalgo asked them to be councilmen in place of the Gachupines. They begged off for fear of Spanish reprisals but were
not at all happy when he found willing candidates among
their poorer neighbors.

Fifty thousand men marched on Valladolid, where Abad
Queipo wore his miter proudly under the rose-tinted Cathedral towers and commanded that the great bell be brought
down and melted for cannon. The onetime champion of
"those who have nothing" now accused Hidalgo of promising the Spaniards' land to the Indians and declared him and
his companions excommunicated for diabolic sedition. But as
the avalanche came nearer, he fled the city. A war was on,
dividing all groups, including the clergy. Before it was over,
hundreds of priests and friars would become Insurgent leaders. Other hundreds would support Spain. And some would
live as best they could with either side, like the canons at
Valladolid who tore down their bishop's excommunication
edicts and sang a Te Deum to welcome Hidalgo.

Whole companies of Royalists passed over to the revolution at Valladolid and fell in with the eighty thousand Insurgents who wound their way through pine forests toward
the capital. Moving with them were food carts, droves of
cattle and sheep, and women with babies in their rebozos,
coming to bake tortillas for their men. Volunteers came,
offering their services to Hidalgo, among them future leaders
like José María Morelos and Ignacio López Rayón.

At the end of October, the sprawling army, loosely formed
into regiments, reached Monte de las Cruces, at the pass
leading into the Valley of Mexico, and disputed the fir-clad
slopes with a small Royalist force. Allende ordered the
Indians to the rear, but they would not be denied their glory

and rushed upon the enemy with pitiful weapons, even thrusting their straw hats into the cannon's mouth. Lieutenant Iturbide mowed them down in a Royalist counterattack that earned him a captaincy. But the Insurgents gained the higher ground at last and sent the enemy reeling into Mexico City.

At the sight of the shattered remnant, the Gachupines began fleeing with their treasure. Viceroy Francisco Xavier Venegas, fresh from the wars in Spain, calmed them with the help of the Virgin of Remedios. She was a figure no larger than a doll, with blue eyes and a pale complexion, as pleasing to Spaniards as Guadalupe to Indians. After a procession to the Cathedral, the viceroy laid his baton at her feet and made her a general. By tradition, Remedios had fought beside the Spanish conquerors, throwing dust into the eyes of the Indians. What she had done once, she could do again.

There was nothing else to stop the Insurgents from sweeping into Mexico City. But their ammunition was nearly spent, and they had to reckon with the Spanish commander Félix María Calleja, already marching south from the Bajío with a formidable army. Allende hoped that a swift descent upon the capital would rally the Creoles to the revolution, civilians and soldiers alike. But Hidalgo was not so sure that Calleja's men would come over. He saw the city as a trap where the Insurgents could neither fight nor flee. While the chiefs debated, the men nursed their wounds and shivered in the cold mountain pass. They thought of the corn ripe for harvesting and began slipping away. After three days, when the Insurgent column turned away from Mexico City, it had shrunk by half.

The new plan was to occupy Querétaro as Calleja left it on his way south, then mark time while the regulars trained a disciplined fighting force. But at Aculco, the Insurgents ran into the army they were so anxious to avoid. Taken by surprise, and no match for the men in tall shakos and their flashing bayonets, they scattered to the barrancas, losing their treasure chests, powder kegs, and Spanish prisoners. Allende, bitter over this new disaster, salvaged what he could and marched off to Guanajuato without Hidalgo.

Muffled in his riding coat, Hidalgo made his way into Valladolid at night with a couple of companions. To his surprise, he was well received. The fires he'd lighted were spreading to many provinces. He issued a reply to the accusations of Spanish bishops and inquisitors, affirming that he had not departed one iota from the faith. "Our enemies," he said, "are Catholics only for politics. Their God is money." Then, with seven thousand recruits, he marched to Guadalajara, which had fallen to El Amo Torres, one of his commissioned agents.

Here Hidalgo formed the nucleus of a government and resumed the title of generalissimo of America, given him by his followers when it seemed the revolution might spread even beyond Mexico. Perhaps it would yet. Zacatecas had fallen without a shot. Two lay brothers had taken San Luis

Potosí. Morelos was at El Veladero, overlooking Acapulco. A priest and his Indian followers had captured the harbor guns of San Blas. The mine foreman José Mariano Jiménez was raising Coahuila and Texas in revolt.

Until an elected congress could make wise use of the abundant resources which "the Sovereign Author of Nature has bestowed on this vast continent," Hidalgo sought to remedy glaring evils through decrees abolishing slavery, tribute, and crown monopolies. He welcomed Allende to the city. Guanajuato was lost, and more blood had flowed at Granaditas. While Allende was leaving and Calleja entering, the Indians made sure before they died to finish off the Gachupín hostages. The Spanish general's terrible vengeance was to order the city decimated. Indians and half-Indians, the innocent and the guilty, were rounded up, and every tenth man, chosen by lot, was hanged in the public square.

The events at Guanajuato foreshadowed a long series of reprisals and counterreprisals. There were nights in Guadalajara when an execution squad, bronze-faced and impassive, took a score of Gachupines to the barrancas and strangled them without remorse. To the Creoles this was more frightful than the burning of an Indian village. So many made common cause with the Spaniards that Hidalgo in a manifesto asked, "Is it possible, Americans, that you will take arms against your brothers? This war would be finished in a day if you would not help the Europeans fight."

In Orozco's mural painting in the state capitol at Guadalajara, you may read the anguish of the Father of Our Country in his eyes, averted from horrors that have made his dream a nightmare. Yet he sweeps on with his freedom torch, for there is no turning back.

In January, he had to face Calleja. Ninety thousand Insurgents massed by the stone bridge of Calderón to defend Guadalajara. Some few had guns; the rest had ox goads, hunting bows, or slings for hurling small flasks of powder. Allende placed the artillery clumsily, but the defenders held out six hours and looked like winners until an ammunition cart blew up. A stiff wind carried smoke and flames through the dry grass. The Insurgent line broke and was unable to re-form in the face of a cavalry charge. Guadalajara was lost, and the first phase of the war, when victory seemed attainable by numbers, was over.

Allende and his fellow-officers now took full charge and started north with a few companies and a string of silver-laden mules. They were bound for the Texas borderlands to buy guns from the Anglo-Americans. Hidalgo was with them, though stripped of authority. The enemy followed behind, reoccupying Zacatecas and San Luis Potosí. The viceroy offered to pardon the Insurgent chiefs if they'd lay down their arms, but they replied, "Pardon is for criminals, not for the country's defenders."

López Rayón was assigned to hold Saltillo, and the expedition continued northward by stony mountain defiles. Each night, huddling by a fire in the March wind, they were closer, without knowing it, to the mouth of a trap. San Antonio and Monclova, ahead of them, had fallen to the other side. A Royalist captain sent his spies among them and prepared an ambush at Norias de Baján. The travelers fell into it, a few at a time, as they rounded a bare gray hill.

Allende was in a carriage with his son and the informer Arias. As the men came for him, he cried, "I'd rather die!" and fired, but missed. The return fire killed his son and Arias, but Allende was taken. Hidalgo was in the saddle when surprised. He reached for his pistol too late and was bound with the others. In Monclova, a blacksmith forged manacles for the leaders, and they went under heavy guard to Chihuahua, the seat of the military command, a month's journey over waterless plains.

Hidalgo was confined in a dark pit, but his jailers were kind, especially the Spaniard Melchor Guaspe, who brought him home-cooked delicacies at every meal. The military and religious authorities who conducted the proceedings against Hidalgo allowed him no defense except what he cared to say when questioned. May 8, his fifty-eighth birthday, passed under heavy examination. He took full responsibility for the uprising, neither asking mercy like Allende nor shifting the blame like Aldama. No one knows exactly under what pressures he signed a retraction, written in words unlike his own and asking his followers to lay down their arms. He desired, of course, the consolations of religion, for which repentance was demanded, and may have believed that the revolution was now a lost cause.

From time to time he heard muffled shots that signified some companion's execution and foretold his own. The court, passing sentence, regretted only that there was no iron strangling collar in Chihuahua. Spanish churchmen stripped off his vestments and symbolically scraped the power of consecration from his fingers. In his last hours, he scribbled some verses on the wall, thanking his jailers for favors received. Before dawn on July 30, he stood before the firing squad and raised his hand to his heart for a target. They fired three volleys in the dim light before he lay still. An Indian received twenty pesos for cutting off his head. It was taken, with the heads of Allende, Aldama, and Jiménez, to Guanajuato and hung in an iron cage outside Granaditas. Ten years the heads remained on display, while the struggle continued.

HOW INDEPENDENCE CAME
⊙⊙⊙⊙⊙⊙⊙⊙⊙   10

AFTER the Insurgent chiefs were captured, López Rayón fought his way from Saltillo to Michoacán and established a supreme junta at Zitácuaro, still using King Ferdinand's name. His craggy hideaway was a convenient retreat for ungovernable guerrilla leaders like Albino García, whose weapon was the lariat. He could unseat a Royalist colonel as easily as he roped a calf. Disrespectful of kings and commanders, he recognized "no highness but the hills and no junta but the coming together of rivers."

As Hidalgo's torch passed to unmanicured hands, Creoles

of good family looked for careers with the Royalists. Calleja kept enlarging his army, "but if it ever turns against us," he told the viceroy, "it can give us plenty of trouble."

Right now the trouble spot was the Southern Sierra and the coastlands about Acapulco. Morelos was operating here, a short stocky man of Indian, Spanish, and African descent, wearing a kerchief to shield his aching head from the tropical sun. He had come to know this country as a muleteer and later as a priest. Some of his parishioners were riding with him in cowhide jackets, with strips of dried beef hanging down the flanks of their horses. Whole towns were ready to follow Morelos, but he took only as many men as could be armed, creating larger units as guns were captured from the enemy.

After sealing off the Spanish fort at Acapulco, Morelos moved toward the highlands. Late in 1811, he was in striking distance of cities along the volcanic belt. Had López Rayón been able to resist Calleja longer, Morelos might have advanced through Toluca to Monte de las Cruces. But in the first days of 1812, the Spanish general took and burned Zitácuaro, put the junta to flight, and turned on Morelos.

They had a test of strength at Cuautla, where Popo's melted snow waters cane fields and citrus groves. Calleja came with heavy batteries and seasoned soldiers, including two regiments from Spain. Morelos's aim was to hold the town till the rains bogged down the enemy's artillery and spread fever among the unacclimated troops. The siege of

Cuautla, from February to May, is an epic of our independence war, marked by courage and endurance.

Morelos ran into an ambush while reconnoitering. "Don't run," he shouted to his men, "you can't see the bullets with your backs!" Hermenegildo Galeana, a tall rancher with blue eyes inherited from some English castaway, slashed a path to Morelos's side and led him to safety. "Quicker, sir, at a faster pace!" urged Galeana, but Morelos replied, "My horse has no other pace."

Leonardo Bravo had fortified Cuautla's convents and plazas. Calleja tried to carry the position by assault. During the battle, twelve-year-old Narciso Mendoza leaped to a cannon whose gunner lay dead and lighted the fuse, holding an important position until Galeana and Father Mariano Matamoros rode up. After six hours, Calleja retired and dug in for a long siege.

For seventy-two heroic days, Cuautla held out, soldiers and civilians. Dropping to the ground when bombs fell, they gathered the fragments for the gun-repair shop. The enemy cut the aqueduct, but Galeana's men repaired it under fire and enclosed the water outlet in masonry walls. The shelter became a popular gathering place. People forgot their woes when the three sisters sang and danced: María, Teresa, and Luz, whom they called La Xocoyota because that means "the youngest" in Aztec. When Morelos praised her gaiety, she promised, "I shall laugh and sing as long as I live." So when a stray bullet hit her, she crept into a thicket and died alone.

No supplies came through the tight siege lines. People ate lizards, iguanas, and the bark of trees. April passed without the showers that were counted on to make Calleja lift the siege. Even so, his sick list was long. On May 1, he offered the Insurgents a pardon for surrender. Morelos returned the message with another: "I concede the same grace to Calleja and his men." But it was impossible to hold Cuautla longer. That night the Insurgents cut their way out, though many were killed or, like old Leonardo Bravo, taken prisoner.

Cuautla rubbed off the magic from Calleja's name. When he paraded his sickly troops and battle trophies in the capital, people said, "He came back with the Moor's turban, but the Moor got away." Morelos regrouped his forces and won fame as the Thunderbolt of the South. Going to the relief of Valerio Trujano, under siege at Huajuapan, he took a thousand enemy guns. In a swift raid on Orizaba, he burned the stores of tobacco on which the viceroy depended for revenue to pay his huge army.

The Insurgents disrupted communications so that nothing moved without a military escort, and not always with one. Leonardo Bravo's son Nicolás captured a mail convoy and two hundred Spanish soldiers. Morelos offered these prisoners and many more for Don Leonardo, but the viceroy preferred a public spectacle and had the old man strangled on a high platform for all to see. Morelos then ordered a reprisal on the Spanish prisoners. Nicolás Bravo was a son with a father to avenge, but knew that these men were not personally guilty. After a sleepless night, he went before them while they waited to be shot and said, "Spaniards, my vengeance consists in pardoning you. Go, you are free." A shining deed in a cruel war — but Morelos did not fully appreciate it and often had to harden his heart against an enemy who neither exchanged prisoners nor spared their lives.

Late in the year, Morelos led ten thousand men against Oaxaca and made the city a source of supplies and a springboard for a leap into the north. Now that the south was largely in Insurgent hands, it was time to think of the nation's future. Morelos is said to be the author of a revolutionary plan for confiscating the property of rich Spaniards and their allies as towns were taken, giving half to the poor and using the other half for war expenditures. He favored dividing the vast holdings of idle land among those who would cultivate small tracts by the sweat of their own brows.

Even the capital was drawn into the revolution. There the Insurgents called themselves Guadalupes and worked in secrecy to supply the guerrillas in the hills. Many a pamphlet blasting them came from the pen of a lawyer named Agustín Pomposo Fernández de San Salvador. He was a grieving father whose son had joined López Rayón and whose law clerk, Andrés Quintana Roo, was with Morelos. He was also the uncle and guardian of the rich and lovely Leona Vicario, whom he adored until he learned she was running an underground post office and sending pistols to the Insurgents. What could he do but put the willful girl in a convent and notify the Royal Junta for Security? The investigating judge was merciful, telling Leona she'd be confined for life, nothing more, if she named her confederates. Otherwise nothing could save her.

Leona's lips remained sealed, and next evening six Guadalupes in black capes rode up, some covering the entranceway while others burst in and carried her, laughing, to a waiting horse. Sometime later a mule train arrived in Oaxaca with an interesting cargo. The fruit crates held printers' type and paper for the Insurgent press; the pigskins, ink instead of pulque; and the ragged girl in blackface disguise was, of course, Leona Vicario.

Leona was married soon after to Quintana Roo, whose name heads the list of signers of the Act of Independence, approved at Chilpancingo on November 6, 1813. "It's time to rip the mask from independence," Morelos had told López Rayón. No more talk of Ferdinand VII. Soon the king would be back, for the French were on the run. A constitution was waiting for him, drafted by Spanish deputies and a few from overseas, like the Mexican Miguel Ramos Arizpe. A good constitution, guaranteeing Spaniards a free press and other liberties but not very helpful to Mexican editors who were still jailed at the viceroy's whim.

The deputies who came to the Congress of Anáhuac at Chilpancingo were strong for independence — and for Morelos, who had just captured the Acapulco fort. They gave him full power to govern while they worked on a constitution. They addressed him as Your Highness, but he insisted he was merely the Servant of the Nation. As such, he outlined the Sentiments of the Nation as he understood them: that sovereignty stems from the people and should be exercised through a government of separate legislative, executive, and judicial powers; that there should be laws moderating the extremes of wealth and poverty, and that Americans of all races should be eligible for public office.

While the sessions continued, Morelos left to invade the north, hoping to bring the war to a close. His first objective was Valladolid, later to be called Morelia in his memory. After he occupied the hills, and Galeana and Bravo stormed the gates, the city seemed about to fall. But the situation changed when Colonel Iturbide arrived unexpectedly. Disobeying his superiors, he attacked without waiting for them. He intercepted a secret order from Morelos, telling his men to blacken their faces in order to recognize one another in battle. Iturbide made his men do the same and galloped into the Morelos camp at nightfall. The Insurgents were so confused that they battled among themselves and finally broke into disorderly flight. This happened on Christmas Eve in 1813, a tragic night when independence was set back for years.

Matamoros, whom Morelos called his right arm, made a desperate stand in the hot country but was captured and taken to Valladolid for execution. The Insurgents dissolved into separate bands. Calleja, now viceroy, picked off the leaders one by one. Galeana was beheaded, and Morelos cried, "My two arms are destroyed, now I am nothing!" He was in disgrace with the Congress. Its members were hiding in the sierra, writing their constitution while Acapulco and Oaxaca were lost.

Ferdinand returned to the Spanish throne and proved to be not a hero but a tyrant. He repudiated the Spanish constitution and imprisoned its authors, including the Mexican Ramos Arizpe. No one was safe, not even Abad Queipo, who was called to Spain to report on the revolution and was delivered to the Inquisition for the books he'd read thirty years before.

Mexico's first constitution, proclaimed by the Congress at Apatzingán in October, 1814, was a brave gesture of defiance. It affirmed the rights of free men and declared that "no nation has the right to impede another in the free exercise of its sovereignty" and that "a claim based on conquest cannot legalize the use of force." The saddle-weary deputies who had written it were forever on the move to avoid arrest. In 1815, they selected Insurgent-held Tehuacán for a capital. Though they'd often complained of Morelos, he was the one they trusted to lead them there.

Morelos could muster only a small escort to protect the Congress on the perilous journey along tropical rivers and into the highlands. To confuse his pursuers, he had campfires built along various routes. But Calleja had a dozen commanders hemming him in and, toward the journey's end, two of them overtook the caravan at the mouth of a canyon. Young Bravo hurried on with the Congress. Morelos fought a delaying action till the last bullet was fired, then cried, "Every man for himself!"

A pursuit group came upon Morelos alone in the cliffs, removing his spurs for faster climbing. A gloating officer asked, "What would you do if I were in your place?" Morelos replied, "I'd give you two hours to confess, and shoot you." Forty-six days passed while Morelos was conducted to the Inquisition's prison in Mexico City, tried for offenses against the king and the faith, and carried to neighboring Ecatepec for execution. He was shot in the back on December 22, after saying his final prayer: "Lord, if I have labored well, Thou knowest it, and if ill, I take refuge in Thy mercy."

Two days later, the Congress for whose safety Morelos gave his life came to a melancholy end. The deputies had reached Tehuacán, but their long-winded arguments so annoyed Insurgent chief Manuel de Mier y Terán that he sent them home on Christmas Eve. The only Insurgent government after that was one or another junta in the marshes and hills. Guadalupe Victoria levied tolls on merchants coming from Veracruz and disputed the road with the young Royalist officer Antonio López de Santa Anna. In the southern mountains, Vicente Guerrero's men fought with clubs until they captured guns.

Iturbide policed the roads to the mines. He bought convoys

of quicksilver at his own price — who could say no? — and resold the precious flasks at a profit that brought screams of protest to Calleja's ears. The viceroy at last suspended him from duty. When Calleja returned to Spain, Juan Ruiz de Apodaca came in his place and let Iturbide continue to cool his heels.

Viceroy Apodaca's first law was that children mustn't fly kites from rooftops lest they fall. He was a gentle man when he had his way and pardoned Insurgents who laid down their arms, as many did. The flame seemed to be flickering out, until the young Spanish guerrilla Javier Mina landed on the coast below Texas in April, 1817, with three hundred soldiers of all nations. Mina had fought for Ferdinand the captive and fled from Ferdinand the tyrant. In London, the Mexican Fray Servando Teresa de Mier had shown him how America's silver paid for the bayonets that supported despotism in Spain. So Mina was here to strike a blow for two countries, his own and Mexico. "Tell your sons," he said to our countrymen, "that there were also Spaniards who loved liberty."

In a month's hard riding, Mina crossed San Luis Potosí and Zacatecas to the Bajío, gathering mounted recruits and defeating forces larger than his own. He joined Insurgent chief Pedro Moreno in a summer's bold raiding. To draw the Royalists from a besieged Insurgent fort, he attacked Guanajuato, but his war-weary allies no longer had the dash to see it through. The guerrilla who had defied Napoleon and

Ferdinand hid on a ranch and was captured while sleeping. Mina was shot as a traitor but lies today with our patriots under the Independence Column.

The firing squad or a pardon, which would it be? That was the choice Apodaca put to the Insurgents. Victoria hid in the mountains, abandoned by all but the Indians who brought him food. Guerrero fought along the Balsas River, retreating when necessary into the mountains or beyond them to the coast. He was the last obstacle to peace. Apodaca searched out Guerrero's father and sent him on a mission to the Southern Sierra. His son embraced him and heard his message, then turned to his men and said, "This venerable gentleman is my father. He comes from the Spaniards with offers of reward and position. I have always respected my father, comrades, but my country comes first." The rugged country where he persevered in fighting for independence is now the state of Guerrero.

In South America, the liberation struggle was flaring up again, but Mexico with its mines was heavily occupied by Spanish troops. Yet the king's own soldiers despised him and came to Mexico with more good words for constitutional reforms than the Creoles dared speak. Early in 1820, rebellion broke out in Spain among the troops that Calleja — none other — was embarking to put down rebellion in America. When the revolt spread to Madrid, the king begged for another chance and promised to abide by the Constitution. A Cortes was elected and proceeded, among other things, to

abolish the Inquisition and limit the clergy's ancient privileges.

The news reached Mexico in the spring. Alarmed and influential Spaniards interrupted their Lenten observances at
La Profesa temple to form a junta. Among them were a
judge, a canon, an inquisitor, and one or another marquis,
general, and mining magnate — all well connected. Their
apprehensions increased as Apodaca was obliged against his
will to proclaim the liberal Spanish Constitution. A free press
sprang up, championing every reform short of independence.
To the junta, this was as bad as independence. Even worse.
For ten years these men had branded independence as trea-
son, but now, to safeguard their privileges, they were willing
to cut the ties with the mother country, especially if Ferdinand or one of his brothers would come to Mexico and rule
in the firm old-fashioned way.

Looking for someone to execute the daring plan, the junta
found a man with ruddy sideburns, restless eyes, and lips
from which persuasion flowed like honey. Iturbide. In his
hands, the Royalist army, seasoned by ten years of war,
would be a powerful instrument. So, without letting Apodaca in on the secret, the junta brought influences to bear and
Iturbide was assigned to mop up the guerrillas in the south.

Iturbide talked his way into the viceroy's confidence and
rode off late in 1820, with the fittest troops and with orders
to beat Guerrero into begging for a pardon. However, Guerrero refused to stand still and be shot at. His way was to hit

and run, cutting off and destroying small Royalist units in the desolate country he knew so well. So Iturbide fired letters at him instead of bullets. They arranged a meeting, and Iturbide, so long a great enemy of independence, joined with Guerrero to achieve it. The two leaders embraced under the tamarinds at Acatempan before their cheering armies, then put their names to an independence plan at Iguala on February 24, 1821.

The Plan of Iguala declared Mexico to be a constitutional monarchy. Ferdinand or another European prince would come to rule, and the religion would be Catholic and no other. Clergymen would keep their lands and privileges, officers their military rank, Europeans their positions and property. Europeans or Americans of any race could hold public office. The plan was the junta's, slightly sweetened but far short of what Guerrero wanted. But it would achieve independence, and the rest, he hoped, would come later.

An independence flag was raised at Iguala — white, green, and red, standing for religion, independence, and the union of Americans and Europeans. An appeal went to the Royalist commanders to serve under this banner in an Army of the Three Guarantees.

The viceroy went purple with rage, but Iturbide was in the driver's seat, and the Royalist officers climbed aboard for the ride. At Guanajuato, Anastasio Bustamante seconded the plan, took down the heads of Hidalgo, Allende, Aldama, and Jiménez, and buried them with military honors. At

Orizaba next day, Santa Anna woke up a captain, fought guerrillas and became a lieutenant colonel, then switched to independence and went to bed a full colonel. Even Spanish commanders joined the stampede. The Insurgent Victoria came out of a cave, all skin, bones, and beard, and declared for the plan in Veracruz. Iturbide campaigned in Michoacán and the Bajío, and by July the game was in the bag.

In August, Juan O'Donojú, sixty-third and last viceroy, came ashore at Veracruz and sought a peace that would untie the bonds between Spain and Mexico but leave them friends and allies. At Córdoba, on the 24th, he signed a treaty with Iturbide recognizing an independent Mexican empire. It was like the Plan of Iguala, with one exception. If no Spanish prince accepted the throne, the Mexican congress might choose an emperor. Nothing was said about royal blood. Iturbide did not mind a bit.

On September 27, 1821, the Army of the Three Guarantees entered Mexico City, ending Spanish rule after three hundred years, one month, and two weeks. Arms shining, the battalions paraded under a cloudless sky to drums and trumpets. Iturbide rode ahead on a coal-black horse, taking bows with sweeps of his plumed hat. It was his thirty-eighth birthday.

The balconies were decked out in the national colors, and even the señoritas' hair ribbons were green, white, and red. The applause showered on the sixteen thousand marchers became a rain of *vivas* and flowers when Guerrero's sun-scorched Insurgents passed in sandaled feet.

Iturbide reviewed the procession from what was now the National Palace, then went to the Cathedral to occupy the viceroy's chair and hear a Te Deum in his honor.

No great day is complete without a proclamation. In the afternoon, Iturbide's went up with some memorable words: "Mexicans, you are now free and independent. It is for you to find happiness."

GROPING FOR NATIONHOOD
ⓞⓞⓞⓞⓞⓞⓞⓞ **11**

INDEPENDENT MEXICO looked for happiness among the ruins of eleven turbulent years. Behind fire-blackened hacienda walls, the magueys had flowered and withered. Fields lay untilled, passing armies having stripped them of tools, animals, and hands, leaving only mortgages on which years of back interest were due. Roads and bridges were out. Mines were flooded. Footloose soldiers were turning to banditry.

Iturbide appointed a governing junta of thirty-eight — not an Insurgent among them — and they named him chief regent. He needed money for deserving patriots who expected rewards and promotions, but the Spaniards were in possession of the Veracruz customs house and would not leave. The chief cities, in a roundabout undemocratic way, elected deputies to a congress. Largely Spanish by birth or sympathy, they looked forward to the pleasure of kissing the hand of whatever Spanish prince might come to rule them. Imagine their confusion when Spain rejected the Córdoba treaty and insisted that Mexico was still a colony! Where did their loyalty lie now? And whom could Iturbide trust?

There had to be a complete break with Spain and the royal family. One May night in 1822, Sergeant Pío Marcha led his comrades from the barracks, shouting, "Long live Agustín I!" Windows lighted up, bells rang, cannon were fired, and Iturbide, whose first name was Agustín, made out he was surprised. The Congress, menaced by noisy demonstrators, had no choice but to elect him emperor. A bitter pill for the Gachupines — and for the Insurgents, too, though they preferred a native emperor to a Spanish prince.

At the coronation, Iturbide was arrayed in splendor, though the crown jewels were from the Monte de Piedad, so the gossip ran. Fray Servando, now a deputy, likened the affair to a comic dance by the *huehuenches,* the little old men. "We want liberty as well as independence," he declared. The emperor locked up the outspoken friar and dismissed the whole Congress. To meet his imperial expenses, he imposed forced loans on the Spanish merchants. Iturbide was so unpopular by the year's end that Santa Anna proclaimed a republic in Veracruz. Iturbide gave up the fight in the spring and sailed for Italy. He returned the next year, unaware that the Congress had declared him a traitor, and was shot on landing in Tamaulipas.

We lived our first independent years under the threat of Spanish invasion and became saddled with a large army which ended by tyrannizing the country it was supposed to defend. To dislodge the Spaniards from Veracruz harbor, we bought a dozen small but costly ships with money borrowed in London. How the interest ran up!

The cry of "Death to the Gachupines!" rang out again. Whenever feeling reached a peak, a shipload or two of Spaniards were deported, many of them not only harmless but needed for their skills. Fortunately, exceptions were made. Hidalgo's verse in praise of his kindly jailer was remembered, and Guaspe lived out a long life in Chihuahua, a leading citizen.

The Insurgent Guadalupe Victoria became our first president in 1824, when the Constitution of the United Mexican States was proclaimed. It was a federal constitution, like yours, though for a different reason. Central America had broken away from Iturbide's misrule, and no outlying state would stand for a strong central government. Ramos Arizpe headed the committee on the Constitution and put in safeguards against the abuse of power. He had learned much while sitting in the Spanish Cortes and in Ferdinand's dungeons. And he knew that people in his native Coahuila liked to run their own local affairs. A smart Mestizo boy could study law and acquire influence in his state but was no match for the great Creole families on the national scene.

Titled gentlemen no longer passed in a receiving line to kiss a viceroy's hand, but they still placed their sons in positions of privilege and power. More than half the population were Indians, suffering the old wrongs and the new one of being led off, tied together, to fight for a republic they hardly knew to exist.

Foreign complications were added to our domestic problems. Our imports now came from England instead of Spain, but other nations wanted in on the trade. Looking for influential friends, United States Minister Joel R. Poinsett was caught in the crossfire between Conservatives and Liberals and went home with nothing to show but the Christmas Eve flower, which you call the poinsettia. But he had given us a bad scare. He wanted to buy Texas.

Spain had neglected Texas, which had neither gold nor docile Indians. Independent Mexico opened the sparsely inhabited land to Catholic colonists like the Irish who settled at San Patricio. Many Louisianans came, too, not just Latins, as was expected, but Anglo frontiersmen who were Catholics in name only, and, after them, Anglos from everywhere, with or without permission.

In 1828, General Mier y Terán was sent to Texas to see what was going on. The Mexicans, he reported, were ignorant and spoke horrible Spanish. The poorer Anglos had fled from their debts in the States or were branded on the cheek as thieves. The more prosperous had a few black slaves and were clearing the woodlands for cotton. Thinking to flatter the general, they told him he must be French or Spanish, surely not Mexican. They wanted schools, their own state capital, and duty-free trade with New Orleans. Knowing these people would never be Mexicans, Terán urged his government to strengthen the defenses of Texas at once and bring in more Mexican and European settlers.

The recommendations reached the capital during a political campaign marked by the pillaging of Spanish shops. The old Insurgent Guerrero came to the presidency. The treasury was empty. Three thousand Spaniards under General Isidro Barradas invaded the coast near Tampico. Terán closed in from Texas, Santa Anna from Veracruz, and the mosquitoes did the rest, driving Barradas from our shores. Santa Anna took the credit and became the hero of Tampico. But the immediate winner was Vice-President Bustamante. He raised an army to fight the Spaniards but used it to overthrow Guerrero and put himself in power. His chief minister was Alamán, the one who still had cold sweats remembering the Insurgents in Guanajuato. The Bustamante-Alamán government pursued Guerrero into the south, where he waged guerrilla war. At Acapulco, he was lured onto a ship, delivered to his foes for fifty thousand pesos, and shot.

Nothing much was done about Texas. The famished soldiers stationed there only provoked the Texans against

Bustamante. Lorenzo de Zavala, governor of the state of México, said, "Send farmers and artisans to Texas instead of unproductive soldiers, and Mexico will have nothing to fear." But General Terán was not so hopeful. "What Texas is coming to, only God knows," he wrote in a parting letter, then died by his own hand.

Texas was one of many places smoldering under centralist rule. The more rebellious states organized popular militias to safeguard their constitutional rights. Governor Francisco García Salinas put the long-abandoned mines of Zacatecas into production and raised money to pay for schools and buy land for the landless poor. Santa Anna made himself a champion of federalism and rode into the presidency in 1833, promising better times. He loved to march at the head of a parade or make a patriotic address but left the tough problems to Valentín Gómez Farías, the vice-president.

No problem was tougher than marking a line between the authority of the clergy and the civil authorities. Churchmen ran schools and hospitals, married the living, buried the dead, searched baggage for forbidden books, and sat as judges when other clergymen were involved. There were two governments — ecclesiastical and civil — both composed of good Catholics but often stepping on each other's toes. The king and the viceroy had kept them working in harness because they controlled the appointment of ranking churchmen. After independence, however, the Spanish bishops and their successors denied the Republic this privilege.

By law and custom, a tenth of the harvest belonged to the Church. This was once a simple way to pay the parish priest, but now, if a Puebla farmer tithed his wheat before shipping his flour to Yucatán, he couldn't meet the price of the New Orleans heretics. Gómez Farías and the young Liberals in the Congress enacted a law making tithes voluntary instead of compulsory. They made plans for public schools and opened California's mission lands for settlement. When cholera swept Mexico that year, it was plain to the Conservatives that Gómez Farías had stirred the divine wrath. He also made enemies in another quarter by weeding out untrustworthy army officers. Santa Anna took back his presidential powers and broke with his former allies. Gómez Farías found refuge in New Orleans, Zavala in Texas. The president then set out to impose his military authority on the states and provinces. After conquering Zacatecas, he marched on Texas.

He'd been there before. As a young officer in the king's service, he'd fought smugglers and cattle thieves and learned in the hard school of the frontier that dead prisoners make no trouble. Now, in 1836, Santa Anna was back, a coarse-featured man of forty-one, with melancholy eyes that pleased the ladies. To him the rebels were "land thieves" and the volunteers sailing from New Orleans to aid them were "pirates." He led his troops to San Antonio. You know the sad story of the Alamo — the bugle's death call as old as the Moorish wars; assault columns scaling the mission walls; shooting and fighting with knives and rifle butts, no quarter asked or given, and the sacrifice of Travis, Bowie, Crockett, and all the others who'd pledged never to surrender.

Mexicans in Texas faced an agonizing choice. They were Federalists, most of them, yet if they fought Santa Anna they were helping the Anglos against their own country. Zavala was a refugee. He shared the colonists' grievances and met with them in convention during the Alamo siege. When they declared Texas independent of Mexico, he voted with them, perhaps with a sigh, and they acclaimed him vice-president. But he found himself a man without a country, unlistened to by the Anglos, and went into seclusion in his home by the San Jacinto River.

Close by, Santa Anna lost the Texas campaign. Overconfident after the Alamo, he let Sam Houston draw him into the bayous where marksmen counted for more than cavalry. He awoke from a nap on April 21, and saw Texans all over his camp, shooting and clubbing. Riding off for reinforcements, he lost his way and was captured. Houston found him more useful alive than dead, for Santa Anna wrote begging his subordinates to withdraw from Texas "for the safety of the prisoners and especially of your affectionate friend and companion, who kisses your hand."

Whose tragedy was greater? Santa Anna's, for putting himself above his country? Or Zavala's, writing a friend, "I cannot live in Texas," and dying before the year was out of malaria and a broken heart?

Bustamante's star was rising again when Santa Anna came

back and retired to country life. He might have stayed there, breeding game cocks, but for the Pastry War. That is what we call the French naval attack on Veracruz in 1838. Its purpose was to collect a bill of six hundred thousand pesos, of which thirty thousand were said to be for the pastries that tipsy Mexican soldiers had upset in a French bakeshop. That's a lot of French pastry, but no more exaggerated than other claims that foreign powers made on us for the real or imaginary losses of their citizens in those unhappy years.

We were unprepared for war — but how could Bustamante say that to a nation smarting over the loss of Texas? He contented himself with token resistance, while the fort at Veracruz crumbled under the pounding of enemy frigates. Santa Anna saw his chance and rushed to the scene, breathing defiance. The French sent a landing party after him, but he slipped away, collected a few men and came to the dock as the enemy was reembarking. A spray of French grapeshot killed nine of his men and wounded him in the left leg. While surgeons sharpened their knives to amputate, he wrote a manifesto telling the nation how he'd driven the enemy into the sea at the point of a bayonet and now faced death serenely, asking only to be buried on his native soil. People read it, weeping, and forgave him Texas, not even asking why, after such a victory, it was necessary to submit to the French demands.

Santa Anna was now sure to return to power, considering the general discontent. The states had been reduced to departments of an all-powerful central government. Yucatán was shaken by agitation for independence. So bitter was the factional strife in that remote peninsula that first one side, then the other, recruited Indians to fight, giving them fire-arms and promising them land. The promises were not kept, but the weapons were. Early in the 1840's, the New York writer John L. Stephens visited Yucatán to explore the for-gotten cities of the ancient Mayas. Sugar planters were moving in among the modern Mayas, taking their land and paying them twelve and a half centavos a day to harvest and crush the cane. Stephens wrote, "The two races move on harmoniously together, with nothing to apprehend from each other, forming a simple, primitive, and almost patriarchal state of society."

After some maneuvering among the generals, Santa Anna emerged on top. No one knew better how to put together a winning military combination. In those days, officers won advancement, honorable exceptions aside, by knowing when to "pronounce," when to rise against the ins and for the outs. Each switch brought a promotion. By picking the winners, a man could go from lieutenant to general in six pronounce-ments.

No government lasted long without paying the army. Most of the revenues went for this purpose. Sometimes it was necessary to borrow from foreign moneylenders and pay back twice as much from future customs receipts. Civil employees often received warrants instead of cash and sold them to speculators for as little as ten centavos on the peso. Nevertheless, applicants kept pounding on the doors for government jobs because there were so few others.

It cost so much to hold the army's loyalty that Santa Anna put a tax on windows and doors. The poor had to brick up the openings that gave them light and air, but their ruler gave them pageants, including a magnificent state funeral for his sacrificed leg. His Immortal Three Quarters, as people called him, beautified the city with statues of himself. Texas was his eternal excuse for forced loans and higher taxes. In 1844, he demanded the enormous sum of ten million pesos to reconquer Texas, and the usually docile Congress at last rebelled. Lesser people took their cue and began pulling down the great man's statues. A colonel or even a general could see it was time to pronounce, so the army stood by while a mob pulled the sacred leg from its marble tomb and dragged it through the filth of the streets. Santa Anna took his other three quarters into hasty exile.

José Joaquín de Herrera, the next president, knew it was too late to recover Texas. He hoped it would remain independent, a cushion between Mexico and the United States, but it was too late even for that. When Texas became part of the great North American Union, he found himself boxed in. If he agreed to annexation, he'd be accused of surrendering Mexican soil. Mexicans were very touchy about what north-of-the-border orators called Manifest Destiny. It meant United States expansion from ocean to ocean and even from pole to pole. Already there were signs of California's becoming another Texas, for the Anglos were going west in covered wagons, some of them turning off to California. The Texans were reaching south, claiming the cattle range in Tamaulipas between the Nueces and the Río Grande, or Bravo. Would the United States support them in this claim?

Herrera ordered General Mariano Paredes to the disputed borderland but, hoping for peace, agreed to discuss the Texas question with a commissioner from the United States. John Slidell was named for this mission. Texas was ancient history to him. What he wanted was to buy New Mexico and especially California. All this leaked to the newspapers before Slidell reached Mexico City in a bumpy stagecoach during the Christmas posadas of 1845. Herrera's enemies saw in it a plot to sell out the country. Paredes had an excuse to pronounce. He turned back from the Texas road and, early in the New Year, shot his way into the presidency.

Naturally, Paredes could not bargain over California or anything else. Slidell notified Washington, "Nothing is to be done with these people until they shall have been chastised." He was sailing home when Mexican cavalry clashed with a United States patrol near the Río Grande.

What follows, you call the Mexican War and we the North American Intervention. It would be courteous to pass in silence over this conflict between our countries. But I have promised to tell you our story and cannot in friendship omit such an important if unhappy event. You have read of it in

your schoolbooks, I in mine. If my story seems different,
remember: as they taught it to me, I am telling it to you.

We are taught that your great Abraham Lincoln, among
others, opposed the war, believing it would lead to the
spread of slavery. We read of a United States lieutenant who
considered the war unjust and expressed regret in his memoirs that he had lacked the moral courage to resign his
commission. It seemed to him that the war with Mexico had
led to the tragic Civil War in which he, Ulysses S. Grant,
commanded the armies of the North.

We are also taught some painful truths about ourselves:
that we went to war without the means to wage it, without
unity and discipline, fighting little civil wars among ourselves and toppling one government after another while a
foreign invader was on our soil. Paredes had set a fateful
example. He was backed by monarchists like Alamán, who
believed that a king would find us allies in Europe to protect
us from the United States. That was not of much immediate
help when United States warships were sealing off our ports
and General Zachary Taylor was smashing through our
defenses in the north.

Taylor's army included many Irish from the old San Patricio colony in Texas. They faced a problem of conscience.
Some had joined to fight marauding Indians, and it saddened
them to see Catholic refugees streaming from Mexican towns
as their parents had fled before the British in the old country.
A hundred or so deserted to the Mexican side and formed the

Saint Patrick's Battalion. They must be traitors in your books, if they are mentioned at all. In ours they are the Irish Martyrs. Who knows what they were to themselves after living under three flags on a disputed frontier.

Santa Anna's conscience was flexible. From Havana he was communicating with generals and bargaining with politicians. Many Mexicans believed that, for all his faults, he'd get rid of the monarchists and know how to organize the war. At the same time the crafty Santa Anna was also negotiating through agents with United States President Polk. Paredes was overthrown, and Santa Anna passed through the naval blockade with the United States' permission and returned to Mexico. Did he promise to bring about a peace agreement? Whom did he sell out, his country or Polk? Historians are still not agreed. That is how devious Santa Anna was. There wasn't a medal on his chest when he rode into the capital. He left his presidential powers with the Liberal Gómez Farías and hurried to San Luis Potosí to regain his lost reputation. Taylor was in Monterrey, and the invaders' flag had been raised in Santa Fe and California. Santa Anna worked the near-miracle of raising eighteen thousand troops and bombarded Gómez Farías with anguished appeals for money to provision them.

Unfortunately, no one had that kind of money except the religious bodies. They'd lent Paredes a million pesos for the war, and it had melted away in revolutions, and so they were not happy when the Congress voted to raise fifteen million more by mortgaging and selling church property. Demonstrators took to the streets, crying, "Long live religion, and death to the government!"

While the capital seethed, Santa Anna's ill-clad soldiers marched north against icy winds. They engaged the enemy at La Angostura and penetrated behind Taylor's lines as far as the hacienda of Buenavista. Victory seemed within reach, when Santa Anna gave the command to turn back, perhaps because Mexico City was slipping into civil war.

The *polkos,* well-to-do volunteers who danced a graceful polka, hated Gómez Farías like the Devil himself. When ordered to Veracruz, where Winfield Scott was preparing to land, they took up arms against the government instead. Heroic Veracruz fought alone and fell after a week's bombardment.

"Mexicans," said Santa Anna on his return to the capital, "we have brought this tragic misfortune on ourselves by our endless disputes." He took the presidency and made his peace with the clergy in return for two million pesos for continuing the war. It did not go well. Santa Anna failed to stop the invaders at Cerro Gordo, on their way from the coast, and they advanced to Puebla. Disputes continued in the capital, and some states gave little or no support to the war. Yucatán went so far as to declare herself neutral and touched off a race war at home by executing a Maya chief for conspiracy against the *blancos,* or whites.

Scott, on entering the valley, found the eastern defenses

tight and sent Captain Robert E. Lee to map a path over the
lava bed to the south. General Gabriel Valencia spied a
Yankee column advancing on Padierna. Santa Anna ordered
him back to Churubusco, but the jealous and mistrustful
Valencia stood his ground, and suffered defeat. Santa Anna
was unwilling or unable to help him. The enemy now con-
centrated on Churubusco, whose defenders held out till the
last round was fired. The United States commander came and
took over, and asked where the ammunition was. General
Pedro María Anaya replied, "If I had any ammunition, you
wouldn't be here."

We remember Churubusco for Anaya's answer and the fate
of the men from San Patricio. Thirty-five of them died at
their artillery posts. Fifty were captured and hanged. Ten
were let off with fifty lashes laid on the back and a brand
mark on the cheek — and their descendants live among us,
like the blue-eyed Kellys of Puebla and the O'Connors of
Nayarit, as copper-hued as any Mexican.

Best remembered of all are the Boy Heroes of Chapulte-
pec, cadets of thirteen and up, in double-breasted long coats
and plumed kepis. They were at the military college in the
Castle when the war swept upon them from Molino del Rey.
The white-haired Insurgent Nicolás Bravo begged Santa
Anna for reinforcements to defend the Castle. He sent the
San Blas battalion so late that the commander Santiago
Xicoténcatl and most of his men died on the slopes below.
The enemy swarmed to the esplanade. At the school door, a

boy sentry cried, "Halt!" He shot one invader and stabbed another before being cut down. His companions resisted from behind mattresses in the dormitory and on the stairs to the high tower. Six of these young eagles gave their lives. Each September 13, we parade with our school banners and lay wreaths on the monument to the spotless patriots who taught us that Mexico is our country: Juan de la Barrera, Vicente Suárez, Agustín Melgar, Juan Escutia, Francisco Márquez, and Fernando Montes de Oca.

After Chapultepec fell, the enemy smashed through the city gates with picks and crowbars. A United States marine battalion occupied the National Palace and raised the starry flag over the "halls of Montezuma" on September 14, just before the independence holidays, a time of humiliation in 1847.

Our government — what remained after Santa Anna's flight — moved on to Querétaro. Chief Justice Manuel de la Peña y Peña, taking over a job no one wanted now, said, "I go to the presidency as to the grave." Peace negotiations were well along when gold was discovered in California, though neither side knew of it. Not that it mattered. California was lost forever, like the untapped oil of Texas, and the province of New Mexico, from which several states have been formed. More than half our territory, sacrificed because, in the agony of unsolved conflicts, we were unable to people and develop it!

A treaty fixing the new boundary was ready in February,

1848. After it was ratified, the young senator Mariano Otero wrote his wife, "I feel we have signed the death sentence of our children." He had spoken against the treaty and scorned the fifteen million dollars we were to receive as indemnity. We could not sell our countrymen like sheep! We should wear down the invaders by destroying their convoys, he declared, and hold out for better terms. But others said it was necessary to sacrifice part of the country to save the rest. Otero, outvoted, served loyally as foreign minister under Herrera, who returned to the presidency after having sought peace in vain three years before.

Many believed it was Mexico's destiny to vanish as a nation, coming under the sway of the United States or a European monarchy. Which it was to be did not matter to the governor of Yucatán in March that year, when he sent messages to Spain, England, and the United States, offering the peninsula free of charge to whichever nation should come and rescue the whites from the "Indian savages," as he called them. But you could not give Yucatán away in that terrible spring when the planters were fleeing to Mérida from their burning plantations. A priest tried to mediate between the races. One Maya chief offered to settle for abolition of the head tax, free use of public land, baptisms for thirty-eight centavos, and marriages for one and a quarter pesos. But other caciques said, "No more broken promises; everything the blancos have done to us, we shall do the same and more." In May, a hundred thousand whites were waiting at the coast to take ship and leave forever. The Mayas, believing themselves victorious, turned back to plant corn. Then the whites received arms from Havana and New Orleans, and regained confidence. They pursued the dispersed Indians, burning their villages and driving them into the southern forest. But the caste war was to go on for more than half a century. Already its effects were felt in other parts of Mexico.

To Otero it was understandable that four million oppressed Indians should have few ties of affection with their countrymen. But why was there so little unity among the other three million Mexicans? How was it that ten or twelve thousand foreign invaders could cross three populous states and meet resistance in only a few places? He set down the answers, as he saw them, in a pamphlet. We are passing, he said, from one age to another. The old order is dying and unable to defend us. The new one is in its infancy. Independence was only the first and easiest step in the destruction of the colonial system. We have tried every form of government but have not undertaken the great reforms demanded by the century in which we live. Taught that it is degrading to serve a master, we prepare our sons for idleness or find them military commissions or government employment. The arts and trades are so neglected that the best carriage maker or blacksmith, even the best shoemaker in a Mexican city, is a foreigner.

A small group engaged in trade, industry, commerce,

agriculture, and mining supports three times its number, including an army incompetent to defend the nation's honor, the religious corporations that have accumulated the larger part of the real estate, and a mass of ignorant and often corrupt officeholders. The productive classes carry the burden of taxes, duties, and forced loans but are unable to work in peace or move their goods with security. The cleavages run so deep in our society that unity of action is impossible even in the country's defense. "In Mexico what is called national spirit does not exist because we are not a nation." That was the bitter conclusion Otero reached, though he believed regeneration would come if the abuses and privileges of the colonial system were destroyed. The brilliant young statesman died of cholera soon after and was unable to participate in the task that lay ahead.

THE REFORM

◎◎◎◎◎◎◎◎   **12**

HE IS VERY UGLY but very good." That is how Margarita Maza, teen-age daughter of a well-to-do Oaxaca family, described her novio, Benito Juárez. Though he had the clean-chiseled features of a Zapotec god, these were not signs of beauty then. He had to be *very* good to win Doña Margarita's hand and heart.

Benito had come from the hills, an orphan speaking an Indian tongue, and found shelter with Antonio Salanueva. Father Salanueva, they called him, for his Franciscan robes, though he was a lay brother who bound books for the clergy and such others as could read. Benito helped him and went to a school where children "without reason" like himself were taught apart from sons of the "decent people." He no sooner learned Spanish than he entered a seminary and started on Latin.

We like to compare Benito Juárez with Abraham Lincoln — one born in an adobe hut, the other in a log cabin; both always reading, Abe sprawled before a fireplace, Benito crouched under a pitch-pine torch. Lincoln tried storekeeping before reading law. The one path young Juárez knew led back to the hills, where he would recite the mass to his own people and live on their fees for baptisms, marriages, and burials. He had earned high grades in philosophy and theology but came to realize that he lacked a true vocation for the priesthood. So when the Institute of Sciences and Arts was opened, he changed to law.

Juárez and Lincoln are pictured in the black coats and tall hats worn by men who believed that justice should be administered equally and fairly to all. Juárez had to contend with special privileges dating from colonial times. A dispute over a tailor's bill was tried in a military, ecclesiastical, or civil court, depending on whether the customer was a colonel, a canon, or plain Pepe Gómez. To Juárez a bill was just or unjust and had nothing to do with religion or military honor. Law was a stepping-stone to politics for Juárez, as for Lincoln. Both were congressmen when their countries were at war. Afterwards, Juárez was governor of his state, saving it from bankruptcy and building schools besides.

Oaxaca was fortunate, for the country's general mood was despairing. After the United States indemnity was spent, the generals returned to pronouncing. Apaches raided into the north, rebel Mayas from the southern forest. In the parched lands beyond the Bajío, the young Indian Eleuterio Quiróz formed an Army of Regeneration that fought for the right to plant corn on idle land and gather firewood and prickly pears. General Bustamante captured Quiróz and shot him for a "communist," a word then coming into use from restless Europe. The ex-Royalist general, always a favorite of staid Conservatives like Alamán, was too near the grave to be president again. Who should warm the chair until a proper throne could be set up for a Spanish prince?

There was always Santa Anna. Alamán promised to curb his flamboyance, and brought him from exile to head a strong but respectable government. After a few weeks, Alamán died and Santa Anna went out of bounds, assuming the title of His Most Serene Highness and costuming his Indian guards as Cossacks with fierce whiskers. He encouraged the blancos in Yucatán to sell Maya war captives into slavery in Cuba at twenty-five pesos a head, and shared in the profits. He received seven million dollars from the United States for what is now the southern strip of Arizona and New Mexico, and spent it in seven months.

Santa Anna had his political enemies banished to remote

villages or snatched from their families and sent out of the country. Juárez was one of them. He went into exile in New Orleans and there, among others, he met Melchor Ocampo, past governor of Michoacán. While Ocampo sold pots, Juárez rolled cigars. They ate for as little as ten cents a day but had plenty of food for thought. Juárez, when not working, steeped himself in constitutional law, while Ocampo's boundless curiosity was like Thomas Jefferson's, but the chief concern of all the exiles was to end their country's ruinous colonial system.

In 1854, rebellion flared in and about Acapulco. Juan Alvarez, who had fought beside Morelos and Guerrero, joined with General Ignacio Comonfort and others in a Plan of Ayutla that called for a return to popular government. They won adherents up and down the coast. Some of the New Orleans exiles moved to the border to spread the flames in the north. In the summer of 1855, Juárez went via Panama to Acapulco and reported at the rebel barracks, a travel-stained, ragged Indian, unrecognized at first. "Knowing that here you fight for liberty, I have come to see how I can be useful," he said. General Alvarez made him his private secretary. The revolution of Ayutla was near flood tide, and Santa Anna fled into exile, never to return to power. Before the year was out, Alvarez was acting president, and Juárez his minister of justice.

Alvarez, a leathery old rancher with graying sideburns and an inferiority complex, turned the presidency over to the more polished Comonfort. And that was a pity, for Comonfort was everybody's friend and had a habit of putting off hard decisions. He must not have foreseen the consequences of a little law he signed for Juárez. It provided that civil lawsuits should no longer be tried in military and ecclesiastical courts, and became the spark that kindled the fire of the Reform.

The Conservatives immediately raised the battle cry of "Religion and privileges!" Comonfort was in the field a month, putting down the rebellion, and went so far as to exile the fiery bishop of Puebla. But his mother's reproaches caused him torments of conscience, and he pardoned his enemies generously.

Juárez became governor of Oaxaca again. Seeing danger ahead, he strengthened the state militia with local boys whose mettle he knew, and urged other governors to do likewise.

All during 1856, the nation's destiny was debated in a constitutional convention. Ponciano Arriaga, one of the New Orleans group, wanted to set a limit on large holdings of uncultivated land. "Are we to have popular government while the people are hungry, naked, and miserable?" he asked — but he was sixty years ahead of his time. To most of the deputies, the evil was not large holdings but rather the "dead hand" that accumulated real estate without ever selling it or paying taxes. By this they meant religious corporations chiefly but also Indian villages. Such bodies, they decided, must sell their holdings, giving first choice to their tenants. It turned out that few of the poor could buy land, even on payments, least of all Indians ignorant of the real estate business and fearful of losing the common lands on which their solidarity rested.

For six days the convention occupied itself with freedom of worship. Some argued that Mexico being wholly Catholic, nobody wanted it. Others held that tolerance would attract needed immigrants. More likely, snapped a deputy, it would revive human sacrifice to Huitzilopochtli. The decisive argument was that religion remained the only tie that united all Mexicans when so many others were broken. And so freedom of worship was voted down, though many other freedoms were written into the Constitution of 1857, including a declaration that slaves treading on Mexican soil become free by that very act.

On February 5, feeble old Gómez Farías knelt before a crucifix and swore to uphold the nation's new charter. He administered the oath to the deputies and the president. But in March, when the civil and military authorities were called on to take the oath, a storm broke. Certain high churchmen declared that the Constitution illegally deprived them of their rights, besides permitting impious books to circulate and young children to attend nonreligious schools. With Spanish tenacity, they went back a thousand years in the canon law to prove that anyone who took the oath was in mortal sin.

In Europe, Church and State had come to new arrangements with the changing times, but Mexico was closer to the
age when warrior-priests did battle with Moorish infidels —
and so change came hard. Put yourself in the shoes of a
government clerk with seven children to support. Do you
refuse the oath and quit your job? Probably not, if your padre
is as easygoing and discreet as many were. But the saints help
you if he's unbending. Your great-uncle Don Maclovio, may
he rest in peace, obtained Christian burial only by retracting
the oath on his deathbed.

Thousands of Mexicans were torn between loyalty to their
country and their bishops. President Comonfort himself had
to face his mother's tears every night for the course he was
taking. In Holy Week, the public officials who went in procession to the Cathedral for a traditional ceremony found the
doors locked. They were chagrined, but when something
similar happened to Governor Juárez in Oaxaca, he made no
issue of it and thought it well that the civil authorities should
take no official part in religious ceremonies.

That year Juárez was elected chief justice of the Supreme
Court. The campaign against the Constitution mounted in
fury, and Comonfort lost faith that it could be made to work.
At the end of the year, he and others pronounced against it.
Juárez refused to go along and was locked up in the Palace.
After three weeks, an ambitious general took the presidency
for himself. Comonfort had to flee but, repentant now,
stopped long enough to let Juárez out.

A few days later, the capital received a bulletin from Guanajuato that read: "An Indian is here who says he is President of the Republic." Juárez *was* president, according to the Constitution, having been chief justice when Comonfort abandoned the post. He had reached the Bajío by foot and mail coach and was telling the rebels to lay down their arms and respect the law. Behind him stood a league of Liberal state governors, pledged to use their militias to defend the Constitution. They installed Juárez in a temporary capital at Guadalajara, and he selected a cabinet that included Ocampo and the poet Guillermo Prieto.

The Liberals lost the opening battle, and the officers at Guadalajara began switching sides. The commander of the guard at the state capitol sent a company of riflemen to shoot the members of the Liberal government. Juárez stood in the doorway of the hall of justice, head up, as they approached and took aim. The poet Prieto flung himself in front of the president, drowning the command to fire with his words: "Brave men do not assassinate!" He went on to say more than he later remembered, but it must have been eloquent because the soldiers, one by one, lowered their guns, then filed away, some weeping.

Juárez and his companions escaped from Guadalajara in a carriage with drawn curtains. "A sick family," the driver explained at the town gates they passed. They took ship at Manzanillo, crossed Panama, and eventually reached Liberal Veracruz, which became the capital of the sick but legal government. To Juárez, legality was "the only guarantee of a lasting peace in our country."

Caciques, or political bosses, ruled the northern states and, though Liberals, fought only when it pleased them. The enemy's western campaign had shattered the league of friendly governors. The armed defense of the Constitution rested on the frail shoulders of War Minister Santos De-gollado, a nearsighted accountant from the Morelia Cathedral. He remained in the danger zone to cross swords with young Miguel Miramón, who had fought beside the Boy Heroes and was the rising hope of the Conservatives.

Against Miramón's regulars, Degollado recruited peasant boys in Michoacán and Jalisco. *Chinacos,* ragged ones, their enemies called them. They returned the compliment, calling their foes *mochos,* hypocrites. Liberals against reactionaries, patriots against traitors. Or seen from the other side, decent people, respectful of religion, against impious demagogues. This was the lineup in the War of the Reform.

Degollado shared the hardships of his men and struggled to overcome his military ignorance. He operated boldly in the country below Guadalajara, retreating into the tropics when necessary and advancing into the highlands when possible. He was the Hero of Defeats, losing more often than not but gaining time and always trying again.

Miramón assumed the presidency of the Conservative regime. Juan N. Almonte was in Spain, bargaining for a Bourbon prince and a naval squadron that would blast the

Liberals from Veracruz. French and British warships came on bill-collecting expeditions, threatening to put troops ashore. No one recognized Juárez in 1858, not even the United States. His task was fourfold: to gain the United States' friendship, prevent European intervention, win the civil war, and bring his country through it whole and free. An agent came from Washington and reported that Juárez was incorruptible but not as smart as his cabinet. Wasn't the same later said of Lincoln? Anyway, the United States decided to recognize the Juárez government. It was a warning to Europe to go easy.

In the spring of 1859, Miramón attacked Veracruz. Degollado saw a chance to march on the capital but was disastrously defeated in the suburb of Tacubaya. As the battle was ending, Miramón returned from the coast, his unacclimated men ravaged by fever. Peevishly he ordered General Leonardo Márquez to shoot the captured officers. Márquez finished with them all, including the doctors. Even a twenty-two-year-old medical student, dressing an enemy officer's wounds, was shot. Márquez, after that, was called the Tiger of Tacubaya.

It was going to be very costly to rebuild the army broken at Tacubaya. One way to get money was to let the United States build railroads on Mexican soil and buy Lower California, as the United States minister wished. But to concede rights on our soil to another country was dangerous, while to surrender territory was more than honor could bear. So the negotiations dragged on.

The only other source of funds was the property of the religious corporations. The Conservative Miramón had been squeezing loans from the clergy and was at the point of mortgaging their remaining wealth to foreign speculators. The northern caciques, on the Liberal side, were seizing church properties in their states. Roving commanders were stripping temples of silver vessels and gold candlesticks in the name of liberty or religion or for their own account. Degollado pleaded with Juárez to take what remained, for the good of the nation. It was argued in cabinet meetings that, by Spanish custom, the clergy held these riches in trust for the crown, which might use them in time of national danger. Finance Minister Miguel Lerdo de Tejada said nothing less than using them now could save Mexico. Juárez hesitated. Lerdo threatened to resign.

Juárez was up against a problem that Lincoln would soon face. To save the nation it was necessary to sweep aside long-accepted property rights. Both men, when they believed the time ripe, took measures that transformed society. Lincoln made the slaves "forever free." Juárez, in July, 1859, declared that the worldly goods administered by the clergy "have been and are the property of the nation." He followed with a series of measures aimed to create "perfect independence" between civil and religious affairs, and known as the Laws of the Reform.

Wherever the Liberals ruled, the religious corporations surrendered houses and lands. Public officials began keeping a register of births, marriages, and deaths. Cemeteries were opened to saints and sinners alike. Marriage became a civil contract in the eyes of the law. Melchor Ocampo wrote the service our judges still use. It explains that a man, being courageous and strong, owes his bride protection, food, and guidance. And she, whose best qualities are beauty, tenderness, and self-sacrifice, owes him obedience, consolation, and good counsel, the latter given without provoking his rude and irritable nature. These are fine sentiments, though most couples don't feel fully married without orange blossoms and a nuptial mass. That's why we are married twice.

Separating Church and State must have come easier in your country, with its many forms of worship. Here a common faith was woven into our daily life. The stroke of a blade cut the fabric apart. Separation came during an impassioned struggle and strongly affirmed the nation's civil authority. Street processions and the ringing of church bells were regulated. Rich endowments were taken over and monasteries closed. Convents might admit no more novices. Parish fees were made voluntary. Freedom of worship was proclaimed.

Mexico, with untold heartbreaks, set her face toward a world in which telegraph lines and harbor installations were more important than pearls and rubies for the Virgin. But the Church has not lacked for offerings, and most Mexicans remain Catholics, though sometimes we lie on the beach at Acapulco during Holy Week instead of making a circuit of seven churches as our grandparents did.

Ocampo favored dividing the church lands into small holdings for independent farmers. But the nationalized property had to be sold quickly to pay for food and clothing for the soldiers. Most buyers with ready cash were foreign merchants and moneylenders or wealthy Conservatives seeking to enlarge their haciendas. Some eventually paid a little conscience money to the Church, though not too much. More became Liberals and paid nothing. But this was later. At the end of 1859, the Conservatives were winning. Almonte had just signed a treaty with Spain. United States friendship was so essential that Foreign Minister Ocampo consented to the building of United States railroads in the north and across the narrow waist of Tehuantepec. Though the agreement yielded no territory, it raised fears of future intervention. But Ocampo and Juárez saw no other way to prevent immediate intervention by Spain.

The agreement never went into effect, being voted down by antislavery forces in the United States Senate, but it helped us when we needed help. In the spring of 1860, Miramón attacked Veracruz again, this time hoping for Spanish support from the sea. He had two armed steamers, purchased in Cuba, to carry bombs and grenades to the besieging force. They sailed past Veracruz harbor without displaying a flag, and Juárez declared them pirate ships and fair prey for all nations. The commander of the U.S.S. *Saratoga* took the hint and captured the vessels. No Spanish help came, and Miramón, unable to run arms by sea, spent his strength in the shallows and dunes. He was never himself again. It was a turning point of the war.

Degollado, too, showed the strain. Determined to get the war over, he took responsibility for seizing a convoy with a million pesos in silver. The other side had no scruples about such "war loans," but Degollado brooded — and all the more when he learned that some of the silver belonged to Englishmen. This he gave back, and the British minister showed his appreciation by proposing a plan to heal the wounds of war. Let the foreign diplomats in Mexico choose an acting president, neither Juárez nor Miramón, he said, then elect a congress to write a new constitution on which everyone could agree.

Poor weary Degollado came out for the plan without so much as consulting the civil government. Juárez had to relieve him of his command and make it clear that the nation's destiny could not be placed in foreign hands. "If the question were whether I should continue in power," he said, "the decent thing would be for me to withdraw. Such is not the case. The nation is fighting for its fundamental law, as enacted by its elected representatives."

In the army for which Degollado had all but sacrificed himself, new leaders were rising, like Jesús González Ortega and Ignacio Zaragoza, as good as the professionals or better.

They took Guadalajara about the time Lincoln was elected and fought their way to the capital for a victory parade on Christmas Day. Miramón took refuge on a Spanish warship, Márquez with a gang of kidnapers and horse thieves in the western hills.

Juárez returned to the capital for a day-long ovation. "Nothing by force, everything through law and reason," he counseled. I wish he might have met Lincoln, as our minister Matías Romero did a few days later. Your president-elect was in Springfield, about to depart for Washington. He expressed friendship for Mexico, reported Romero, "in an explicit and even vehement manner." Poor Lincoln, with a civil war only three months away! Had your country been spared that agony, ours might not have been plunged into new misfortunes.

RESPECT FOR OTHERS' RIGHTS

◉◉◉◉◉◉◉◉◉ **13**

WHEN YOUR civil war began, ours seemed over, except for some marauding bands. A newly elected congress met and counted the presidential votes, Juárez winning narrowly over General González Ortega.

Then in June, 1861, Márquez, the Tiger of Tacubaya, went on a manhunt. By his orders, a band of outlaws kidnaped Ocampo from his country home and carried him off to be shot as one of the authors of the Laws of the Reform. "I die having done for the service of my country what in conscience seemed good," said Ocampo. The killers strung his riddled body from a dead limb of a pepper tree and left it for the zopilotes.

The crime raised the capital to a fury. A mob clamored for reprisals against the Conservatives. The young commander Leandro Valle risked his life to protect his war prisoners. Degollado burst into a heated session of the Congress and won a chance to redeem himself by going in pursuit of the assassins. He led a flying column to Monte de las Cruces and was slain in battle. Then Valle went with a larger force. Márquez captured him and had him shot and hanged.

There was nothing for the government to do now but mobilize in full strength and clean out the rebel bands, which it did, though the sly Márquez found another lair. The costly campaign forced Juárez to suspend payments on the foreign debts. The news reached Madrid, Paris, and London at the same time as the reports of the Battle of Bull Run, in which, as you know, Lincoln's green recruits ran away from the rebels. Wise old heads saw the United States breaking up and Mexico ripe for picking. The mochos in Europe assured them that unhappy Mexico wanted nothing so much as a foreign king. Having lost the War of the Reform, their only hope lay in foreign intervention. Miramón begged Isabella II for a Spanish general's uniform and promised to march triumphantly to Mexico City and put one of her relatives on the throne. The queen thought that would be nice. Her ministers did, too, but considered some French help necessary.

France was then ruled by Louis Napoleon, dapper nephew

of a famous uncle. He not only agreed to go along with Spain but lined up England for a three-power expedition. Each power, however, had a different purpose in mind. Britain wanted us to pay our enormous debts. Isabella wanted to tie us to the apron strings of the mother country. In Louis Napoleon's crafty mind, other bees were buzzing. He dreamed of an empire in America, a Latin empire, strong enough to hold off the Anglo-Saxons and therefore under French, not Spanish, leadership. Having no relatives to send us, he hit upon Maximilian of Hapsburg as the right emperor for Mexico. Maximilian, an unemployed brother of the Austrian monarch, said he'd come if the Mexicans wanted him. But he started studying Spanish without waiting to know, prodded by his wife Carlota, an ambitious Belgian princess.

The hostile squadrons arrived at half-abandoned Veracruz in December and January. While drawing up their demands, the commissioners of the three powers fell to quarreling. It was one thing to ask full value for Santa Anna's worthless warrants but another for the French to expect Juárez to repay twelve million pesos for a million lent to Miramón. The Spanish general Juan Prim became suspicious of Napoleon's motives. He obtained permission for the foreign troops to come up out of the fever zone to Orizaba while the claims were negotiated, but they were to return if agreement failed. This was not as foolish on Mexico's part as it sounds. The Spanish and English commissioners saw with their own eyes that there was no popular support for a monarchy and that they might as well be patient with the republican government. And they resented being duped when the monarchist Almonte appeared, under protection of French arms, and proclaimed himself Maximilian's representative. Thanks to Prim, the three-power expedition broke up and only the French remained. We have a street named General Prim for this invader courageous enough to admit a mistake. He inaugurated an era of better feeling between Spain and Mexico.

Count de Lorencez led the French on, breaking his word. He wrote the war minister in Paris: "We are so superior to the Mexicans in race, organization, morality, and elevated sentiments that I beg Your Excellency to tell the Emperor that at the head of six thousand soldiers I am already master of Mexico."

Proud words, put down a week before May 5, 1862. On that memorable *Cinco de Mayo,* the count stood before Puebla. His monarchist friends told him, "You will enter in a rain of flowers," but then a cannonball whizzed by from Fort Guadalupe on a nearby hill. Zaragoza, the Texas-born Mexican commander, passed the morning there and at Fort Loreto, examining the defense works through his iron-rimmed spectacles. Looking like an earnest young professor, he told his men, "Your enemies are the first soldiers of the world, but you are the first sons of Mexico, and they are trying to take away your country."

Baggy-trousered zouaves and French marines led the assault on Guadalupe. Near the crest they fought with Indians in sleeveless wool jackets and cotton pants tied below the knee. These sandaled soldiers from Zacapoaxtla matched their machetes against French bayonets and pushed the enemy into the crossfire between Guadalupe and Loreto. Three times Lorencez sent his brave men up through the chaparral to die on the slope or tumble from scaling ladders at the fort's stone walls. The rains came early that year, and at five P.M., the bugle sounded retreat. The invaders fell back, pelted by hailstones and harassed by Mexican cavalry.

Zaragoza telegraphed the capital: THE ARMS OF THE NATION ARE COVERED WITH GLORY. Lorencez used the slower mails and asked Napoleon for twenty thousand more soldiers. They came, along with a new general, but the invasion timetable had been set back a year. Juárez gained a breathing spell — and so did Lincoln, according to our historians.

The destinies of your country and mine were closely linked during that week of May 5. Lincoln, my teacher says, was with a convoy in Virginia waters, investigating why the campaign against Richmond was lagging. He was worried that unless the North got on with the war, France and England would recognize the Confederacy and blast their way into the blockaded Southern ports to get cotton for their famished mills. The Confederate agent Slidell was in Paris — the same Slidell who once came asking us for California. That summer he promised Napoleon a hundred thousand free bales of cotton if he'd send a war fleet for them. The

French ruler said he'd run the blockade if England would, as seemed quite likely at the time. Two weeks before, he'd told General Elie Forey why he was sending him to Mexico: to build an "impassable dam" against the United States and to spread "our beneficent influence" north and south.

Suppose Mexican resistance had crumbled at Puebla, allowing the French to advance to the Texas border and make common cause with the Confederacy. Would Napoleon have respected the cotton blockade? Would Lincoln have had time to win the world's sympathy by freeing the slaves, and to prepare for the victory that made "one nation indivisible" of the United States?

Among us, the Cinco de Mayo inspired an upsurge of national feeling. May 5 was and is a patriotic holiday, exalting nonintervention, or the right to be free of foreign interference in our domestic affairs and the duty of respecting that right in other nations.

After Puebla, Maximilian was not sure he wanted to be a Mexican emperor. French deputies spoke out against Napoleon's risky adventure. Forey spent the fall and winter moving from the coast to the mountains, for the countryside had been stripped of mules and wagons. Zaragoza died while on a reconnaissance, and the second defense of Puebla was entrusted to González Ortega, along with command of twenty-four thousand men. Forey came with an equal force. Avoiding last year's mistakes, he constructed siege works before attacking. Then in eight days he occupied seven blocks — and there were 158 blocks in Puebla! Every street was blockaded, every house and convent was a thick-walled fortress. After a two-month siege, the defenders yielded, but only to starvation. A council of war ordered the guns smashed and the arms destroyed. The officers delivered themselves over as prisoners of war, refusing parole. Five hundred were deported to France, but González Ortega, Porfirio Díaz, and others escaped before reaching Veracruz and were free to fight again.

Juárez and his advisers chose not to sacrifice everything in a brief and glorious defense of the capital. Instead, they traded space for time in which to wear down the enemy. The Congress, not knowing when it might meet again, gave Juárez full power to wage a second war of independence. At dusk on May 31, 1863, before a multitude in the Zócalo, he pressed the lowered flag to his lips and cried, "Viva México!" Then he took the road to San Luis Potosí, a refugee for the third time.

When the French marched into the capital, they came upon a newly opened avenue bearing the name of Cinco de Mayo. They shot holes in the street signs, but the name remained in our hearts. Things had been done that Forey himself couldn't undo. He showed respect for religion by sending his regiments to military masses but failed to return the church lands. How could he do so when a third of the buyers were French? The bitter-enders who would be satisfied with nothing less than the uprooting of the Reform impatiently awaited the emperor's coming.

A delegation of monarchists now formally offered Maximilian the throne. He was reassured by the taking of Mexico City but still insisted on a popular vote. This caused the French no end of bother. General François Bazaine, campaigning in the west, had to stop at every town square for an "act of adherence" to the empire. Many people were unable to sign, even with a bayonet at their ribs, so names were forged and invented. All to please Maximilian.

Bazaine reported, "Where we are in occupation, peace reigns and the population declares for intervention and the monarchy. Everywhere else there is war and a dismaying silence." Juárez put it this way: "When the enemy concentrates in one place, he is weak in the rest. When he spreads out, he is weak everywhere."

Taking care to elude capture, the president moved farther into the north in 1864. The carriage in which he rode with his ministers was temporarily the National Palace. To some, however, it was a shabby vehicle carrying a lost cause into dusty oblivion. At Saltillo, a committee representing González Ortega and others asked the president to resign, saying it would then be easier to reach a settlement with the French. At Monterrey, a regional cacique objected to turning over the federal customs receipts. Juárez surmounted such difficulties. His firm will and lawful authority were the threads holding the resistance together.

In these days, Maximilian's Mexican friends came with armfuls of papers and told him he'd received six and a half million votes for emperor. He was glad to be so popular, and Carlota was happy to be an empress. They sailed from their castle by the Adriatic, the French emperor having made them a loan and promised to keep his army in Mexico (at our expense) while Maximilian organized one of his own. Already the costs were great, but Napoleon expected to pay himself back with the mines of Sonora, which he imagined were richer than California's.

The imperial couple reached Mexico shortly before General Sherman began marching through Georgia. It was plain that a puppet emperor on an American throne was not going to be popular in your country or mine. Tears came to Carlota's eyes when irreverent Veracruz ignored her. There was curiosity, at least, in the capital, the rich going in their carriages to the city's edge to mix with real royalty and the poor lining the sidewalks to look, as they would at a giraffe or an elephant. They saw a blue-eyed man of thirty-one with silky, neatly parted whiskers, his fair wife of twenty-four, holding herself proudly and, with them, an array of counts and countesses.

We have good reason to detest Maximilian, but it's hard to hate anyone who's so well-meaning and friendly, at least in television serials. Wanting to be loved as the number one Mexican, he often rode about dressed as a rich cattleman. The Liberals grinned, the Conservatives hid their embarrassment, and people in general thought that an emperor who cost so much should *look* like one. Maximilian had no money sense, none whatever. He filled Chapultepec Castle with marble statues, did over the National Palace, and invited all the world to banquets and balls. Carlota demolished scores of

Indian huts to make way for a boulevard linking the Castle with the city. She named it for the emperor, but we call it the Paseo de la Reforma.

Maximilian paid himself a big salary and his wife a small one, but she knew she had the better head for running an empire and gladly took charge while he traveled about, meeting "his people." He signed the visitors' book at Dolores Hidalgo on September 15, and wrote a tribute to the brave padre who'd raised the grito in 1810. Dead heroes get more praise than live ones. Juárez was then by the Nazas River in mountainous Durango. He'd sent his family to New York, and gone into the desert with his ministers and a small escort. As the moon cast its beams on the rain-fed stream, they celebrated the independence anniversary with guitar music and tortillas with beans. They reached Chihuahua the following month, after what seemed like a steady retreat, but Juárez kept saying, "We shall win, you'll see."

They'd win because in Jalisco, Oaxaca, Tamaulipas, Coahuila, and half a dozen other states, guerrillas were harassing the enemy, destroying his convoys, wasting him in marches and countermarches. They'd win because Juárez had taken Maximilian's measure: "He is not the one who can work miracles and sustain a long struggle, as we are doing."

Troubles were indeed crowding in on the fair-haired intruder. To the ultra-Conservatives, he was a Juárez with a yellow beard, if not worse. Maximilian accepted the Reform in large part and looked for support among moderate Liberals who lacked faith in a Juárez victory and appreciated a well-paying government job. But how long would the money last? Maximilian ran through one French loan, then another. A year of his rule proved more costly than forty years of Santa Anna and Bustamante. Napoleon had made a bad investment. He was afraid to take Sonora once the United States civil war was over and decided to "get out of that nest of eggplants," as he called Mexico. Slowly he began calling his troops home. Maximilian was supposed to replace them with Mexicans and foreign legionnaires, but with money running out, that was a problem. When problems weighed on him, he went to Cuernavaca and watched the hummingbirds in their nests.

Before leaving, the French made a mighty effort to drive Juárez from Mexican soil in the hope that the United States would then recognize Maximilian. Juárez retreated as far as Paso del Norte, now Ciudad Juárez, but nothing would induce him to cross the frontier, not even the governor's concern for his safety. "No one knows this state as you do, governor," he said. "Show me the highest, driest, most inaccessible mountain, and I will climb to the top and die there of hunger and thirst. But leave the Republic? Never!"

Lincoln's tragic death deprived Mexico of a friend when many looked for early help from the north. Juárez spared no effort to get arms from beyond the frontier but was wary of foreign troops and reminded his friends, "What Mexico does not do for herself in order to be free, she should not expect other nations to do for her." Bazaine tried to extinguish the resistance by terror and prevailed on Maximilian to sign a decree that all prisoners would be shot as bandits. As a result, some of our bravest officers and men died, and Maximilian sealed his own fate.

By May, 1866, Juárez could say, "Time and our steadfastness have exhausted the enemy." His guerrilla bands had grown into armies. Napoleon speeded the withdrawal of his troops, nudged by the United States. Maximilian had the sensible idea of abdicating, but his wife's sharp tongue put him to shame.

Carlota then went to Europe and tried to shame Louis Napoleon whose big worry now was not Mexico but Prussia's rising power. Tears were all he could spare for Carlota — no money, no troops. She flew into a rage and fell prey to delusions of persecution. Napoleon became the Devil in person, sending his demons to poison her, even to Rome, where she fell at the Holy Father's feet, imploring his protection. Poor mad Carlota! She lived with her fantasies for sixty years, confined in a Belgian castle.

Before Carlota's tragedy became known, her journey inspired a song, "Adiós, Mamá Carlota, adiós, my tender love." Armies marched to its rollicking rhythm, down from Monterrey with Mariano Escobedo, across Oaxaca with Porfirio Díaz, into Guadalajara with Ramón Corona. Juárez began his return in a whirl of parades and banquets.

Maximilian, floundering, turned to the Conservatives as his last hope, but on learning of Carlota's breakdown he set out for the Gulf, homeward bound. At Orizaba, a letter came from his mother. "You are a Hapsburg," she reminded him. "It is better to perish in the ruins of your empire than to return with the baggage of the French army." Wavering, he turned back to the capital and appointed Miramón, Márquez, and Tomás Mejía as his commanders. His hopes rose when Miramón raided Zacatecas and all but captured Juárez. They fell when his commanders pulled back into Querétaro. He put out feelers to the Liberals for permission to leave the country but had a change of mood and assured the Conservatives that a Hapsburg never deserts his post in time of danger. They told him his post was in Querétaro, commanding his army in person, and there he went in February, 1867.

Escobedo, then Corona, closed in. Between Maximilian's indecision and his generals' rivalries, the siege lines tightened. The wily Márquez broke out before it was too late, promising to return with aid but going to Mexico City instead. There Díaz had him under siege after taking Puebla on April 2.

At Querétaro, Maximilian suffered the torments of dysentery and bedbugs, while Miramón lunged in vain against an encircling ring of fire. On the morning of May 15, the city surrendered. Maximilian handed his sword to Escobedo, a black-bearded ex-muleteer. He asked for an escort to the coast, where an Austrian warship was waiting. To a Hapsburg, descended in the tenth generation from the great emperor in whose name this land was conquered, it seemed a reasonable request. But Mexico was now a republic with an

Indian president who believed that all men were equally subject to the law. Maximilian remained a prisoner, accused of usurping power, ordering the execution of patriots, and serving as an instrument of French intervention against the independence of the nation.

A military tribunal of seven young officers tried the fallen emperor. Rejecting the plea that he was merely a party chief in a civil war, they voted to convict and, by four to three, fixed the punishment as death. They passed the same sentences on Miramón and Mejía. Juárez and his minister Lerdo declined to interfere with the course of justice, saying that firmness was necessary for the nation's peace and security.

June 19 dawned to the sound of drums and trumpets. "Miguel, is that for the execution?" asked Maximilian. "I cannot say, sire," replied Miramón, "this is the first time I have been shot." The question was sufficiently answered when Maximilian, Miramón and Mejía were escorted in carriages to the Hill of Bells. It was a fine morning. Maximilian, dressed in severe black, remarked, "I have always wanted to die on just such a day." He died a good death, comforting the grief-stricken priest who was there to console him and ceding the middle position in the line of fire to Miramón. Asking that his face be spared disfigurement, he made his heart an easier target by pushing the halves of his handsome beard behind his shoulders. His country claimed the body some months later. It was well preserved, considering the season, and the wasting eyes had been replaced by fine orbs of glass taken from a Virgin in a Querétaro church.

In this fashion, Maximilian of Hapsburg returned obediently to his mother.

Porfirio Díaz had the glory of recovering the capital. Márquez fled the country, and it must be true that the good die young, because he lived to be very old. Benito Juárez was the Well Deserving of the Americas, a title conferred by the Colombian congress for his persevering defense of his country's liberty, but the Mexican people's affectionate name for him was El Indio, the Indian. He returned on July 15, gray locks setting off his dark Zapotec face, riding into the capital in his black carriage without military display, always a civilian.

The great Indian, granite-willed and patient, had affirmed his country's true independence, rooted in the Reform and the resolute defense of Mexican sovereignty. At his homecoming, he begged his countrymen to work for the nation's prosperity, obeying its laws, and spoke his most famous words: "Among nations, as among individuals, respect for the rights of others is peace."

THE DAYS OF DON PORFIRIO

◎◎◎◎◎◎◎◎◎ **14**

FELÍCITAS RAN to her father in tears. Her husband, named in a lawsuit, had insulted the judge. "Papá," she sobbed, "he's in jail, but a word from you will arrange everything." It was not forthcoming. "We most of all must set an example of respect for the law," said her father, who was President Benito Juárez.

Don Benito had refused a political favor even to the war hero Porfirio Díaz, who went away complaining, "The president is cold and severe, a man who never laughs." But the strollers with whom Juárez mingled evenings on the Zócalo found him cordial and democratic, always in his lawyer's black, with Doña Margarita beside him, correctly but simply dressed, without jewelry, the two of them fitting symbols of a poor but self-respecting country.

Once the Republic was restored, the president sought to bring primary education to every child, besides sponsoring a National Preparatory School, where future leaders were grounded in mathematics, science, and logic before entering upon professional studies. The school's motto was Order and Progress. Lacking order, Mexico had made little material progress in half a century.

Men schooled only in war could not easily make a living. There were desperadoes who shot the pink plaster angels off stagecoaches in the mountain passes and stripped the passengers even of their clothes. Most ex-soldiers, however, sat at home, grumbling that an ungrateful country gave its defenders no honest work. They looked back on heroic days and, when Porfirio Díaz ran for president, many were ready to vote — and fight — for him.

Don Porfirio lost the 1871 elections to Juárez, and rose in arms. "Indefinite reelection endangers our national institutions," he proclaimed. "Let no citizen perpetuate himself in power and this will be the last revolution." Juárez replied, "To sacrifice law and order for the plans of one man, however deserving, would plunge us into endless anarchy." He drained his strength crushing the revolt, and when his strong heart faltered, the doctors shocked it into action temporarily by dousing his chest with boiling water. The muscles twitched involuntarily, but no sign of pain crossed the Indian face. Juárez did his work to the last and expired on a summer night in 1872, with the peaceful expression you see on his death mask.

The new president, Sebastián Lerdo de Tejada, continued the Juárez policies. Never had Mexico been so free as under these Liberal presidents. Lerdo did what even Juárez wouldn't and let Santa Anna return to die in Mexico. His Most Serene Highness, eighty and nearly blind, drowsed away his last days in poverty, his chief necessity being a public. His patient understanding wife gave pennies to beggars to clamor at the door for an audience. "How many are in the waiting room?" the great man would ask, and when told, "About a dozen," he'd mumble, "Let them wait," and go back to his slumbers.

Lerdo inaugurated Mexico's first important railway line. It ran from Mexico City to Veracruz. Concerning one to the United States frontier, he said, "Let there be a desert between the strong and the weak." His immediate problem was his army, which perhaps no civilian could have held in check after Juárez was gone.

Porfirio Díaz had retired to raise sugar without, however, abandoning politics. Though he looked like a plain countryman, with his bronzed Mixtec face and drooping Spanish mustache, he was quietly making friends among the aristocracy, even with generals who'd served the French, promising

them forgiveness in return for support. In the election year
of 1876, Don Porfirio raised the cry of No Reelection again
and pronounced against Lerdo. Defeated at first, he slipped
over the United States frontier, returned in disguise, raised a
new army in his native Oaxaca, and won a decisive battle
near Tlaxcala after his compadre Manuel González rode up
at the crucial moment with fresh cavalry. Don Porfirio then
proclaimed himself president, ushering in a period that
lasted till 1911 and is called the Porfiriato. His supreme aim
was to stay in power. Going by the maxim that "two cats
can't stay in the same sack," he pulled the claws of rival
generals, giving them gambling-house concessions and
governorships or shifting them to small isolated commands.
When rumors of a plot to restore Lerdo came from Veracruz,
Porfirio wired the governor: KILL THEM ON THE SPOT, and
nine men died, who knows how many of them innocent.

The idea of a desert between the strong and the weak was
forgotten. Railroads would be useful for moving troops
against rebels and, besides, Porfirio had a message from his
minister in Washington, saying that the westward-surging
Yankees were bound to come into Mexico, if not with rails,
then with bayonets. He chose rails and gave the railroad
builders land, money, and all the forced labor they wanted at
twenty-five centavos a day.

Díaz regretted his No Reelection pledge after four years
but let his compadre González be president for a term while
the election laws were changed. Meanwhile he married Car-

men, the refined daughter of an old army pal. It wasn't easy for poor Carmelita to love a man thirty years her senior, who picked his teeth with a goose quill. Grimly she undertook his education. She made him use a fork instead of a tortilla and stop slushing his soup, and he returned to the presidency wearing white gloves as a president should.

Porfirio needed no lessons to impose his will on the civilian government. He made over the Congress into what he called "my herd of tame horses." Four hundred "political chiefs" carried his rule into every nook of the Republic. At their call were the dreaded *rurales,* the rural police in silver-trimmed gray, so given to shooting prisoners for "trying to escape." Porfirio called that "spilling the bad blood to save the good blood," but he'd make an exception when some famous outlaw was captured. Having the prisoner brought before him, he loaded his revolver, chamber by chamber, and while taking aim held out his free hand and asked, "Which will it be, the five bullets or the five friendly fingers?" That's how he recruited his most valued rurales.

A favorite saying of his was *pan o palo,* bread or a club. Bread for friends in the form of government jobs, clubbings for malcontents. All who could read, write, do sums, and find a political sponsor went on the public payroll because, as Porfirio said, "a dog with a bone neither bites nor barks." Unlike Juárez, who always appealed to our thirst for liberty, Díaz held that the Mexican people wanted only a cage with birdseed.

To meet his expenses, Díaz sold mining, lumbering, and cattle-raising concessions. So much of the nation's wealth passed to foreigners that it came to be said, "Mexico is the mother of foreigners and the stepmother of Mexicans."

In 1887, Don Porfirio dedicated a monument to Cuauhtémoc, who, the inscription ran, had "struggled heroically in the country's defense." Cuauhtémoc had been dead three and a half centuries; Cajeme four months, shot by the rurales while struggling heroically in defense of his Sonora homeland. There in the northwest, speculators were swarming into the rich Yaqui river bottom lands, cutting them into plots, big ones for themselves and little ones for the Indians, who protested, "God gave the river to all the Yaquis, not a piece to each one."

Cajeme was one of many nineteenth-century Cuauhtémocs who fought in defense of their peoples' common lands, consisting of forest, water, meadow, and cropland. Drawing on these varied resources, each householder gathered firewood for his hearth and prepared charcoal to trade in the market for candles and salt. He hunted ducks by the stream and had pasture for his goat, the poor man's cow. The elders assigned him his corn patch. No legal fees to pay.

This age-old system was under attack by men who claimed that every meter of ground must be covered by an individual title of ownership. Such a title shut an Indian off from his woods, streams, and kinsmen. If, innocently, he accepted a small loan, he lost even his land. And once strangers obtained a foothold in the neighborhood, they might boldly remove the boundary stones and add the Indians' fields to their own. In the Morelos sugar bowl south of the capital, Emiliano Zapata saw this happen when he was twelve. Shaking with rage, he vowed, "When I'm a man, I'll make them give back our land."

Most feared of all were the men who came with rod and chain. They worked for surveying companies, owned by great families and foreigners, and were privileged to bound "unowned" land along the coasts and in the north. This, they explained, was so that European farmers could settle on it and make Mexico prosperous like the United States. As it happened, few such immigrants came, being neither rich enough to buy an hacienda nor poor enough to grub like an Indian. But the companies took a third of the land for their work and bought as much more for a trifle. What could the Indians say when asked to show a land title? That their ancestors were planting corn here when the Spaniards came? That was no title at all. Indian villages that had survived the colonial centuries were stripped of fields, forests, wells, gardens, and houses. Not even the Mestizos were safe. Any small rancher unable to call a political chief his compadre would spend more defending his title than buying back his land. Up to a million families were dispossessed, and a fifth of Mexico passed to the surveying companies.

But do not think of Don Porfirio as unfeeling. Tears rolled down his cheeks when he was told of a village leveled or when, on his saint's day, he gave silver pesos to widows and orphans. They flowed even more abundantly every four years when important gentlemen with silk hats in hand insisted that he accept one more reelection for his country's sake. They called him the Hero of Peace, the man who was bringing progress to Mexico.

It was true that peace reigned — except for Indians put down, students clubbed, and editors jailed. There were now new ways of recovering silver and gold, and tall chimneys poured yellow smoke into Monterrey's clear sky. The United States was a growing market for beef cattle, sugar, coffee, copper for transmission wires, and henequen to bind the sheaves in the spreading wheatfields.

Doña Carmelita had Porfirio in white tie and tails that harmonized with her golden tea set and the pearls her father was said to have robbed from the Cathedral during the War of the Reform. If he did, Carmelita's piety had washed away the guilt. Porfirio could refuse her nothing. When a secret convent was to be raided, he let her give warning, and the police found no one, unless it was the gardener. Reconciliation became the watchword. The sons of Conservatives and Liberals studied law together and became bureaucrats, or playboys squandering the rent from Papacito's land.

There were lawyers by thousands, doctors by hundreds, engineers by scanty tens. To fill the gaps and hasten progress, Porfirio showered more favors on foreigners, and they came to own half the nation's wealth and a third of its land. Some of them blended in with our people as New Creoles and have passed on such Mexican surnames as Duret, Herzog, O'Gorman, Poniatowska, and Aboumrad. But the English-speaking foreigners liked to keep to themselves and return with their money to the lands of their birth.

Our native-born rich had roots nowhere. Disdaining to be Spaniards or Mestizos, they made believe they were French and built mansions such as they'd admired in Paris, with sloping mansard roofs waiting for snow that never fell. Everything came from Paris: velvet drapes, Haviland china, tall mirrors, even babies — or so inquisitive children were told until old enough to ask, "Where's the box?"

For Mexico to look like Paris was progress. But Mexico was not France, where a peasant lived as well as a government clerk. A Mexican peasant was twelve times poorer than the lowliest bureaucrat. Yet with three or four years' schooling he'd be equally deserving of a government job and would surely want one, as Porfirio well knew. So he praised education as the road to progress but was careful to build few schools, and three-fourths of the people remained illiterate.

Cheap prints were woven in the mills, but the owners wore imported fabrics. The railroads, instead of spreading over the countryside, made for the seaports and border towns, carrying tropical products and mineral wealth out of the country. Traces of green were visible on the mountainsides, where villagers scratched in the thin soil, but the valleys lay unplanted, there being little sale for hacienda produce. A

Mexican with only a sleeping mat and the clothes on his back
was a poor customer for anything.

In the Jockey Club, pompous gentlemen with scorpion-tail
mustaches sat talking of science. They agreed it was Nature's
law for the rich to prosper and the poor to succumb, especially if the poor were Indians. Because of their twisted
notions, they were mockingly called *científicos,* or scientists.
First among them was Finance Minister José Yves Limantour, who as a result of the mining boom won credit for
restoring Mexico's good name in the money markets and was
talked of for president. Now nothing alarmed Porfirio so
much as an underling's success. Seeing a rival in the pearly-
toothed Limantour, he fed the ambitions of Bernardo Reyes,
a northern general with an untamed beard. Each longed to be
president, and they intrigued and slandered each other for
years on end, while Porfirio rode the storm in full command.

The old man had come to call the presidency "my eternal
companion." He liked foreigners to appreciate his beautiful
capital and kept the principal streets free of *pelados,* or
peeled ones, meaning his barefoot countrymen in short cotton
breeches. Their place was in the slums of Tepito, where
Juventino Rosas grew up, playing the violin at saint's day
parties. On a country walk he captured the rhythm of a
rushing stream and wrote "Over the Waves," selling it for
seventeen pesos. Soon all the world was waltzing to it. It was
taken for granted that the composer was a European. No
one, unless in Tepito, believed a Mexican capable of a

masterpiece. Only after Rosas died a pauper in another land was he brought home and laid to rest in the Rotunda of Illustrious Men.

It was left for the engraver José Guadalupe Posada to appreciate his countrymen in life and death. He sat in his shop in a leather apron, doing covers for lives of saints and outlaws, and eye-catching illustrations for ballads on tinted paper that told of the calamities besetting the people. Posada often drew his figures as skeletons dancing, feasting, or fighting like living persons. The art student Diego Rivera, bursting from his boy's clothes, liked to look in on his way to San Carlos Academy. It was more fun watching the maestro than imitating European painters.

Long after Posada had joined his lively skeletons, Rivera painted a mural in which you see the fat boy and his master arm in arm with Death, joined for all time. "Posada," said the artist, "showed me the beauty inherent in the Mexican people and their struggles and aspirations. He taught me the supreme lesson of all art: that nothing can be expressed except through the power of feeling." The same painting shows a policeman ejecting a peasant family from the Alameda. You see the young son's helpless rage and, farther on, you see him returning, older now, with the Zapatistas. But that runs ahead of our story.

During Cuba's independence struggle, when the world was hungry for sugar, thirty families took over Zapata's home state of Morelos and planted even the village squares.

Zapata headed angry protests and wound up as an army conscript, but because he was the best horsebreaker in the state, a wealthy horse fancier secured his release and put him in charge of a stable of thoroughbreds. The pampered animals enjoyed tile floors and marble baths, and Zapata dreamed of when people would fare as well.

Another who dreamed was Ricardo Flores Magón, who became an opposition newspaper editor and was sent to a dark cell to spend a year with spiders and rats. Unable to publish in his own country, he crossed the frontier and lined up railwaymen to smuggle his paper into Mexico. Porfirio had Flores Magón shadowed everywhere — in San Antonio, St. Louis, and Los Angeles. A Pinkerton detective supplied this description: "5 feet, 8 inches; 225 pounds; dark eyes; black, curly hair; complexion dark brown; good typist; never gets drunk; inspires respect but is a dangerous fanatic."

The Madero family of Coahuila owned vineyards and wineries, cotton plantations, cattle ranches, flour mills, smelters, and mines. Don Evaristo Madero had thirty-four grandchildren, the girls marrying well, the boys sturdy and ambitious — all but little Francisco, who was given to daydreaming. The family sent him to France to make a banker of him, and he came back a vegetarian and a spiritualist. After a course at the University of California, he took up farming but spent what he made sending poor children to school. Even worse, he went into politics and tried to restore self-government in his hometown. But no one even remembered the election laws — a whole generation had grown up without political experience.

In 1904, Porfirio was so old that to get a foreign loan he had to accept a vice-president. There was nothing he wanted less, so he chose Ramón Corral, a hated científico grown rich on Yaqui lands. "Who is going to assassinate me," asked Porfirio, "knowing that Corral will take my place?" After making his nephew Félix Díaz a police chief to keep an eye on Corral, the aging dictator raced about the city in his new Mercedes at ten kilometers, or six miles, per hour, frightening the horses. How could he know that his gasoline-consuming toy would lead to a great industry? He gave priceless oil concessions to smooth-talking promoters, and they went their reckless way, bringing in gushers that flowed unchecked or caught fire and burned for months.

In 1907, United States Secretary of State Elihu Root was a guest at Chapultepec Castle. Doña Carmelita had rubbed the Indian completely off her husband at last. He was a white-haired gentleman of stately presence, and Mr. Root went away saying, "I look to Porfirio Díaz as one of the great men to be held up to the hero-worship of mankind." Did he know of a recent tragedy before the mill gates at Río Blanco? Hardly. Not even the Mexican papers told how Porfirio's troops had fired upon the strikers there, killing two hundred or more. The bodies, piled on flatcars, were fed to the sharks at sea. Or so it was whispered — anything is believable when the press is silent.

The working day in textile mills was thirteen hours, and the miserable wages were reduced by fines for breaks in the yarn or spots on the cloth. Store clerks were on duty twelve hours and had, as their employers pointed out, no time to waste money and get into trouble. In the Cananea copper mines, Mexicans were paid in silver pesos, United States miners in gold pesos worth twice as much. A strike committee seeking equal pay for equal work was drenched by fire hoses. A gun battle followed, and the governor of Sonora rushed in with troops — not Mexican soldiers but Arizona guardsmen. The strike leaders were cast into the dungeons at Veracruz, but the governor, and Porfirio with him, bore the shame of bringing foreign soldiers onto Mexican soil.

Soon after, a refugee group met in St. Louis as the Mexican Liberal Party, Flores Magón presiding, and called for an eight-hour day with Sundays off, a minimum wage, compensation for work injuries, no more debt bondage, and land for the landless. All this and more is now written into our constitution, but then there was no free ballot, no right to strike. Flores Magón and his companions took the path of revolution. They made forays over the border to arouse the Mexican people and were pursued by the authorities of both countries. In 1908, Flores Magón was sitting in the Los Angeles County Jail. He'd mapped out plans for a general uprising but was too closely watched to pass them on to his Mexican visitors. So Ethel Duffy Turner, the wife of a friendly newspaperman, came to see him with two other young ladies. One of them obligingly spilled her handbag before the cell. While the guards were picking up hairpins, Flores Magón handed Ethel the master plan for the 1908 revolt, which turned out to be the biggest one up to that time.

Ethel's husband, John Kenneth Turner, had heard the refugees declare that slavery, real slavery, existed in Mexico. Surely an exaggeration, he thought, but he decided to find out for himself and went to Yucatán in the guise of a wealthy investor. Henequen planters with haciendas for sale promised him unlimited workers at sixty-five pesos a head. Every month five hundred Yaquis were placed on sale. They were brought here from Sonora after being robbed of their fields and houses. Turner saw some of them cutting and shredding the sawlike leaves with nimble, bleeding fingers. Two thousand leaves was the daily stint. They worked not for money or freedom but to escape the lash. Adults survived about a year, children a little longer. A planter advised Turner to buy children. The writer went home and put what he'd seen into a book called *Barbarous Mexico*. A million of your countrymen read it in 1909, and understood why we had to have a revolution.

By then, most of Mexico's cropland belonged to eight or ten thousand haciendas. Only three of each hundred rural families owned any land, the rest being sharecroppers or laborers. A man's daily wage of twenty-five centavos was less than the rent of a burro. It had not changed in a century, but he was poorer now and could buy only a fourth as much corn. Sometimes he was paid in metal tags, good only in the hacienda's store. In colonial times there were places of refuge, but now four-fifths of the villages had been absorbed or surrounded by great estates. A peon running away from his eternal debts was hunted down by the rurales. It was his destiny to rise before the sun, sing a hymn of praise on his knees, toil for a master who believed that "an Indian hears only through his back," and pass on his debts to his children.

Labor was so cheap that landowners seldom bought farm machinery. Despite the peons' ceaseless toil, the hacienda system was so inefficient that, as Andrés Molina Enríquez pointed out in *The Great National Problems,* Mexico often imported corn and wheat from the United States. The great families paid taxes on a tenth of their property's value, while the small farmer was taxed to the limit.

Molina Enríquez was the Mestizos' champion. They, and not imaginary European immigrants, could put idle land to productive use. The Mestizos, he wrote, are a blend of all the Indians, modified by the Spaniards. They are alike in origin, customs, language, and hopes of betterment. They make up nearly half the population and are constantly increasing by absorbing the Indians. They can live on salt and tortillas, if need be, and outwalk a horse. They are self-reliant, not leaning on foreigners as the Creoles do. Their endurance and fortitude have created the nation and maintained its independence. They are the largest, strongest, and most patriotic element in Mexico. No one before Molina Enríquez had spoken so well of the Mestizos or seen so clearly that we were to be a Mestizo nation.

Everyone was reading his book in 1909, as well as *The Presidential Succession in 1910*, by Francisco I. Madero. There was hope that year that the seventy-nine-year-old dictator might at least permit the free election of a vice-president. Madero wrote that a little democracy now would save bloodshed later. His grandfather warned him, "Don't get in the way of the horses' feet." But for the moment Madero passed as harmless and was even useful to General Reyes, who hoped to be elected vice-president in place of Corral. The Reyistas wore red carnations; the Corralistas, white. Porfirio saw more red carnations than he liked, and ordered Reyes to surrender his command. Reyes wavered. The moment for rebellion passed, and he went meekly to Paris, an exile.

The amateur Madero now remained the only one challenging Díaz and Corral. He spoke to small audiences, using nervous gestures, his voice rising to a treble: a little, stubby-bearded man, measuring five feet, face radiant, heart overflowing with kindness. Early in 1910, he toured the west and the north, finding sympathy among those who'd gone to the frontier in search of a small ranch, only to find that everything belonged to the cattle interests. What stories they told in Chihuahua of Luis Terrazas, owner of the world's biggest cattle ranch! "Is your ranch in Chihuahua?" he was asked while traveling, to which he replied, "No, Chihuahua *is* my ranch." That's the story. In justice to Don Luis it should be stated that the ranch itself was not much larger than New Jersey. But he'd ruled the whole state with an iron hand for thirty years, and people wanted a change. A Chihuahua merchant named Abraham González was the first to insist that Madero run against Díaz for president.

Only a few weeks before, this idea would have seemed fantastic, but now they were acclaiming the little crusader as the Apostle of Democracy. In April, a hundred delegates gathered in the capital and made him their David to fight Goliath. They turned against Porfirio the No Reelection slogan he'd used against others so long ago. Soon Madero was addressing tumultuous meetings in city after city. Porfirio became alarmed and had him dragged from his train and locked up. From a prison cell, Madero wrote the dictator: "We welcome a contest at the polls, but if unfortunately the public peace is disturbed, the responsibility will be yours before the nation, the civilized world, and history." Díaz ignored the letter and, after awarding himself ninety-nine percent of the votes, gave Madero the city of San Luis Potosí "for his jail," which he might move about in but not leave.

Don Porfirio was preparing a colossal birthday party for September 15, 1910, when he'd be eighty and the nation a hundred years old. The celebration grew and grew, and lasted a month. Delegations from all the world were told that under Don Porfirio's wise rule Mexico had achieved lasting peace and prosperity. On the night of the grand ball, he led the march, magnificently erect despite the weight of his medals. Few knew how his mental powers were failing. It did not matter: he looked like a president. Two thousand guests dined and danced the night away, enjoying ten courses on gold and silver plates and consuming ten carloads of champagne. The party cost twenty million pesos, more than twice what Díaz spent that year on schools.

Meanwhile, Madero's friends were laying plans for his escape, having learned that his life was in danger. On October 4, his saint's day, he rode out hunting to the edge of San Luis Potosí without attracting the attention of the police. Two days later, he ventured to the first flagstop on the northbound railroad. A fiesta had been arranged there as a cover. Madero shaved off his beard and put on a railroad-man's attire. Someone flagged the Laredo Express, and the crew, already alerted, took the Apostle of Democracy aboard. Not till the next day was Madero missed. He was then crossing the international bridge to join the San Antonio refugee group and organize the Revolution.

THE SOCIAL REVOLUTION

ⓞⓞⓞⓞⓞⓞⓞⓞⓞ   **15**

IN A SAN ANTONIO HOTEL, his companions about him, Madero put into the Plan of San Luis the conclusions he'd reached while a prisoner at San Luis Potosí. He wrote, "It would be a betrayal of those who have put their trust in me not to place myself at the head of my fellow-citizens and oblige General Díaz by force of arms to respect the will of the nation."

The proclamation called for a general uprising on November 20, 1910. Its contents were soon known, and arrests began. The gun runner Aquiles Serdán reached Puebla undetected only by wearing a black dress with a heavy veil. "I am taking my wife her widow's outfit," he said. Once home, he passed out arms, but on November 18, the police battered at the door and troops blocked off the streets. Serdán and a few companions held out four hours, firing from windows and the roof, his sister Carmen reloading the rifles. The house where most of them died stands with its bullet-pierced windows as a shrine to the Revolution's first martyrs.

The Revolution got off to an uncertain start, except in Chihuahua, where Abraham González raised a force from the sierra. They were men of "many britches," hard as nails, like the lean and moody Pascual Orozco, who ran a packtrain from the mines, and Pancho Villa, an ex-cattle rustler who'd taken to the hills after shooting his landlord over a question of family honor. Orozco was uncommunicative, though they say he did send Porfirio Díaz some bloodstained Federal uniforms with a message: "Here are the leaves in which the tamales I ate were wrapped. Please send me some more." Villa was different. Enemies saw the flash of anger in his eyes; friends, the dimple on his cheek. Don Abraham harnessed his restless energy for the Revolution. Pancho hated the rich in general but loved the rich Madero, sight unseen, for helping the poor.

As Madero crossed into Chihuahua and took command of the Revolution, men sprang to arms at the mention of his name. "Who is Madero?" a correspondent asked a peon recruit. "Who knows, señor," was the reply, "but my captain says he is a powerful saint." The cattle baron Terrazas imagined his own men loved him like a father but found them unwilling to fight Madero, "even though I offer to pay them two pesos a day and mount and feed them at my own expense."

Not that everyone accepted Madero's leadership. In Los Angeles, Flores Magón wrote that for Mexico to be really free its fields, shops, and mines should belong to those who worked them. He sent an expedition into Lower California. Though unsuccessful, it spread such alarm that the United States put Flores Magón back in jail. A great forerunner of the Revolution, Flores Magón was fated to be in prison at the crucial moments when he might have assumed its command.

His slogan of Land and Liberty was taken up by the Zapatistas. They called themselves the Liberating Army of the South and, by Holy Week of 1911, were on the march with prints of the Virgin of Guadalupe on their high-peaked hats. Soon their campfires on Ajusco, south of the lava flow, were visible in Mexico City. The capital newspapers likened them to the hordes of Attila.

For fighting these revolutionary fires, and others in Durango and Sinaloa, Porfirio had generals of eighty, captains of seventy, and lieutenants of sixty-five, it being his policy to discourage younger and possibly rival talents. He himself was growing forgetful. And how horribly his tooth ached!

Finance Minister Limantour made peace overtures to the

Maderistas, encamped near Ciudad Juárez, offering to sacrifice Vice-President Corral, though not Don Porfirio. Madero was torn between the counsels of old Venustiano Carranza, who warned, "A revolution that compromises is a revolution lost," and his timid relatives, who wanted no trouble. And being so close to the border, he was afraid that a stray bullet might bring on complications with the United States. Orozco and Villa, not being diplomats, provoked the Federals into combat and took Ciudad Juárez, almost before Madero knew it. The revolutionists now had a port of entry for guns.

Limantour now promised to get rid of Porfirio. An agreement was signed for a provisional government, pending elections, and the disbanding of the revolutionary forces. Don Porfirio resisted to the end, talking only of his toothache to Limantour, who hovered over his bed with pen and paper. Crowds marched outside, crying, "The resignation! The resignation!" and many were mowed down by machine-gun fire before Porfirio, delirious from an infected jaw, finally signed and was hustled off to a ship at Veracruz.

The capital welcomed Madero like no one since Juárez. His election to the presidency was sure, but his enemies had an interval of five months in which to regroup and sow mistrust among his friends. His promise to disband the revolutionists did not sit well with the Zapatistas, who insisted, "First return the common lands of which we were robbed." "All that will be done by lawful means," promised Madero. He arranged a truce, but when the Federal commander Victoriano Huerta broke it and began pillaging peasant villages, Zapata took to the hills, believing Madero had betrayed him.

In November, 1911, President Madero moved into the National Palace. Zapata was hiding near the village of Ayala. He summoned his chief officers, and they signed the Plan of Ayala, calling on the people to take the woods, waters, and fields that were rightly theirs and hold them with arms in hand. It was a sign that Madero's mild program of Effective Suffrage and No Reelection would have to make way for a social revolution.

Madero was all sympathy when peasant delegations came asking for land. A commission was studying the problem, he explained, but it would take time and the laws would have to be changed. He meant well but felt no need to hurry. Urging everyone to work together for the country's good, he even brought old Porfirians into his cabinet. His former companions protested, "You are governing with your enemies against your friends."

Though Madero exasperated the revolutionists, he failed to gain the confidence of the other side. General Reyes came back to deliver the Revolution a counterblow but, finding his popularity faded, went to prison. Pascual Orozco then rose in arms, resentful, he said, over Madero's slow pace but actually going into the pay of the Terrazas cattle interests. General Huerta defeated him with Pancho Villa's help, but the two men fell out over a horse, and Pancho barely escaped the firing squad. He was sent to prison in Mexico City and found himself among generals of all stripes, including a Zapatista who taught him to read and write better. While Villa was struggling with *Don Quijote,* Porfirio's blundering nephew Félix issued a call to arms in Veracruz. No one responded, and Félix was sentenced to die, but Madero spared his worthless life. The busiest place in the prison was General Reyes's cell. Officers with epaulettes of high rank came and went, and it was no secret that new plans were afoot to topple Madero. "If I could see him alone," thought Pancho, "I'd tell him many things that his enemies keep from him." But all Villa could do was save himself. On a cold day toward Christmas of 1912, he cloaked and muffled himself like a visiting lawyer and, walking past the guards, escaped to the north.

Madero's ears heard more than Villa imagined, but his generous heart rejected ugly insinuations. The press vilified him daily. His loyal brother Gustavo protested, "They are biting the hand that unmuzzled them." But the president replied that the press must be free.

United States Ambassador Henry Lane Wilson went around saying that Madero should be in a madhouse. They were so different: the idealistic, even visionary Madero and the frosty Wilson, practicing what was then called "dollar diplomacy." If we have harsh words for your countryman, you will find, so my teacher says, that your country's historians treat him no better. Porfirio had spoiled him with favors. So when Madero put a tax of three centavos a barrel on oil — less than in the United States — Wilson threatened and blustered. And his animosity turned to personal hatred when Madero let President-elect Woodrow Wilson know that a more understanding ambassador would be welcome.

Before President Wilson took office, we suffered Ten Tragic Days. On Sunday, February 9, 1913, worshipers coming from early mass in the Cathedral stepped into a burst of machine-gun fire and fell dying on the paving stones. Close by, a struggle was on for the National Palace. It changed hands twice, but then the rebel prisoners were freed and General Reyes rode to the attack. No turning back this time. "You'll be shot!" cried his friends. "But not in the back," he replied, just before he fell dead from his horse.

Félix Díaz preferred to risk his back and took refuge a dozen blocks away in the Ciudadela, a thick-walled arsenal. Madero, on being alerted at the Castle, rode down Reforma and Juárez avenues to the cheers of the throng but on the way made the terrible mistake of putting the Palace and himself under the protection of the bullet-domed Huerta. By the next day, Huerta was already having secret talks with Félix and making sure that the projectiles directed at the Ciudadela fell short of their mark and killed only civilians. Félix returned the courtesy. The mock battle went on for days, with brief truces when carts collected the dead. Ambassador Wilson lined up diplomats and senators to insist that

Madero resign, but the president stood his ground, saying, "Foreigners have no right to interfere in Mexican affairs."

By the ninth day, Huerta's treachery was so apparent that Gustavo disarmed him at pistol point. The president rebuked his suspicious brother and freed the general. On the tenth day, Huerta made both of them his prisoners and met with Félix Díaz at the United States Embassy. They agreed that Huerta would be president temporarily, but Félix put his friends into the cabinet and expected to step into his uncle's shoes. Ambassador Wilson called in the diplomatic corps and announced the new government. Then he offered a toast: "Long live General Díaz, the savior of Mexico!"

It was the night of February 18, last of the Ten Days, but the tragedy was not over. Félix returned to the Ciudadela, where his drunken followers were calling for Madero's blood. Unable to get Huerta to release the president, they took Gustavo and tortured him to death.

Huerta had his own reasons for holding President Madero and Vice-President José M. Pino Suárez. He wanted them to resign and promised them a safe departure from Veracruz for doing so. Not even Madero trusted Huerta now, but an intermediary agreed to keep the resignations until the prisoners were at sea. Oh, if he had done so! Instead he gave them to Huerta right away, all because the old scoundrel pulled a Guadalupe medal from under his shirt and cried, "This was hung around my neck by my mother, and by it I swear to respect the lives of Madero and Pino Suárez."

With the resignations in hand, Huerta bullied a frightened

congress into recognizing him as president. Now he had no further need of the prisoners. The ever optimistic Madero told a friendly visitor, "If some day I govern my country again, I shall do it with men of firm purpose, not the wishy-washy sort." But his wife realized he was in mortal danger and begged Ambassador Wilson to use his influence to save his life. Wilson turned her away, saying, "I will be frank with you, madam, your husband's fall is due to the fact that he never wished to consult me."

It was Thursday. On Saturday night, while Huerta was at a merry Washington's Birthday party in the Embassy, two carloads of uniformed rurales pulled up at the National Palace. They went inside, came out with Madero and Pino Suárez, took them to the rear of the penitentiary, pumped them full of bullets, and left them dead. No one believed Huerta when he said they were killed during a rescue attempt. But he had another story, putting the blame on Félix Díaz, and this gave him an excuse to clean out the cabinet and make himself dictator.

The cold-blooded assassinations shocked the world. In the United States, courageous newspapers spelled out Ambassador Wilson's role in bringing down the Madero government. In Mexico, we forgot Madero's indecision as president and remembered his democratic faith and martyrdom. Teen-agers by thousands, my grandfather among them, made their way north to join a revolutionary band and fight against Huerta the Hyena.

Venustiano Carranza was governor of Coahuila now.

He refused to recognize the usurper and rallied a small force that in time grew into the Constitutionalist Army. Don Venus had blue glasses and a snowy beard and, though fifty-three, was a tireless rider. He was called the First Chief and sometimes The Stubborn Old Man, affectionately or otherwise. The younger element argued for a program of land reform and labor laws, but the old man insisted that all that mattered now was unity against Huerta. "Do you want the war to last two years, or five?" he asked. "We are young enough to fight five years, or ten, if necessary," replied Francisco J. Múgica, who was twenty-eight.

Soon after, Múgica had the pleasure of helping the even younger Lucio Blanco to divide Félix Díaz's Matamoros hacienda among the peons who worked it. Carranza frowned on hearing of this revolutionary measure. He was a land-owner himself, but in a speech at Hermosillo, he faced the facts and said, "When the armed struggle is over, a social struggle will begin, like it or not. We shall have to change everything and create a new constitution."

One revolutionary division was moving toward Monterrey and Tampico under Pablo González. Another was rolling down the Pacific coast with Alvaro Obregón, a stocky teacher-farmer with a big mustache. He'd started out with a handful of Yaquis armed with bows and arrows and was now sweeping into Sinaloa.

The Zapatistas were giving Huerta trouble close to home. These gentle-spoken, sandal-footed little men would wreck a troop train and silently melt away. Anyone asked about them knew nothing. To the exasperated Federals, the nearest peasant plowing with his oxen might be one of them. So, before leaving, they would string him and a few others from the trees and burn a village or two. No one knew where the Zapatistas would strike next. They were everywhere and nowhere.

On the northern plateau, between the eastern and western ranges, Pancho Villa came riding on Seven Leagues, and bronzed men whom he called his Race Brothers enlisted in the Division of the North. They were from the sierra and the range, and the caboose and the roundhouse, too, for this war traveled on wheels as well as hoofs, and whole families moved with it. In old photographs you see the freight cars they lived in, the laundry drying on the roof, the cook pot boiling by the right-of-way. Juan, the rank-and-file soldier, joined around the campfire in melancholy songs like "La Valentina," with its refrain, "If they are going to kill me tomorrow, let them kill me right away." But Juana, his woman, was with him to bind his wounds and pick up his rifle if he fell.

Villa was out to avenge Madero and, more particularly, his beloved chief Abraham González, whom the Huertistas had thrown under the wheels of a moving train. In his first major victory, Pancho rode into Ciudad Juárez at midnight in a captured train and took the border town by surprise and, with it, three hundred thousand pesos from the gambling houses. He outmaneuvered the Federals at Tierra Blanca, capturing fieldpieces and additional trains. In the spring of 1914, he moved against Torreón, the communications center of the north, with ten thousand men. In seventeen epic days, he blasted the Federals from their commanding positions in the Coahuila-Durango lake country and entered the city over heaps of his dead. They, and not the lawyers with their books, are the true heroes of the Revolution, he told himself.

The Torreón victory led indirectly to a misunderstanding with the United States. The spreading civil war was paralyzing business, and President Wilson was as anxious to get Huerta out as Ambassador Wilson had been to put him in. Now seemed the time to speed his downfall. Huerta's undemocratic behavior in having congressmen jailed and murdered shocked Wilson, and rightly so. Only this was not a funeral, as we say, in which he had a candle. Such a scholar as Wilson was in his own country's history, how could he know so little about Mexicans as to invade our soil, all because of a dispute with Huerta?

On April 21, 1914, Veracruz — thrice heroic Veracruz, we call it — was surprised to see infantrymen leaping ashore from launches and taking over the customs house and the railroad station. The Huertista commander abandoned the city, but part of his men joined with civilians and naval cadets to defend the nation's honor. In two days of fighting, four hundred good men fell, your countrymen and mine. The naval school crumbled under the pounding of offshore guns, but cadets like Virgilio Uribe remained at their stations and took a place in history beside the Boy Heroes of Chapultepec.

The resistance astonished Wilson. He'd assumed we'd be grateful for this supposed blow at Huerta. What he overlooked was that Veracruz belonged not to Huerta but to Mexico. Actually, its occupation let Huerta pose as a patriot defending the motherland. Volunteers enlisted to oppose the invaders — and were sent north to fight the revolutionists. Carranza called the occupation an offense to Mexico's dignity and independence and said that anyone who came to power through foreign intervention would be unworthy of the nation's trust.

Villa was alone among the revolutionary chiefs in not protesting, perhaps because a stream of arms was flowing to him from over the border. Wilson had an agent with each of the factions, and his favorite at the time was Villa, a good man, so the reports said, who neither drank nor smoked, and bet only on cockfights. Surely he'd make a better president than Carranza, whom everyone found so headstrong. Between bossy Don Venus and impulsive Pancho there was bound to be trouble. It came during an angry exchange of telegrams over the plans for taking Zacatecas. Villa was provoked into resigning, but his fellow-officers wouldn't let him step down and vowed to take Zacatecas with or without permission of "Old Goat Whiskers," meaning Carranza.

Zacatecas is a mountain-rimmed city. Each peak was a fortress. In the crags of La Bufa, commanding the city, the enemy was lodged as in eagles' nests. Such positions could be taken only under cover of artillery fire, perfectly timed. Fortunately, Felipe Angeles was the best artilleryman in Mexico. And Villa was the Centaur of the North, the idol of his twenty-two thousand Dorados, golden brown of skin and uniform. For a week, troop and artillery trains rolled south; then on June 23, at ten A.M. the roar of cannons echoed from the cliffs. Each time a position was taken by assault, it was necessary to drag the fieldpieces to a new emplacement under a rain of lead. Villa drove the gunners on with words and, when they failed, at pistol point. The power of his will carried men up even steep La Bufa. On that memorable day, he embodied the Revolution.

The back of the Federal Army was broken there at Zacatecas and soon after at Guadalajara by Obregón. Pablo González was at San Luis Potosí, and the Zapatistas were raiding the suburbs of Mexico City. Huerta read the signs and fled the country.

Who would lead the victorious Revolution? Where was it bound? These were the questions now. Commissioners for the divisions of the North and the Northeast met and agreed that the Revolution was a struggle of the disinherited against the privileged few. They recommended a convention, one delegate for each thousand fighting men, to draft the needed changes. And they made a truce between Villa and Carranza, though they feared it couldn't last.

The man with the balance of power was Obregón. He

dissolved what remained of the Federal Army and entered the capital, his Yaquis dancing and beating their drums and frightening the "decent people." He had a poor opinion of the big city. During a ceremony at Madero's grave, he gave his pistol to the revolutionary teacher María Arias, saying she was more worthy of bearing arms than men who'd not known how to defend their president. After that, she was called María Pistolas.

The revolutionary tide was running high, so high that local commanders raised wages on their own authority and canceled the peons' debts. The convention met, holding most of its sessions at Aguascalientes, away from Carranza's influence. Obregón and Villa exchanged an abrazo. The delegates cheered. They sobbed with Villa when he tried to speak. The Zapatistas told how they were already taking the land, cutting saplings for stakes and using their lariats for measuring rods. The Convention, spelled now with a capital C, was swept into voting for the Plan of Ayala.

None of this pleased Don Venus. He broke with the Convention, and it deposed him as First Chief and named General Eulalio Gutiérrez acting president. Carranza replied by ordering all commanders to their posts. Obregón wavered, then finally obeyed. And so the lines were drawn for a new struggle.

Now there were two governments. Carranza moved into Veracruz as the United States occupation forces at last moved out. The Convention took over Mexico City. Into the capital poured the Zapatistas, not looting and killing, as was feared, but knocking softly at kitchen doors and asking politely for provisions. The freight yards filled with trains bearing Pancho Villa's Dorados. The Mestizo hero of the north and the Indian hero of the south embraced at Xochimilco. They agreed that Carranza, sleeping on his soft pillows, was unable to understand the sufferings of the poor. "Such men love land and will die before giving it up," said Zapata. Villa made a prediction: "With the help of God, the men of the south, and my forty thousand Mausers and sixteen million cartridges, a new day will dawn." Villistas and Zapatistas paraded together on December 6, thirty thousand men in Texas hats and cartwheel sombreros, while pretty señoritas showered them with flowers.

It was too good to last. The Convention was a shaky alliance of men with contradictory aims. Some were scheming with the Carrancistas to undermine Villa's influence. Pancho's agents were quick to punish double-dealing, or the suspicion of it, before the firing squad. President Gutiérrez couldn't get along with Villa, or without him. So he just slipped away.

While the Convention debated, the single-minded Carranza wasted no words but rebuilt his strength. Since reforms were bound to come, he decided he might as well get credit for them. His law of January 6, 1915, made it possible for villages to apply for an *ejido,* consisting of fields, woods, and waters for community use. It became the basis of the land reform.

Obregón recaptured Mexico City and bid for the workers' support. Printers, tailors, and streetcar conductors marched as Red Battalions with the Constitutionalists, organizing unions, making speeches, fighting. Some were in the Bajío with Obregón when he matched his strength with Villa in the bloodiest conflict ever fought on our soil. The Constitutionalists entrenched themselves in Celaya's wheatfields and withstood repeated cavalry charges. Then they enveloped Villa's flanks and pushed him back toward León. From April to June, the battle raged so far and wide that only the hungry-eyed circling zopilotes could see it all. Obregón steadily wore down the Division of the North with his superior arms and strategy and drove it into the desert, broken but not destroyed. He paid with his own right arm, which was torn away by shrapnel, and he was known after that as the One-armed Man of Celaya.

This was the most tragic period of the Revolution — fifty thousand men with the same revolutionary ideals warring on their brothers. Its horror came out in stories. An officer found a soldier caught in a tangle of barbed wire and pierced through with a bayonet. "Does it hurt much?" he asked. "No, my general," was the reply, "only when I laugh." Perhaps the sacrifice of these humble men secured the gains of the Revolution. For it was the Convention's challenge that made the Constitutionalist leaders raise their goals higher.

The Red Battalions returned to Mexico City and moved into the House of Tiles, the Jockey Club's former home. Their union emblem was a picture of Obregón's hand in a jar of alcohol: it meant justice for the workingman. For all that, 1915 was a hungry year. The capital was changing hands between Constitutionalists and Zapatistas. Paper money became so nearly worthless that shopkeepers rolled down their shutters. The poor demonstrated, holding up empty baskets, and the rich hung out signs offering pianos for food.

President Wilson was in misery over Mexico. Foreign residents complained of their hardships in the capital and worried about their mines in the north, where Villa still ruled, and their oil wells in Carranza-held territory. Wilson insisted that the two enemies agree on a compromise government, but Carranza replied, "No nation has a right to interfere in the internal affairs of another nation." Said Wilson, "I have never known a man more impossible to deal with." But the First Chief was winning, and at last the stubborn Wilson had to recognize the equally stubborn Carranza as head of the Mexican government.

Villa took this action as a betrayal. His hopes of United States support had been raised so high, and now suddenly he received no more arms, while Carranza got all he wished. The code of the mountains called for vengeance. One March night in 1916, Villa rode into Columbus, New Mexico, and shot up the town, starting fires and paying special attention, so his friends say, to a certain establishment that neither delivered the guns and cartridges he had paid for nor refunded his money. Pancho Villa's was not the first raid over the border, Mexico often having suffered from filibusters coming the other way. President Wilson, however, did what a Mexican president can't do: he sent a punitive expedition after the invaders. It was led by his number one general, John J. Pershing, and spent a year searching Chihuahua and brushing with civilians and Carrancista troops but never picking up Villa's trail. Then Wilson sent Pershing to France, and the man who couldn't catch Pancho Villa turned the victory tide in World War I.

Villa fought on as a guerrilla, then went into ranching and, in 1923, was shot down by enemies. For long years he was an outlaw officially, though always a popular idol. Finally, in 1966, his name was placed in letters of gold in the Chamber of Deputies among our national heroes. There Villa keeps company with Carranza, his mortal enemy. "A man's virtue," as we say, "lies not in being perfect but in being heroic." Villa, the ex-bandit, is forgotten, and we remember the superb leader of men who assured the Revolution's triumph at Zacatecas. Carranza is not so much a testy politician of limited social vision as a patriot who defended the cherished principle of nonintervention as tenaciously as Juárez and prepared the way for the Constitution of 1917, under which we live.

Carranza had in mind some small reforms to the Constitution of 1857. But the elected delegates who came to Querétaro were not so much old-fashioned lawyers as teachers, journalists, and peasant-soldiers risen to high command. General Múgica, who'd been ready to fight ten years if necessary, presided over the constitutional committee. The resulting constitution was the most advanced of its time. Article 27 embodies the land reform and declares that the mineral resources lying under the soil belong to the nation, while Article 123 is labor's bill of rights.

When the constitution went into effect, on February 5, 1917, the Revolution had cost a million lives, counting the slain and those who'd perished from famine and disease. Hacienda buildings were in ruins. The owners had fled, and their peons, after campaigning through many states, meeting their countrymen, were now more Mestizo than Indian.

Carranza became the constitutional president but was plagued by unemployment, rising prices, and all the problems of a war-weakened country. The land reform moved slowly, wages lagged, and people looked to Obregón for leadership. Carranza was grooming a civilian to be his successor, but as yet the real power lay with the armed forces of the Revolution. This meant Obregón, unless General Pablo González should perform some remarkable feat. In 1919, González conceived the idea of making himself the "pacifier of Mexico." He'd finish off Zapata, who was still fighting for land and liberty, distrustful of promises. González sent a pretended deserter to win Zapata's confidence and draw him to an ambuscade, where hidden marksmen shot him from his handsome sorrel horse. Zapata's body was laid out in Cuautla for all to see — the great peasant leader who, the ballad says, "was born among the poor, lived among them, and fought for them, always saying, 'I don't want riches, I don't want honors.'"

The treacherous assassination did González no good. Obregón remained in control of the army, and Carranza of the government, and between these two forces no fair election was possible. Obregón, facing arrest early in 1920, hid among the Zapatistas and promised if elected to speed the land reform. His military friends in Sonora issued a call to arms. The generals began rising. Carranza, hoping to make a stand in Veracruz, loaded his government — officials, papers, money — onto special trains. The cars creaked along, pursued by rebels. When water and fuel gave out, Carranza and his chief aides took to the Puebla sierra by horse, while their foes paused to pick up gold pieces beside the tracks from the abandoned treasury. The president took shelter in a mountain hut. That night the rain beat down, the wind swept in, a hostile band shot a volley through the thin boards, and Carranza met his tragic destiny, as did all the chief leaders of the Revolution.

After an election under a provisional government, Obregón became president. He made a start toward dividing the great estates, though the owners considered them priceless and refused payment at the value they'd put on them for tax purposes. Foreigners had much of the best land and made trouble through their governments, especially when the presence of oil was suspected. A poet has called our oil wells "those springs of the Devil" for the grief they've caused us. These were flush production times. British, Dutch, and United States combines had long since taken over from the pioneering prospectors. The Revolution did not stop their operations. They made deals with generals of any faction, even with bandits. They formed their own armies and enforced their own law. Their oil claims reached into vast areas not even explored. To keep peace, we had to stretch our laws to the breaking point.

Obregón is remembered for encouraging schools for the people. Education Minister José Vasconcelos saw a "cosmic race" emerging in Latin America and gave the National University its motto, "Through my race the spirit will speak." Artists like Diego Rivera, Clemente Orozco, and David Alfaro Siqueiros painted the walls of public buildings, creating a Mexican Renaissance and dignifying our people and their arts, crafts, dances, and revolutionary aspirations. Yucatán's governor, Felipe Carrillo Puerto, set out to give every village a school. His love for Alma Reed of San Francisco inspired our well-known song "La Peregrina," or "The Pilgrim." During a military uprising, he was executed for his loyalty to the government. Today schools all over the Republic bear his name.

After Obregón came Plutarco Elías Calles of Sonora, a teacher turned general. He scowled even while campaigning, but when really angry, as his pupils knew, he half shut his eyes. Once, when a hostile crowd closed in on his moving train, his aides wanted to go faster, but Calles said, "No, if they are coming to kill me, they are too many, and if they are coming to scare me, they are too few."

The modern Mexico of highways and dams begins with President Calles. He started building automobile roads and took the first steps to irrigate the arid north. He taxed incomes, set up the Bank of Mexico to regulate the money supply, and opened technical and agricultural schools. "Missionary teachers" went into the countryside, instructing children and adults and making the schoolhouse the House of the People. Not since the teaching friars had there been such activity.

Men who'd joined the Revolution as boys were coming to the fore. The young officer Lázaro Cárdenas, a Tarascan weaver's grandson, went to restore the government's authority in the Tampico fields. The oil companies sent him a shiny new Packard. He refused the gift and bought a Dodge, paying for it himself, a hundred pesos a month. In the oil camps, he saw foreign employees living in comfortable bungalows and his own countrymen in hovels, carrying water from the stream in oilcans for lack of a water hydrant.

Calles, like Obregón before him, was prejudiced against the Spanish-born clergy for their opposition to the Revolution and the land reform. He began, with his rude energy, to enforce the Reform laws, which Don Porfirio had treated lightly. The opposition was equally determined — and the clash led to what one side has called the Cristero Rebellion and the other the religious persecution. Many of the faithful removed their children from public schools. The government sent foreign priests out of the country and told others to register. The clergy, in protest, withdrew from the temples. In the Bajío and Jalisco hills, armed groups paraded with banners reading, "Long live Christ the king!" and resorted to guerrilla warfare. A circle of young zealots in the capital undertook to assassinate Calles. But their victim turned out to be Obregón, who in 1928 was elected president for the second time. One of the terrorists trailed the president-elect to a victory banquet, elbowed his way to the head table with pad and pencil, did a quick sketch and showed it to the smiling Obregón, then suddenly drew a pistol and killed him.

The young fanatic was tried and executed. His deed left Calles as the only leader strong enough to hold the revolutionary regime together. But unlike Obregón, Calles did not violate the principle of No Reelection. Others might sit in the presidential chair if he remained *Jefe Máximo,* or Big Chief, until a government of laws and institutions was firmly established. He believed that for this to happen the revolutionary family must unite in a single political party, strong enough to keep its members in line and map a course for the nation. Otherwise, the end of each presidential term would see a civil war over the next president, and soon the Revolution's gains would be lost.

Calles took his ideas to the nation by radio. The outcome was the National Revolutionary Party, which has continued to guide the nation's destinies, though now it's called the

Institutional Revolutionary Party. Other parties have their campaigns and even win local elections, but by and large the official party rules. Rival interests clash and resolve their differences within its framework, and it has come to provide a means of peaceful transition from one administration to another.

Do-it-yourself justice is the mark of a backward and disorganized society. In 1929, men went armed to the office, the bullring, and the concert hall. Diego Rivera wed his fellow-artist Frida Kahlo, wearing a cartridge belt and pistol about his ample waist. Gradually, this was to change. Highways were drawing the nation together, people were buying, selling, and producing for a larger market, and orderly development called for internal peace. Moderation on both sides cooled the religious dispute, and once more little girls in white dresses were seen going with their godmothers to first communion.

TRANSFORMATION

ⓞⓞⓞⓞⓞⓞⓞⓞⓞ   **16**

THERE BEING NO ILL from which good does not come, the depression of the 1930's brought great presidents to your country and mine. At his inauguration, Franklin D. Roosevelt announced a Good Neighbor policy toward Latin America, saying, "The neighbor who respects himself respects the rights of others." In that spring of 1933, General Lázaro Cárdenas went campaigning for the presidency of Mexico. A sure winner, chosen by Calles and his party, Cárdenas nevertheless traveled twenty-five thousand kilometers — sixteen thousand miles — by plane, train, and car, and by horse into mountains where not even a cart had been. He spoke softly and listened intently, squatting like an Indian in a circle of peasants, eyes smiling, face long and grave. Everywhere he asked the people what they needed, and they told him: a school, a pump, and water fit to drink, or a power mill to grind hominy into dough and save the village women seven hours' daily toil before the *metate,* the grinding stone.

In office, Cárdenas continued his field trips, saying, "Only by constant travel can the authorities know the problems of the people." It was a standing joke at the National Palace that "the President is out teaching the Indians to grow lettuce." Often he listened all night to their problems. "They need so much, at least patience I can give them," he'd say. But he also gave them seedlings for orchards; clinics and hospitals; and ball parks where formerly the only recreation was pulque drinking.

Cárdenas did not drink, smoke, or go to bullfights. The Castle was not for his simple tastes, and he changed it from a presidential residence into a history museum. He set aside an hour each day when anyone in the Republic with a complaint could send him a telegram free. A barefoot peasant was admitted to his office as quickly as an important politician. His sympathy went out to labor. Calles, the Big Chief, by way of reminding Cárdenas who was boss, declared in a press interview that there were too many strikes. Cárdenas accepted the challenge. While strikes might cause temporary inconvenience, he said, they helped the country by putting a fairer share of the wealth into the hands of the people. Meanwhile he was checking the loyalty of the army commanders, removing or reassigning those who might side with Calles. Peasant and labor organizations called pro-Cárdenas rallies. When senators and deputies began switching to the president, Calles knew he'd lost. "I am a slave to my own device: institutional government!" he exclaimed — and went away, the Big Chief no longer.

Cárdenas distributed twice as much land as all his predecessors — and better land, too, much of it irrigated. To him an ejido was not a place to grow corn while looking for work: it was cooperative farming as a way of life. He transformed the cotton plantations around Torreón into ejidos for thirty thousand farmers and supplied the irrigation works and technical assistance. The land reform moved on to the henequen of Yucatán, the rice of tropical Michoacán, the sugar of Sinaloa, and the coffee of Chiapas. In the wheat-fields of Sonora, Cárdenas met with the long-suffering Indians. "Fellow-Yaquis," said the chairman, "former presidents have never left their thrones to see us. This is the first who has come." Cárdenas made sure the Yaquis received generous land and water rights.

In the face of these sweeping reforms, big landowners organized "white guards" to assassinate peasant leaders and government agents. Cárdenas gave the people arms to defend their land. He cut military expenses and used the money for rural schools that taught the dignity of work and denied the right of any race or caste to live by enslaving others. He founded normal schools and the National Polytechnic Institute.

Signs of change appeared. Fewer pole-and-thatch huts, more houses of concrete, with separate cooking and sleeping quarters and beds instead of mats. Clinics to combat tuberculosis and pneumonia, medical graduates doing a stint in the countryside for the people whose sacrifices made their education possible. Playgrounds, basketball courts, a new generation parading in sports clothes on November 20, the anniversary of the Revolution.

We were casting off the fetters of our colonial past and the misery of peonage. We were building a nation strong enough to impose that respect for the rights of others which, as Juárez said, means peace. Cárdenas went to San Luis Potosí with only twenty soldiers and faced down the last general to rise in arms against the government.

The greatest test of his leadership — and of our independence — came in March, 1938, on the Gulf coastlands, the conquerors' path. Yesterday it was gold, now it was oil. Cárdenas faced a hard decision. Miners and railroadmen were living better, but oil workers' wages lagged behind rising prices. For sixteen months the foreign oil companies had resisted settling with the union. The dispute had been arbitrated, as the law provides, and the workers had been awarded a third of their demands. The companies refused to pay, appealed to Mexico's Supreme Court, and lost their case.

Still they refused to pay. The money difference between the award and their last offer was small, but they were determined not to submit to government regulation.

A strike was imminent. The companies could afford to wait until hunger broke the workers' ranks and a fuel shortage paralyzed the nation. If Cárdenas let the oilmen defy the laws and the courts, then they were stronger than the government. A nation too weak to make foreigners respect its laws was no better than a colony!

On March 18, in a memorable broadcast to the Mexican people, Cárdenas announced the nationalizing of the oil industry in the public interest. He recalled how the oil interests had interfered in Mexican affairs over the years and accused them of indifference to the people's welfare. "In what town near the oil fields," he asked, "is there a hospital, a school, a social center, a waterworks, an athletic field, or a light and power plant such as might be fueled with the millions of cubic meters of gas now wasted?" As he told of his decision, he asked for the support of a united nation.

The response was overwhelming. For hours people marched by the National Palace where the president stood on the balcony under the bell of Dolores. They bore themselves with the dignity of citizens of a country that had declared its economic independence. Along Madero Avenue, women lined up with gifts to pay for the oil properties, rich ladies with their jewels, the poor with chickens. But the oilmen wouldn't discuss payment. They left the country, boasting they'd be back in three weeks because Mexicans were children unable to run anything complicated like a refinery. All over the world they made propaganda against us, scaring away tourists, preventing us from buying spare parts, tying up our boats with lawsuits in foreign ports. My father remembers what dreadful things were said here in the foreign colony about Cárdenas, and about Roosevelt, too, but they must have been a level-headed pair because they settled this, and other disputes besides, like good neighbors.

The oilmen have long since been paid for their properties. Why were they so cocksure we'd fail to run the industry? Did they never notice how we keep our *carcachas,* our jalopies, running year after year? We don't work such miracles without being mechanics of a sort. So it was in the oil fields. The foreign generals left, and we promoted the native sergeants. It wasn't easy at first, but union committees helped, and gradually our government-owned oil company took shape: Petróleos Mexicanos, or Pemex for short.

It was about the best thing that ever happened to us. Petroleum has been the making of Mexico. It supplies nine-tenths of our energy: industrial gas, electric power, and fuel for motor vehicles, diesel locomotives, and farm machinery. Pemex served us as a training ground for technicians in every industry. Many of its sixty thousand well-paid employees are sons of peons who earned practically nothing. When workers and farmers have money to spend, business prospers. What touched off our long-delayed industrial revolution was the land reform and the nationalization of oil.

Cárdenas opened the door to fifty thousand of Spain's best

sons, defeated in their country's tragic civil war. We gained valuable skills and talents when we needed them most, and enriched our cultural life. As allies of the United States in World War II, we supplied materials for your war plants and manpower for your farms. Since imports were scarce, we learned to do for ourselves, building canneries and shoe factories and plants that made cement and steel for dams, highways, and the tall buildings of the booming capital.

The new industries needed literate, healthy employees no less than freight cars and electric power. Schools and social services multiplied. There was so much to do and so little money! The efforts of local and state governments and private individuals were not enough. The federal government came in, putting tax money to work and selling bonds to mobilize the savings of the nation. It continues to do so, and the resulting combination is what we call a mixed economy. Besides providing public services, the government gets needed industries rolling, alone or in partnership with private investors.

Agriculture remains our greatest problem. Though millions of peasants are ejido members or small property owners, many remain without land or have tracts that are too little, too dry, or too steep. Barely half the population lives in the country now, and they earn but a fifth of the nation's income. Young people for whom there is no land flock to the cities, faster than there are jobs. They build themselves shanties in the "belts of misery" and try to live by selling

chiclets or lottery tickets until they find work. In the country
there is hunger; in the city, hope.

Some go north to pick cotton or harvest wheat. Half our
crops are now raised on irrigated land, much of which lies in
the border states. Though our population has multiplied, we
no longer import food as in Porfirian times. Instead, we
export it. All winter long, trailer trucks roll north to the
United States with tomatoes, melons, and strawberries. With
the dollars they earn us, we buy cranes and transformers. But
the Cárdenas dream of prosperous cooperative farming has
come true only in small measure. The big rewards from irrigation farming are for "nylon farmers" in city clothes who
have others working for them.

Experience, money, equipment, and leadership have been
lacking in the ejidos. Woodlands and pasture continue to be
used in common, but usually the cropland is worked in individual plots, averaging twelve acres and seldom irrigated.
Such a parcel once meant freedom from the whipping post
and, if the rains were merciful, enough corn to tide over until
the next harvest. But today a man needs money, and who will
lend it to him except the Widow Lombriz, at six percent a
month, or Don Tiburcio, who gins the cotton or sells the
coffee, and takes most of it for his charges? If a mule team is
costly, a tractor is beyond his dreams. Anyone rich enough to
have a tractor puts together many small plots into a big field
and pays his poor neighbors what he calls rent and wages to
cultivate their own land.

Perhaps among the coming generation there will be more farmers with the schooling and self-confidence to join with their neighbors and set up cooperative machine stations. Already, some second-generation Zapatistas have built a tourist hotel with a fine swimming pool on their common land. It pays better than sugar cane. Some ejidos have turned to cooperative forestry and livestock raising, since only fifteen percent of our land is arable. A shrimp fishermen's coop has channeled fresh water into the salt marshes of Sinaloa and increased its catch ten times.

Land alone does not guarantee a prosperous democratic agriculture. With it must go technical assistance, credit on reasonable terms, cooperative buying and selling, improved livestock, plants that yield more and resist frost and drought, and relentless war on the spotted fly, the boll weevil, the cattle tick, the chahuixtle, and a hundred other pests. Something is being done, but much remains to do.

Natural gas from Tabasco flows to a refinery in the Bajío and comes out as anhydrous ammonia to enrich the impoverished soil. The petrochemical industry produces the building blocks for fertilizers, insecticides, detergents, plastics, paints, fibers, and artificial rubber. To conserve petroleum, we are turning to hydroelectric power. It's hard to generate electricity on a river that goes dry every winter, so in the 1960's we began harnessing mighty tropical rivers of constant flow. Nezahualcóyotl Dam, where the Grijalva comes down from the mountains to the Gulf, supplies power for reducing aluminum ores and refining oil and, by regulating the water flow, is opening the Tabasco floodlands to agriculture. The fifteenth-century Indian engineer would surely admire this dam named for him, with its sculptured figure of the rain god Tláloc, watching mankind use his gift of water for farming and industry.

We have dams bearing other illustrious names: Miguel Hidalgo, Benito Juárez, Francisco I. Madero, Venustiano Carranza, Alvaro Obregón, Francisco Villa. Francisco for Pancho. From Chihuahua, where the guerrilla chieftain once heated and twisted the steel rails in the enemy's path, a railroad line now winds and tunnels through the Western Sierra Madre to the Pacific. The destruction of the Revolution made way for the construction that came after. Ciudad Sahagún has risen in the maguey fields east of the capital to honor Brother Bernardino Sahagún, who tried to convince the Spaniards four hundred years ago that the Indians were brothers and equals. Many descendants of his promising pupils must be there among the men making Renaults, trucks, and freight cars. Our Indian past is everywhere. University City stands on the lava flow that buried Cuicuilco two thousand years ago; Polytechnic, near the hill from which Juan Diego brought a message that Guadalupe was with the Indian people in their sorrows and calamities.

Our first million telephones and our first million automobiles are long since behind us. We have microwave communications, modern airports, and highways reaching from ocean to ocean, from border to border, and to faraway Yucatán. How proud we were of the first cylinder blocks that came off a Mexican assembly line! Now we make refrigerators, washing machines, and television sets, including color sets. Some of our North American friends advise us to buy these gadgets from the United States and remain a land of lovely peasant handicrafts. But experience teaches us that a nation that fails to industrialize remains poor, sick, and ignorant. It sells its sugar or zinc in competition with all the world, stints on education and health, and pays low wages to its workers and high prices for imported manufactures.

A Mexican economist asks, "Can we pay for internal combustion engines with lacquer ware? Electric generators with glass toys? Pumps with handloomed wool? Excavating equipment with straw hats? Automobiles with hammocks? Linotype machines with clay pitchers? Diesel locomotives with guitars?"

No, we must make these things ourselves and save our precious dollars for what we can't yet make. Since the Revolution, our population has doubled and tripled. Soon there will be two million more of us every year. Some will settle in the coastlands, where malaria is all but conquered. But more will come to the cities. For this reason alone, we have to industrialize.

Loans and investments from other countries, especially the United States, help us develop needed industries. But, remembering the past, we like foreign companies to Mexicanize in part, sharing the opportunities for management and ownership with Mexican citizens.

We are on our way. Pessimists say we are still an underdeveloped country. Optimists like my father say we are not underdeveloped but developing. Since he was my age, our farm output has increased by four times, our national income by five or six times, and our electric power capacity and steel and cement production by ten to twenty times. Few tourists used to venture into Mexico. Now they come, some two million a year. We tell them they are in their own home and we mean it. In population, Mexico City has moved into a class with Tokyo, New York, and London. My father learned in school that a Mexican's average length of life was only thirty-nine years. Now it's sixty-five and climbing to seventy. One child in eight used to die before his first birthday. Today half of these "little angels" live and grow into healthy sinners.

A fourth of our federal tax money goes for education. That's two or three times what the armed forces receive. Before the Revolution, it was the other way around. Higher education, formerly limited to a few thousand youths, is the privilege of hundreds of thousands. We are building schools at the rate of a classroom an hour, besides shops and labs. Motorized cultural missions carry education for living into regions where people have grown up with little schooling. In each mission there's a director, a doctor, a nurse, an agricultural engineer, a home economist, and teachers of music, art, recreation, and building techniques. They carry audio-visual equipment, a library, and miniature workshops, and remain two years or so in a place, encouraging community development activities in the surrounding region.

Our social security system began with city workers and is expanding into the countryside. It operates community centers and gives medical care, retirement benefits, home-building loans, brides' dowries, aid to nursing mothers, and widows' benefits. A widow who remarries gets three years' benefits — what you might call severance pay.

These are among the fruits of the Revolution, as my father sees them. We students have our dissatisfactions. We ask why, a generation after Cárdenas and two after Madero, a quarter of the nation is still illiterate. Or why the diet of half the rural population is without the animal proteins found in eggs, meat, fish, and milk. Without our school breakfast program, the children in some places would be too weak to sit up and keep awake.

We have vast housing projects, with schools, playgrounds, and shopping centers. Yet half of Mexico still lives in one-room dwellings, often without water or sewer connections. The Revolution has bestowed its best gifts on the growing middle class and the newly rich, and its next best on the skilled workers and irrigation farmers. Others, while gaining in human dignity and pride of nationality, must tighten their belts while the country industrializes. Their poverty puts a brake on development by limiting what they can buy. But they live in hope of better times — all but the ten percent at the bottom of the heap, who speak an Indian language and cling to ancient traditions, hardly aware of what Mexico means, but suspicious of outsiders who, if not scheming to steal their land, will surely cheat them while buying their straw hats. One of them has said, "I am an Indian, a worm hiding in the grass. Every hand avoids me, every foot crushes me." We ask why Mestizo Mexico, so proud of its Indian heritage, has failed to incorporate these Indians into the nation.

Our teachers concede us justice in our complaints but remind us of our country's background. Though we are smaller than the United States, our history is longer, more tormented and tragic.

We are descended from a disinherited race which fused with its conquerors during three centuries of colonial tyranny and a century more of turmoil. Independence helped a few and left most of us at the mercy of military dictators, the hacienda system, and foreign intervention. Your red men and black men were minorities, whereas a majority of Mexicans have suffered oppression. Land, free and abundant, awaited your pioneers; the oases of our arid frontier were seized upon by caciques and absentee landlords. Your rich natural resources were free from foreign control; ours slipped from our hands during internal upheavals.

After 1925, we built anew. More people gained a stake in the country's future and were unwilling to tolerate constant disorder. But only since Cárdenas have we been free to develop in peace without the threat of military uprisings. "That would not seem long if you could remember what it used to be like," say our teachers. "We hope you will do better."

What, then, do the students propose to accomplish?

First, we are trying to bring all our people into the life of the nation. Isolation is growing impossible as roads and lumbering crews advance into the hills. The Indian communities are bound to be transformed but not, we hope, destroyed. Indian teen-agers are being prepared in National Indian Institute centers to bridge the two worlds, as Sahagún's pupils might have done. They talk to their suspicious elders about the advantages of a sewing room, an orchard, or a herd of pigs. They teach their kid brothers and sisters the Spanish they need to attend primary school and become literate so they will know how to defend themselves when, later on, they buy and sell in the Mestizo towns. We hope to persuade the Indians to come into the larger community of the Mexican nation by their own choice and without giving up their loyalty to their smaller community, their helpfulness to one another, and their arts, crafts, and sense of beauty.

Second, we must press on to a higher stage of industrialization. There will be a hundred million Mexicans before the century ends. A higher percentage than now will be working in factories and producing for home consumption and for export. In what products can we learn to excel, like the Swiss with their watches and the Dutch with their cheese? For the answer, we must tirelessly pursue what you call the know-how, and do more original research. Today as yesterday, more students study law than can practice it, but all their lives, whatever they do, they bear the title of licenciado. I will feel equally honored — and more useful — to be called *ingeniero,* or engineer. And have I told you that my novia Chabela speaks of studying biochemistry? Mexico needs every talent, whether of the beautiful or ugly sex. We are about to generate nuclear power against the time when petroleum runs short. We are searching for cheap ways of desalting sea water. What a garden Lower California, with its long tapering coastline, will be when irrigation comes!

Third, we seek for ways to participate more effectively in public affairs. We feel that as our country becomes the horn of plenty its shape suggests, its fruits should be enjoyed by all. Our president has said, "We are like a large family with only one small blanket. When one person covers himself, he pulls it off another. We must make a larger blanket so no one in Mexico will be cold or hungry or want for a home or a school."

Fourth, we want peace and friendship with all the world and opportunities for a creative life. Chabela and I were in Chapultepec recently. From the Castle we stepped down to the spiral gallery that depicts "the struggle of the Mexican people for their liberty" in vivid dioramas. School children were there with drawing boards, sketching Hidalgo raising the cry at Dolores — Morelos holding out under siege at Cuautla — the Boy Heroes of 1847, and the Zacapoaxtla warriors of 1862, defending the nation when many despaired of its survival — Juárez, the Indian shepherd boy who was to enact equality before the law and topple a Hapsburg emperor — Madero entering the jubilant capital, full of democratic hopes — the people in arms after Huerta's crimes — the domed chamber of marble and lava stone that spotlights the Constitution of 1917, with its promises of political liberty and social justice — and, at the exit, an inscription that tells our role, Chabela's and mine, in our country's destiny:

"We leave the museum but not history, since it lives on and through us. Our country endures, and we are the architects of its grandeur. In the lessons of the past, we find strength to deal with the present and reason to hope for the future. Let us meet whatever responsibilities freedom lays upon us so that we may always deserve the honor of being Mexicans."

FOR MORE READING ON MEXICO

ⓞⓞⓞⓞⓞⓞⓞⓞⓞ

GENERAL HISTORY

Cumberland, Charles C. *Mexico: The Struggle for Modernity.* Oxford University Press, New York, 1968.

Parkes, Henry Bamford. *A History of Mexico.* Houghton Mifflin, Boston, 1960.

Simpson, Lesley Byrd. *Many Mexicos.* University of California Press, Berkeley, 1967.

Wolf, Eric R. *Sons of the Shaking Earth.* University of Chicago Press, Chicago, 1959. The "lifeline of a culture." An excellent study for readers at the college level or beyond.

PRE-HISPANIC TIMES

Bernal, Ignacio. *Mexico Before Cortez: Art, History, Legend.* Dolphin Books, Doubleday, Garden City, N.Y., 1963.

Caso, Alfonso. *The People of the Sun.* University of Oklahoma Press, Norman, 1958.

Coe, Michael D. *Mexico.* Praeger, New York, 1962. From the early hunters to the Aztecs. Also *The Maya,* 1966, an up-to-date account.

Covarrubias, Miguel. *Indian Art of Mexico and Central America.* Knopf, New York, 1957.

Peterson, Frederic A. *Ancient Mexico: An Introduction to the Pre-Hispanic Cultures.* Capricorn, New York, 1962.

Ramírez Vázquez, Pedro, and others. *The National Museum of Anthropology, Mexico: Art, Architecture, Archaeology, Ethnography.* Abrams, New York, 1968. A great museum in photographs.

Soustelle, Jacques. *The Daily Life of the Aztecs on the Eve of the Spanish Conquest.* Macmillan, New York, 1962.

Thompson, J. Eric S. *The Rise and Fall of Maya Civilization.* 2d ed. University of Oklahoma Press, Norman, 1966.

Vaillant, George. *The Aztecs of Mexico: Origin, Rise and Fall of the Aztec Nation.* Revised by Susannah B. Vaillant. Doubleday, Garden City, N.Y., 1962.

Wauchope, Robert, ed. *Handbook of Middle American Indians.* 13 vols. University of Texas Press, Austin, 1964——. Scholarly articles on Indians, past and present, with pictures everyone can enjoy.

Westheim, Paul. *The Art of Ancient Mexico.* Anchor Books, Doubleday, Garden City, N.Y., 1965. Also *The Sculpture of Ancient Mexico,* 1963.

THE CONQUEST

Blom, Frans. *The Conquest of Yucatan.* Houghton Mifflin, Boston, 1936.

Díaz del Castillo, Bernal. *The Discovery and Conquest of Mexico.* Grove, New York, 1956.

Leon-Portilla, Miguel. *The Broken Spears.* Beacon, Boston, 1962. Indian accounts of the Conquest.

Prescott, William H. *The Conquest of Mexico.* Bantam, New York, 1967. The classic and conventional story, first published in 1843, outdated in part by present-day knowledge of Indian sources and culture.

COLONIAL TIMES

Benítez, Fernando. *Century After Cortés.* University of Chicago Press, Chicago, 1965.

Cameron, Roderick. *Viceroyalties of the West: The Spanish Empire in Latin America.* Little, Brown, Boston, 1968.

Denhardt, Robert M. *The Horse of the Americas.* University of Oklahoma Press, Norman, 1947.

Dobie, J. Frank. *The Mustangs.* Little, Brown, Boston, 1952. Also *The Longhorns,* 1941.

Hanke, Lewis. *The Spanish Struggle for Justice in the Conquest of America.* University of Pennsylvania Press, Philadelphia, 1959. Role of Las Casas and others.

Leonard, Irving A. *Baroque Times in Old Mexico: Sixteenth-Century Persons, Places, and Practices.* University of Michigan Press, Ann Arbor, 1959.

Powell, Philip W. *Soldiers, Indians, and Silver: The Northward Advance of New Spain, 1550–1600.* University of California Press, Berkeley, 1952.

Ricard, Robert. *The Spiritual Conquest of Mexico.* University of California Press, Berkeley, 1966.

Schurz, William Lytle. *The Manila Galleon.* Dutton, New York, 1939.

Toussaint, Manuel. *Colonial Art in Mexico.* University of Texas Press, Austin, 1967.

NINETEENTH-CENTURY MEXICO

Calcott, Wilfred Hardy. *Santa Anna: The Story of an Enigma Who Once Was Mexico.* University of Oklahoma Press, Norman, 1936.

Corti, Egon Caesar. *Maximilian and Charlotte of Mexico.* Knopf, New York, 1928.

Fisher, Howard T., and Marion Hall, eds. *Life in Mexico: The Letters of Fanny Calderón de la Barca, with New Material from the Author's Private Journals.* Doubleday, Garden City, N.Y., 1966.

McWilliams, Carey. *North from Mexico: The Spanish-Speaking People of the United States.* Monthly Review, New York,

1961. Border troubles and Mexican influences on mining, cattle raising, and farming in the Southwest.

Reed, Nelson. *The Caste War in Yucatan.* Stanford University Press, Stanford, Calif., 1964. A story of the rebel Mayas who went into the forests to live their own life.

Robertson, William Spence. *Iturbide of Mexico.* Duke University Press, Durham, N.C., 1952.

Roeder, Ralph. *Juarez and His Mexico.* 2 vols. Viking, New York, 1947.

Stephens, John L. *Incidents of Travel in Yucatan.* 2 vols. Dover Publications, New York, 1963. A New York writer's search for the Maya past in 1840 and 1841.

Tolbert, Frank X. *The Day of San Jacinto.* McGraw-Hill, New York, 1959. Houston vs. Santa Anna: a blow-by-blow account.

THE SOCIAL REVOLUTION: CAUSES AND CONSEQUENCES

Beals, Carleton. *Porfirio Díaz, Dictator of Mexico.* Lippincott, Philadelphia, 1932.

Brenner, Anita, and George Leighton. *The Wind That Swept Mexico: The History of the Mexican Revolution, 1910–1942.* Harper, New York, 1943.

Crow, John A. *Mexico Today.* Harper, New York, 1957.

Gruening, Ernest. *Mexico and Its Heritage.* Appleton-Century-Crofts, New York, 1928. Why there was a revolution in 1910.

Guzmán, Martín Luis. *Memoirs of Pancho Villa.* University of Texas Press, Austin, 1965. Told as if in Villa's words by one who knew him well.

Johnson, William Weber. *Heroic Mexico: The Violent Emergence of a Modern Nation.* Doubleday, Garden City, N.Y., 1968.

McBride, George M. *The Land Systems of Mexico*. American Geographical Society, New York, 1923.

Nicholson, Irene. *The X in Mexico*. Faber and Faber, London, 1965.

Padgett, L. Vincent. *The Mexican Political System*. Houghton Mifflin, Boston, 1966.

Ross, Stanley R. *Francisco I. Madero: Apostle of Mexican Democracy*. Columbia University Press, New York, 1955.

Scott, Robert E. *Mexican Government in Transition*. University of Illinois Press, Urbana, 1964.

Simpson, Eyler N. *The Ejido: Mexico's Way Out*. University of North Carolina Press, Chapel Hill, 1937.

Tannenbaum, Frank. *Mexico: The Struggle for Peace and Bread*. Knopf, New York, 1950.

Townsend, William Cameron. *Lázaro Cárdenas: Mexican Democrat*. George Wahr, Ann Arbor, Mich., 1952.

Turner, John Kenneth, *Barbarous Mexico*. Kerr, Chicago, 1911. Pre-revolutionary slavery in Yucatán. Out of print in English but available in some libraries.

Weyl, Nathaniel and Sylvia. *The Reconquest of Mexico: The Years of Lázaro Cárdenas*. Oxford University Press, New York, 1939.

Whetten, Nathan L. *Rural Mexico*. University of Chicago Press, Chicago, 1968.

HOW PEOPLE LIVE IN MEXICO

Cordry, Donald and Dorothy. *Mexican Indian Costumes*. University of Texas Press, Austin, 1968.

Covarrubias, Miguel. *Mexico South: The Isthmus of Tehuantepec*. Knopf, New York, 1946.

Fent, Patricia Ross. *Made in Mexico*. Knopf, New York, 1968. The folk arts.

Fergusson, Erna. *Mexico Revisited*. Knopf, New York, 1955.

Foster, George M. *Tzintzuntzan: Mexican Peasants in a Changing World*. Little, Brown, Boston, 1967.

Gardner, Erle Stanley. *The Hidden Heart of Baja*. Morrow, New York, 1962. The charm of Lower California.

Instituto Nacional de Bellas Artes. *Arquitectura Popular de México*. Mexico City, 1954. Popular architecture in photographs with explanatory text in English and Spanish.

Lewis, Oscar. *The Children of Sánchez: Autobiography of a Mexican Family*. Random House, New York, 1961. A father and his sons and daughters describe life in a Mexico City slum.

———. *Life in a Mexican Village: Tepoztlán Restudied*. University of Illinois Press, Urbana, 1951.

Pozas Arciniega, Ricardo. *Juan the Chamula: An Ethnological Recreation of the Life of a Mexican Indian*. University of California Press, Berkeley, 1962. Reads like a novel.

Redfield, Robert. *The Folk Culture of Yucatan*. University of Chicago Press, Chicago, 1941.

Reed, Alma. *The Mexican Muralists*. Crown, New York, 1960.

———. *Orozco*. Oxford University Press, New York, 1956.

Romero, Pepe. *Mexican Jumping Bean*. Putnam's, New York, 1953. The lighter side of daily life.

Shipway, Verna Cook and Warren. *The Mexican House Old and New*. Architectural Book, New York, 1960.

Smith, H. Allen. *The Pig in the Barber Shop*. Little, Brown, Boston, 1958. Funny stories with serious undertones by one who loves Mexico.

Spratling, William. *A Small Mexican World*. Little, Brown, Boston, 1964.

Toor, Frances. *A Treasury of Mexican Folkways*. Crown, New York, 1947.

Treviño, Elizabeth (Borton). *My Heart Lies South: The Story of My Mexican Marriage*. Crowell, New York, 1953.

GUIDES TO MEXICO

Bloomgarden, Richard. *The Easy Guide to Mexico City.* Anmex Asociados, S.A., Mexico City, 1968.

Clark, Phil. *A Guide to Mexican Flora.* Editorial Minutiae Mexicana, S.A. de C.V., Mexico City, 1964.

Nash, Joe. *A Guide to Mexico City: Then and Now.* Editorial Minutiae Mexicana, S.A. de C.V., Mexico City, 1968.

Norman, James. *A Shopper's Guide to Mexico: Where, What and How to Buy.* Dolphin Books, Doubleday, Garden City, N.Y., 1966.

————. *Terry's Guide to Mexico.* Revised ed. Doubleday, Garden City, N.Y., 1965.

Toor, Frances. *New Guide to Mexico.* Revised by Fredericka Martin. Crown, New York, 1966.

Wilcock, John. *Mexico on $5 a Day: 1968–1969 Edition.* Arthur Frommer, New York.

Wilhelm, John. *Guide to All Mexico.* 3d ed. McGraw-Hill, New York, 1966.

Wright, N. Pelham. *A Guide to Mexican Animals.* Editorial Minutiae Mexicana, S.A. de C.V., Mexico City, 1965.

FICTION

Fuentes, Carlos. *The Death of Artemio Cruz.* Farrar, Straus and Giroux, New York, 1964.

————. *Good Conscience.* Noonday Press, Farrar, Straus and Giroux, New York, 1968.

Guzmán, Martín Luis. *The Eagle and the Serpent.* Knopf, New York, 1930. Vivid glimpses of the Social Revolution.

Lea, Tom. *The Brave Bulls.* Little, Brown, Boston, 1949.

Rulfo, Juan. *Pedro Páramo.* Grove, New York, 1959.

Traven, B. *The Night Visitor and Other Stories.* Hill and

Wang, New York, 1966. Also *The Treasure of the Sierra Madre,* 1967, and *The Bridge in the Jungle,* 1967.

Yañez, Agustín. *The Edge of the Storm.* University of Texas Press, Austin, 1963.

PERIODICALS

Two monthlies, published in Mexico in English, are available in many libraries: *Mexico This Month,* with gay illustrations, tells of things to see and places to go, including summer schools for United States students; *Mexican Life* is full of short stories and enlightening background articles. *Artes de México,* another monthly, carries handsome art reproductions and illustrated reports on places and past events, with text in English and other languages.

PRONUNCIATION GUIDE: PEOPLE AND PLACES

◎◎◎◎◎◎◎◎◎

This list includes the Indian names mentioned in the present volume, along with enough Spanish names to show how they are pronounced.

Acamapichtli	ah-cah-mah-PEECH-tlee
Acatempan	ah-cah-TAME-pahn
Ahuízotl	ah-WEE-sotl
Ajusco	ah-HOOS-co
Allende	ah-YANE-day
Anáhuac	ah-NAH-wahk
Axayácatl	ah-shah-YAH-cahtl
Azcapotzalco	ah-scah-po-TSAHL-co
Aztlán	ahs-TLAHN
Bajío	bah-HE-o
Bonampak	bo-nahm-PAHK
Cajeme	cah-HAY-may
Calleja	cah-YEA-hah
Calles	CAH-yace
Calmécac	cahl-MAY-cahk
Carvajal	car-vah-HAHL
Chapultepec	chah-POOL-tay-PAYK
Chichén Itzá	chee-CHANE eet-SAH
Chichimec	chee-chee-MAKE
Chihuahua	chee-WAH-wah
Chimalpopoca	chee-mahl-po-PO-cah
China Poblana	CHEE-nah po-BLAH-nah
Chumayel	choo-mah-YALE

Clavijero	clah-vee-HAY-ro
Coahuila	kwah-WEE-lah
Coatlicue	kwat-LEE-kway
Copil	co-PEEL
Cortes (parliament)	COR-tace
Cortés (conqueror)	cor-TACE
Cuauhtémoc	kwow-TAY-moc
Cuautla	KWOW-tlah
Cuicuilco	kwee-KWEEL-co
Cuitláhuac	kweet-LAH-wahk
Culhuacán	cool-wah-CAHN
Díaz	DEE-ahs
Gil	HEEL
Guadalajara	gwah-dah-lah-HAH-rah
Guanajuato	gwah-nah-HWAH-to
Guaspe	GWAHS-pay
Guerrero	gay-RARE-ro
Hacienda	ah-see-EN-dah
Hidalgo	ee-DAHL-go
Huejotzingo	way-ho-TSEEN-go
Huémac	WAY-mahk
Huerta	WARE-tah
Huitzilihuitl	wee-tseel-ee-WEETL
Huitzilopochtli	wee-tseel-o-POACH-tlee
Insurgentes	een-soor-HANE-tays
Iturrigaray	ee-too-ree-GAH-rye
Itzcóatl	eets-CO-ahtl
Ixtlilxóchitl	eesh-tleel-SHO-cheetl
Iztaccíhuatl	ees-tahk-SEE-wahtl
Jalisco	hah-LEES-co
Jesús	hay-SOOS
Jiménez	he-MAY-nace
Juárez	HWAH-race
Junípero Serra	hoo-NEE-pay-ro SAY-rah
Junta	HOON-tah
La Corregidora	lah co-ray-he-DO-rah

La Güera Rodríguez	lah GWAY-rah rod-REE-gace
La Malinche	lah mah-LEEN-chay
La Xocoyota	lah sho-co-YO-tah
Maxtli	MAHSH-tli
Maya	MAH-yah
Mestizo	mace-TEE-so
Mexica (Aztecs)	may-SHEE-cah
Michoacán	me-cho-ah-CAHN
Mixcóatl	meesh-CO-ahtl
Mixtec	meesh-TAKE
Moctezuma	moc-tay-SOO-mah
Montejo	mon-TAY-ho
Motolinia	mo-to-LEEN-ee-ah
Múgica	MOO-he-cah
Nezahualcóyotl	nay-sah-wahl-COY-otl
Nuño de Guzmán	NOON-yo day goos-MAHN
Oaxaca	wah-HAH-cah
Otomí	o-to-ME
Peña y Peña	PANE-yah ee PANE-yah
Popocatépetl	po-po-cah-TAY-petl
Quetzalcóatl	cay-tsahl-CO-ahtl
Quintana Roo	keen-TAH-nah RO-o
Revillagigedo	ray-vee-yah-he-HAY-do
Sahagún	sah-ah-GOON
Saltillo	sahl-TEE-yo
San Jerónimo	sahn hay-RO-nee-mo
San Miguel	sahn me-GALE
Sigüenza y Góngora	see-GWEHN-sah ee GON-go-rah
Tajín	tah-HEEN
Tarahumara	tah-rah-oo-MAH-rah
Tarascan	ta-RAHS-cahn
Taxco	TASS-co
Tehuacán	tay-wah-CAHN
Tehuantepec	tay-WAHN-tay-PAYK
Tenochtitlan	tay-noach-TEE-tlahn
Teotihuacán	tay-o-tee-wah-CAHN

Tepexpan	tay-PESH-pan
Tepeyac	tay-pay-YAHK
Texcoco	tess-CO-co
Tezcatlipoca	tess-caht-lee-PO-ca
Tezozómoc	tay-so-SO-moc
Tizapán	tee-sah-PAHN
Tizoc	tee-SOAK
Tlacaélel	tlah-cah-AY-lel
Tláloc	TLAH-loc
Tlatelolco	tlah-tay-LOL-co
Tlatilco	tlah-TEEL-co
Tlaxcala	tlash-CAH-lah
Totonac	to-to-NAHK
Velázquez	vay-LAHSS-case
Villa	VEE-yah
Xicoténcatl	shee-co-TEHN-cahtl
Xitli	SHEE-tlee
Xochicalco	so-chee-CAHL-co
Xochimilco	so-chee-MEEL-co
Zacapoaxtla	sah-cah-po-AHST-lah
Zaragoza	sah-rah-GO-sah
Zócalo	SO-cah-lo

INDEX

⊚⊚⊚⊚⊚⊚⊚⊚⊚